Crime, Public Opinion, and Civil Liberties

Crime, Public Opinion, and Civil Liberties

The Tolerant Public

SHMUEL LOCK

Westport, Connecticut
London

Library of Congress Cataloging-in-Publication Data

Lock, Shmuel, 1969–
    Crime, public opinion, and civil liberties : the tolerant public /
Shmuel Lock.
        p.   cm.
    Includes bibliographical references and index.
    ISBN 0–275–96432–9 (alk. paper)
        1. Criminal justice, Administration of—Public opinion.   2. Crime—
Public opinion.   3. Criminal law—Public opinion.   4. Public
opinion—United States.   I. Title.
    HV9950.L63   1999
    364.973—dc21   98–33606

British Library Cataloguing in Publication Data is available.

Library of Congress Catalog Card Number: 98–33606
ISBN: 0–275–96432–9

First published in 1999

Praeger Publishers, 88 Post Road West, Westport, CT 06881
An imprint of Greenwood Publishing Group, Inc.

Printed in the United States of America

The paper used in this book complies with the
Permanent Paper Standard issued by the National
Information Standards Organization (Z39.48–1984).

10 9 8 7 6 5 4 3

Contents

Acknowledgments

First and foremost, I am deeply indebted to Professor Robert Y. Shapiro. He is not only an advisor and mentor, but a true friend. Without his advice and guidance, this book could have never come to fruition. I would also like to thank Professor Michael Delli Carpini, who also read through numerous drafts, and whose suggestions to better this project were incredibly helpful.

In addition, I would like to thank other professors, who have served as teachers, colleagues, and mentors throughout my academic career. They have also read and commented on parts or all of the text. These include Professors Michael Kahan, Philippa Strum, Dan Kramer, George Cunningham, and William Browne, as well as my new colleagues at John Jay College of Criminal Justice.

Of course, this all would not have been possible without my family. My mother, Miriam, and my siblings Racheli, Elisheva, and Peretz helped with the project in both a professional and courteous manner, under, at times, quite stressful conditions.

Chapter 1

Introduction: Public Opinion, Democratic Governance, and Criminal Justice

This book argues and offers evidence that the public is not as intolerant of civil liberties for criminal defendants in the area of criminal justice as one might expect based upon the continued reporting by the media of the public's strong support for the death penalty, among other more salient issues. Therefore, if the public can be educated in the importance of the protections provided by civil liberties in the area of criminal procedure, they too might be as protective of the rights of criminal defendants as the elites of society. It is true that the mass public is not as protective of the civil liberties of criminal defendants as members of the legal profession, as well as of the decisions of the United States Supreme Court; however, contrary to past literature (McClosky and Brill, 1983), the differences are not as great as many might expect. It is possible that many in the mass public simply might not have the time nor energy nor means of acquiring vital information regarding the importance of civil liberties, and it is this that causes the differences in opinion. In other words, if vital information can be relayed to the mass public by knowledgeable elites, the opinions of the mass public can become as protective of civil liberties as elites.

The importance of educating the public is twofold. First, an informed and active citizenry is the basis for a well-functioning society. If members of the public do not have the information to make informed judgments, nor the time and means to formulate these judgments, the democratic nature of such a society can be called into question. I argue that elites—those within society who have more knowledge, means of acquiring information, and, at times, more time to spend acquiring information—have a duty and responsibility to help provide easy access to relevant information to members of public who do not have the same access (Page and Shapiro, 1992; Fishkin, 1991, 1992).

Another reason for educating the mass public is quite practical. Members of the public elect politicians, who nominate judges, and voters at times elect the judges directly. In a society in which many members of the public do not value protections for criminal defendants, the wishes of an unprotective public will be reflected in court decisions and public policy. Again, this is not to argue that the will of the public should not be followed by policy makers. Rather, I am arguing, it is important for those with the means and ability to acquire information to assure those in society not similarly situated that they can have the ability to make an informed decision.

In law in general, and in the field of criminal justice in particular, lawyers are in the unique position to acquire and understand information concerning these subjects, even when these subjects appear visibly on the nightly news, in newspapers, and elsewhere. They acquire the information in greater frequency, and with more understanding of the issues under discussion, since they have at least had three years of intensive and structured training which enables them to understand the intricacies involved in grappling with the issues within the field of law. This training also gives lawyers the knowledge, background, and confidence to examine all information with a critical eye, as opposed to taking all information distributed by the various media outlets as fact. In other words, lawyers acquire more information, and the information they do receive has very likely been examined for truthfulness and accuracy, as well as critically analyzed, with help from their legal knowledge. Hence, the legal elite are an ideal group of individuals to serve as educators of the mass public. They can educate the public, regarding the facts associated with issues of criminal justice, and thus enable other members of the public to make informed judgments regarding the importance of civil liberties. The methods through which this education can occur are explained later in Chapter 7.

In sum, this book compares mass and elite opinion, specifically legal elite opinion, with each other, as well as with specific United States Supreme Court decisions. Through this exploration, one can see whether the elite are more protective of civil liberties than members of the public. An examination such as the one I have undertaken might help social scientists pinpoint explanations for views of the mass public which might seem intolerant. In addition, this study is timely, since the Supreme Court in recent years has been moving to the Right on many issues, including those cases dealing with issues of criminal justice (LaFave and Israel, 1992). It is possible that past studies that found elites to be particularly tolerant (McClosky and Brill, 1983) might be dated. This might be so, since at the time of those studies the Supreme Court still had an expansionist reading of the rights afforded to criminal defendants. If this recent move to the Right, is in contradiction to public opinion, should the Supreme Court heed public opinion? In general, what role should public opinion have in democratic governance in general, and Supreme Court decision particular?

PUBLIC OPINION AND DEMOCRATIC GOVERNANCE

Democratic theory posits that participation in the decision-making process by the mass public is essential to the well being of society (Rousseau, 1762; Bentham, 1843; Mill, 1849). In order for the public to have some sort of voice in the decision-making process, as well as to assure political accountability, the public must be aware of the issues which are being discussed (Dahl, 1956; Key, 1961). If the public is not knowledgeable regarding these issues, there might be little or no incentive for politicians to adhere to the public's needs. Public policy would reflect the wishes and interests of those in society who are informed. Rational politicians would have no incentive to respond to the wants of an uninformed citizenry.

Unfortunately, many writers have argued and offered evidence that the public is ill-informed on the issues of the day (Berelson, 1952; Schumpeter, 1943; Converse, 1964; Campbell, Converse, Miller, and Stokes, 1960). In fact, some have argued that it is, in fact, those least informed and knowledgeable, many of whom are struggling financially, whose interests are most often ignored (Delli Carpini and Keeter, 1996). Ironically, this is the group that would most need government to be responsive to it. This is also the group within which many criminal defendants find themselves. Thus, an uninformed public is an ignored public.

However, if an informed public would force politicians to support and enact policies that would be disadvantageous to others in society, it is possible to make a normative argument supporting an uninformed public, which could be ignored by the leaders, who would have no fear of retribution at the ballot box. There is, in fact, some evidence that the mass public does not support democratic norms, and is not particularly tolerant of groups they greatly dislike (Stouffer, 1955; Sullivan, Piereson, and Marcus, 1982). In addition, many have found evidence that even in circumstances where the public might support democratic principles in the abstract, there is still less support for these democratic principles when presented with specific situations (Sullivan, Piereson and Marcus, 1982; Schuman, Steeh, and Bobo, 1985; Page and Shapiro, 1992). For example, the public has supported the right for anyone to teach in the public schools when the question is asked in the abstract. However, the public is not as tolerant when asked to support this right for a group it dislikes (Sullivan, Piereson, and Marcus, 1982). Comparing these findings to mass opinion regarding the rights of criminal defendants, it is possible that the public would not support the civil liberties of defendants in specific circumstances, even if they would support the norms of civil liberties in the area of criminal justice in the abstract. For example, members of the mass public might support the right to counsel in the abstract, yet might allow a confession an individual gives concerning a crime, even if there has been a violation of the Supreme Court's interpretation of the constitutional guarantee of counsel.

In addition, if the public is not informed regarding basic political facts, a contention many researchers have argued and brought evidence to support (see

Delli Carpini and Keeter, 1992), it could be argued that logic would not support the idea of public involvement, regardless of the level of tolerance displayed by the mass public. If one defines democracy as a society in which the "will" of the public is carried out by the leaders of society, democracy cannot exist if the public has no informed "will." Another group of researchers has offered evidence to the contrary, showing that the public does indeed have such a will. Many authors have shown that the public collectively holds explicable opinions, responding especially to objective conditions and political events (Page and Shapiro, 1992; Caldeira, 1986; Stimson, 1991). This is true, even though many of the public's opinions are not necessarily deeply held (Zaller and Feldman, 1992). Many also argue and offer evidence that "issue publics" have developed (Elkins, 1993; Popkin, 1991), emphasizing that only a portion of the population has enough of a stake or interest in any given issue to be motivated to follow the information flow on the given issue (Popkin, 1991). The section of the citizenry that does follow an issue under consideration becomes the "public" for that issue. Therefore, the public as a whole should not simply be labeled "ignorant" when it does not have information or opinions on issues, since the public for that issue can act as the guardians for the rest of society who are "rationally" ignorant (Downs, 1957).

However, even if one accepts the notion that the public is able to follow the flow of information through cues and other devices, the fact remains that the mass public is not well informed on basic political facts (Delli Carpini and Keeter, 1992), and it is not becoming more tolerant of the groups they dislike (Sullivan, Piereson, and Marcus, 1982). While the public might hold explicable opinions collectively (Page and Shapiro, 1992), if the elites are generally more tolerant, and have more knowledge on which to base their opinions, would it not be more logical to argue in favor of the "elitist theory of democracy"?

Proponents of this elitist theory have argued that only a relatively small elite is—and need be—informed on the issues of the day. Elites, defined as community leaders, some of the more educated and more active in society, and in the case of criminal justice procedures, the legal elite, are the vanguard for society (Berelson, 1952). Though the idea of noninvolvement by the vast majority of the American public seems contradictory to our tradition (de Tocqueville, 1835), some evidence, as mentioned, supports the practicality of such a system. The notion that the more educated and financially secure within society would be more knowledgeable and active in political affairs is quite logical. With a vast number of Americans working long hours for modest or little pay, it might be irrational for many Americans to spend their few spare moments following and becoming involved in daily political events (Downs, 1957; Popkin, 1991). Hence, there is much practicality for an "elitist theory of democracy."

In short, it is possible to point to evidence that suggests that identifiable elites are better citizens than others in society: they are more likely to adhere to democratic norms in the United States (Nunn, Crockett, and Williams, 1978; McClosky, 1964; Weil, 1985). The most tolerant tend to be the best educated

(Bobo and Licari, 1989), and many hold positions of leadership within the community (McClosky and Brill, 1983).

Some argue that this is the case because elites have helped form and have therefore been most exposed to mainstream values (Zaller, 1992). According to this line of thought, it is not education per se that causes some to be more tolerant; rather, it is that the better educated are more likely to have been exposed to these values and reasoning processes and persuaded by them (cf. Zaller, 1992; Page and Shapiro, 1992). When mainstream norms support democratic norms, those in society most exposed to them will be more supportive of them. However, quite logically, when mainstream values do not agree upon one set of norms, elite opinion will not necessarily converge upon one set of norms. In fact, if mainstream norms oppose democratic norms, it is possible that elites might be less likely than others to demonstrate democratic values.

Others argue that elites with more education and knowledge have more complex thought processes than the mass public (Milburn, 1991; see/compare Sniderman, Thomas et al., 1991). Due to this and other factors, education naturally causes one to be more protective of democratic norms (Stouffer, 1955; Nunn, Crockett, and Williams, 1978). In this case elites are more tolerant than others not because they have been exposed to mainstream norms, but rather because their education will tend to make them more protective of democratic norms, regardless of current mainstream values.

According to the proponents of the elite theory of democracy, elites can act as representatives for the relatively ignorant mass public (Downs, 1957). It is true that democratic theorists have stressed the importance of members of the public to be involved in the workings of the government (Rousseau, 1953; Locke, 1960), but, if it can be argued and proven, that the more knowledgeable and educated can do a better job than the public in protecting the interests of the public, the necessity of the broad involvement of citizens in politics can be called into question. Moreover, a quiescent public, which allows elite opinion to dominate and set public policy, might seem more favorable than more openly democratic processes. The dominance of an informed and tolerant elite opinion, which serves to represent and substitute for an uninformed and intolerant public, would have great virtue. A further possibility, as mentioned earlier, is for the elites to act as teachers. This may occur in the form of elites and experts communicating on the nightly news, editorials in newspapers, or, as some have suggested, through town meetings where ideas can be freely exchanged (Fishkin, 1991, 1992). As far back as Plato's dialogs with Socrates, political philosophers have argued that the truth can only come about through a reasoned debate. Through the modern media (e.g., radio and television call-in shows, "town meetings," the Internet, etc.), it is possible that the equivalent of public education that occurred at Athenian town meetings can emerge once more in a different mass form.

Of course, all this assumes that elites are selfless participants whose intentions are to promote the education of the citizenry as a whole. The problem, of course, is that relatively few members of the public would have firsthand access to information, while others would have to rely on these individuals to provide accurate, as opposed to self-serving, information (Parenti, 1986).

Indeed, over the years, the elite theory of democracy has come under much criticism. Jackman (1972) examined the Stouffer "tolerance" data that elites are more tolerant of deviance than members of the mass public, and found that once one accounts for distinguishing characteristics such as race and education, political leaders were no more tolerant than the mass public. Further evidence challenging the ideas of the elite theory has surfaced more recently. One persuasive study concluded that communist repression of the 1950s in the American states came not from the mass public but rather from intolerant elites (Gibson, 1988). Others have argued that elites are self-interested actors, only passing on information to promote their own advancement, and at times passing on misleading information (Parenti, 1986; Herman and Chomsky, 1988). What role, if any, do elites have in the mass opinion formation within the area of criminal justice? To assess the situation, one must first examine the current state of mass opinion in the area.

PUBLIC OPINION TOWARD CIVIL LIBERTIES AND CRIMINAL JUSTICE

In their book *The Rational Public* (1992, p. 89), Page and Shapiro explained, as McClosky and Brill (1983) had earlier, that "tolerance is unnatural, difficult, an acquired taste." They argue that "the most natural thing in the world is to want to silence people who are offensive, or dangerous, especially in times of peril." In the late 1990s, criminals and criminal defendants might be held, by many in society, as the most offensive and dangerous group.

Page and Shapiro (pp. 90-93) report that "between April 1965 and January 1969, there was a very substantial 26% rise, to 83%, in the proportion of the public who believed that the courts were not harsh enough in their treatment of criminals (Gallup)." In addition "in Autumn 1970, 49% (of the mass public) located themselves on the stop criminal activity (as opposed to 34% on the protect the legal rights of those accused) side of an SRC/CPS seven point scale." In addition "in an August 1970 Harris poll . . . 73% of those queried said that: a person who commits a horrible crime should be compelled to answer questions about it during a trial. This opinion violates the constitutional guarantee against self-incrimination.

They also report (pp. 93-94) that "support for capital punishment declined rather gradually and steadily from the mid-1950s to the mid-1960s, but then jumped up in 1966-67 and, after a pause, rose gradually through the 1970s and 1980s." This corresponds with the public's change in the "perceived purpose of punishment." Also, "between 1970 and 1982, according to slightly varying Harris items, the 78% who said the 'main emphasis' in most prisons should be on rehabilitation rather than punishing the individual or protecting society from future crimes fell to 46%."

Page and Shapiro attribute the increase in the punitive opinions of the American public, beginning in the mid-1960s to "urban riots by blacks, and then protests and demonstrations against the Vietnam War by students and others, together with increased media reports of violent crimes (the reports apparently being more important than crime rates themselves" [see Funkhauser, 1973a, 1973b]).

Bearing on the causes of opinion change, Page and Shapiro speak of three forms of elite influence (pp. 356-357). The first they call elite *education* of the public, when the "public receives useful interpretations, and correct and helpful information—information that can help it move toward the policy choices it would make if it were fully and completely informed." If this occurs the policies implemented might be "better adapted to achieve people's basic values and goals."

The second type of influence is *misleading* the public, which occurs when "the public is given erroneous interpretations or false, misleading, or biased information." This might influence individuals to "make mistaken evaluations of policy alternatives and may express support for policies harmful to their own interests or values they cherish."

The third form of elite influence occurs when there is a systematic *manipulation* of public opinion. This occurs when elites "consciously and deliberately, by means of lies, falsehoods, deception, or concealment" alter public opinion. In other words, the pundits are not merely putting a 'spin' on the information the public receives as is the case when the public is mislead, rather, outright lies are being fed to the mass public.

Consequently, Page and Shapiro (1992, pp. 363-364) argue that a system of collective deliberation is needed to ensure that a true education of the public occurs. They state that "collective deliberation entails dissemination of the results of inquiry to the general public, but not wholesale diffusion, because only a small part of what is said and thought can (or need) find its way to the citizenry: only certain summary information that emerges from an elaborate process of study and discussion in which ideas are tested and filtered." They also argue that "social networks further help transmit political information to individual citizens; these involve political associations and groups, opinion leaders, co-workers, friends, families."

With regard to criminal justice, however, it is questionable as to whether a system of collective deliberation exists in the field of law in general, and in the area of criminal procedure in particular. It can be argued that the same situation exists for criminal justice as for foreign relations in which elites, due to their monopoly on information, have a greater ability, than in domestic matters to mislead and manipulate public opinion (Chomsky and Herman, 1979; Herman and Chomsky, 1988; Parenti, 1989). This problem can become extremely troublesome in the area of criminal justice, as well. Mass indifference has often been quite apparent when it comes to public law. There is significant evidence that the mass public has little information on the decisions of the judiciary as a whole, and of the Supreme Court in particular (Adamany and Grossman, 1983; Casey, 1974, 1976; Kessel 1966; Tannenhaus and Murphy, 1981). This is an area, then, in which there is great reliance by citizens upon elites to help them keep abreast of and summarize and interpret Supreme Court decisions.

In this study, I investigate to what extent the elite theory of democracy is pertinent to criminal justice. The opinions of four groups are examined, three of which are groups within the general population, the fourth being the United States Supreme Court. The public is divided into three groups: lawyers, the attentive public, and the general public. The reason for singling out lawyers, is that members of the legal profession, more than all others, are assumed to have learned about and adhere to "democratic norms" in the area of criminal proce-dure. The second group examined in the analysis is the educated and informed who constitute an elite group in society. This group includes individuals who have not acquired a formal legal education, yet have attained a position in society in which they have both the intellectual and financial ability to enable themselves to become aware of Supreme Court decisions, as well as the posi-tions of experts regarding these decisions. The last group compared in the analysis consists of individuals who do not fall within either of the other upper echelon categories. This group does not have, on average, the time, inclination, and educational background to follow elite discourse very well. Therefore, the information it receives concerning the law and criminal procedures is less direct and systematic than that of legal and educational elites.

If lawyers were highly protective of civil libertarian values, while non-lawyers were not as protective, it might suggest that lawyers have not been edu-cating the mass public regarding democratic norms. This education of the public can occur, for example, when lawyers act as legal experts on the nightly news, or through commentary on various talk shows or in the printed media. Though it is true that some within the public are suspicious of lawyers in their role as advocate, it is still probable that they are respectful of their knowledge of the law. Some research has shown that nightly news commentary, as well as some experts who appear on the news, are related to significant shifts in public opinion (see Page, Shapiro, and Dempsey, 1987; Page and Shapiro, 1992). It should be noted that any education represented here does not necessarily mean forcing one's views upon the mass public, but, rather, providing information to the mass public that enables it to make further judgments (Fishkin, 1991, 1992). Ideally, this would assure that the public has access to multiple sides of an argument, so that a reasoned opinion can be formulated (Page and Shapiro, 1992).

There are good reasons for educating the public. If a large proportion of the mass public disagrees with many major Supreme Court decisions, the Supreme Court's legitimacy may be questioned. Merely having elite support is not neces-sarily enough to ensure the stability of a healthy democracy. As Erickson and

Tedin (1992) note: "if political alienation becomes sufficiently intense and widespread, it may pose a threat to democratic stability" (p. 148). As the issue of crime has become more salient, it is possible that this is the sort of issue, which might cause political alienation, and eventually delegitimization.

While it is true that this delegitimization of the American government has not happened in the past, different generations have different attitudes (Delli Carpini, 1986). It is possible that new adult cohorts born between 1965 and 1980 have attitudes and opinions on many issues on which their parents would have deferred to the experts (*Newsweek*, 1994). This may occur as younger Americans have obtained higher levels of education than individuals who came of age in past generations (Erickson and Tedin, 1992). In addition, the proliferation and pervasiveness of the mass media may have caused many to acquire information, and become more knowledgeable, concerning issues which the public traditionally had deferred to experts (Abramson, Aldrich, and Rohde, 1995). It can be argued that the combination of more education and easier access to information through the mass media has helped cause the lack of strong partisan identification among the younger generation, as well as lower levels of public confidence in government across all generations.

Moreover, if the public does not have enough information on judicial decisions to know whether or not they agree with the court, who is to protect its interests? Politicians who nominate judges might not have an incentive to protect the public, because political repercussions cannot follow from an apathetic mass public. In sum, the elite must, in some way, educate the public about the norms of the court and criminal justice.

However, as with most political issues, members of the public can obtain information from others who have enough of an incentive and "will" to follow the flow of information regarding issues at hand (Popkin, 1991). Some argue that individuals within the mass public, or even from within the elite, who have an interest in court decisions, may be acting as "guardians" for the rest of the public. They may be the "issue public" in the area of criminal procedures.

Regarding most issues, some have argued that only a small percentage of the public is active and attentive, regardless of the issue (Price and Zaller, 1993; Zaller, 1992; Neuman, 1986). The situation might be, however, different in the area of law in general, and criminal procedure in particular. For law, members of the legal profession, due to their legal education, have a larger base of knowledge, and more of an incentive to obtain knowledge, than all other groups. However, the groups who traditionally form the "attentive public," who have more education and knowledge, may be more knowledgeable about criminal justice than the mass public, yet will not nearly reach the levels of the legal elite. This also means that the attentive public will be more greatly exposed to the influence of the "legal elite" (Geddes and Zaller, 1989). The influence can be through media agenda-setting (Iyengar and Kinder, 1987), reports by media experts (Page, Shapiro, and Dempsey, 1987; Jordan, 1993), or possibly outright manipulation (Parenti, 1986; Diamond and Bates, 1992). Since the attentive public follows the flow of information, yet does not have the knowledge to question the opinions of ostensible legal experts (Zaller, 1992), one role of the legal elite is to help truly educate those who have trouble in obtaining and interpreting accurate information regarding the criminal justice system.

The debate over political tolerance and the need for the elites to educate the public is pertinent for law in general, and even more so in the area of criminal procedure. Bobo and Licari (1989) offer evidence that education has led the public toward becoming more tolerant of some groups, but not of "extremely disliked groups." They define "extremely disliked groups" as having histories of violence and harmful activity. Criminal procedure deals with the constitutional rights of those who have been suspected or accused of a crime. Accused criminals are likely to fall within Bobo and Licari's definition of "extremely disliked groups." If the public is intolerant of the constitutional rights of alleged criminals, the primacy of elite opinion and values serves a critical function. However, if the public is as protective as elites when it comes to criminal procedure, there is less clear support for elitist arguments unless it can be shown that the public has in some way been influenced against its interests.

Based on past literature, it is quite possible that the mass opinions may be based on fleeting events of the moment, whereas lawyers, who are well versed in the bases of the law, might examine these issues in a more reasoned fashion. If indeed this is the case, perhaps the legal elite can begin to educate the public on the need to see the "big picture." A form of deliberative democracy (Fishkin, 1991, 1992), wherein lawyers, acting as "experts" at various televised town meetings, might give members of the legal profession a good opportunity to accomplish this task.

PUBLIC OPINION AND THE SUPREME COURT

This study attempts to compare public opinion with the decisions of the Supreme Court, as well as with elite opinion. In recent years, the Supreme Court has more and more been deciding in favor of law enforcement, as opposed to the interests of criminal defendants. It is important to find to what extent this turn to the Right reflects or is otherwise consistent with the opinions of the legal elite and the public. This study distinguished itself from past research in several important characteristics.

Past studies comparing the opinions of the public with those of the Supreme Court have tried to encompass all areas of the law (Marshall, 1987, 1989), or to make sweeping ideological judgments without careful case-by-case comparisons (Mishler and Sheehan, 1993). In contrast, this study focuses directly on the area of criminal procedure, analyzing survey results concerning particular Court decisions.

William Mishler and Reginald S. Sheehan (1993) have argued that the Court has turned to the Right of the mass public. To support this point, they compare the ideological mood of the country with the results of recent Supreme Court decisions based on Segal and Cover's (1989) ideology scores for the justices and Stimson's (1992) measure of liberal-conservative "public mood." I would argue, however, that a more thorough investigation is required, in which one compares the actual opinions of the mass public and legal elite concerning specific policy judgments, not broad ideological predispositions such as gauged by the "public mood" scale. When one creates a mood scale and includes both low and high salience issues, a too general picture can emerge, missing important issue-by-issue variations. As Page and Shapiro (1992) point out, when the public has little information on different issues under discussion, it is quite reasonable for their opinions to change and vary across issues when presented, at times, with new persuasive information.

One of the important factors missed by such generalizing is the effect of prior decisions. As Martin Shapiro (1990) notes, "conservative" decisions may merely be moderating past decisions of the Court, which may have been more liberal than mass opinion. In other words, the mere fact that the Supreme Court has decided a particular case in a more conservative direction than a past court does not mean that the Court has moved to the right of mainstream public opinion.

In addition, Mishler and Sheehan mistakenly assume that a justice always reflects the ideology of the president who appointed him. They assert that "the conservative appointments of Nixon and Ford probably reflected the prevailing public sentiment at that time, the appointments of Reagan increasingly did not" (p. 97). They continue that "because Republican presidents have filled all of the vacancies on the Court during this period (the past 24 years) of their study and have appointed all but one of the current justices, the court can no longer be considered reasonably balanced" (p. 98). President Richard Nixon appointed former Justice Harry Blackmun and President Gerald Ford appointed Justice John Paul Stevens. It can reasonably be argued that neither were conservative. Former Supreme Court Justice William Brennan, a well-known staunch liberal, was appointed by Republican President Dwight Eisenhower. Certainly, it cannot be taken for granted that judges will remain conservatives because a Republican president appointed them. In sum, it is necessary to examine the subsequent behavior of justices in actual cases to establish more conclusive findings.

Another important study that attempted to gauge public opinions in relation to Supreme Court decisions was conducted by Thomas Marshall (1987, 1989) who examined change in public opinion caused by various decisions. I consider Marshall's methodology to be far superior to that of Mishler and Sheehan, since Marshall did compare actual cases with the results of public opinion polls on those particular decisions.

In this study I examine recent decisions. Only twenty of Marshall's 126 decisions examined occurred after 1980. To compare Supreme Court decisions with mass and elite opinion, one must take into account that the Supreme Court is composed of individuals during a particular time period. Each justice comes to the Court with his or her own set of beliefs on how the decision making process of the court should operate (Kluger, 1975; Woodward and Armstrong, 1979). Therefore, researchers should attempt, as I do here, to keep their study of the Court to a particular time period to see how its decision-making process operated while certain justices were on the bench. The results from the cases decided during the 1970s cannot help us in our attempt to discern the Court's decision-making process of the 1990s. Many of the justices who were on the Court in the 1970s are no longer on the bench. The Supreme Court of the past is not the same Supreme Court of the present.

The decisions studied by Marshall did not concentrate on any particular area of the law. Every area of the law deserves separate attention, at least for comparison purposes. As mentioned earlier, criminal procedure cases are more easily understood than other areas of the law. Also, it is easier in this area for the public at large to develop opinions. As Schattschneider (1960) maintained, decisions change when the number of participants grows. This is not to argue that the Supreme Court necessarily takes public opinion into account when rendering decisions. However, the evidence points to the fact that the Supreme Court would hardly ignore a vocal public, whether it be mass or elite (Kluger, 1975; also see Court delaying miscegenation case for fear of public reprisals). Each area of the law should be considered separately, since the public's influence on the Court will depend on the vigor of its opinions in that area. My study focuses, then, on the area of criminal procedure.

RESEARCH DESIGN

To study mass and elite opinion, I conducted a survey on attitudes toward criminal justice procedures as determined by the United States Supreme Court. Though one would not normally expect the mass public to be as knowledgeable as the elites in issues of civic knowledge, with rising crime rates and media reporting since the 1960s, the public has had an incentive and opportunity to become knowledgeable. In this scenario, the opinions of the mass public are as important in policy making decisions as the elites. In order to discern to what extent the mass public and legal elite disagree with major Supreme Court decisions, I administered two parallel national opinion surveys.

I conducted a telephone survey of adults from across the continental United States from December 26, 1994, to January 16, 1995. The survey asked about opinions regarding civil liberties in the area of criminal procedure. The survey questioned respondents concerning their opinions regarding the holdings of recent Supreme Court decisions, root causes of crime, race and crime, sources of information, personal experiences with crime, as well as other matters and independent variables of interest. Random digit dialing was used to assure that a proper cross-section of the population would be guaranteed. At least four return phone calls were made to the respondents to obtain a sufficiently high response rate. Out of 1,241 eligible respondents, 811 completed their interviews, for a completion rate of 65.3% (see Appendix 4 at the end of this volume for more details regarding the survey).

During the same time period, I mailed to a cross-section of lawyers across the United States a comparable questionnaire (see the end of Appendix 4 for details on how the list of lawyers was obtained). All of the questions appearing on the mail questionnaire to lawyers were asked, using identical wording, in the phone survey of the mass public (see Appendices 1 and 2). Out of 931 possible respondents, 410 lawyers (45%) mailed back their completed questionnaires. A more detailed description of the methodology is provided in Appendix 4.

The critical part of the survey consisted of sixteen questions drawn from past Supreme Court decisions which have determined the current law. The questions provide measures of the main dependant variable involving attitudes toward criminal procedures. Also included were questions dealing with general political knowledge, specific legal knowledge, sources of information, and opinions regarding crime and the causes of crime, race, and law enforcement. Based on past studies and theoretical considerations, it is possible that all these variables plus other processes represented by demographic characteristics affect individuals' opinions regarding civil liberties.

I examine specific areas of criminal procedure, including the areas of search and seizure and right to counsel, as will be seen later. A more detailed review of the law is provided in Appendix 3. The relevant court cases are summarized so as to present the current state of the law in the area of criminal procedure included in the survey (see LaFave and Israel, 1992). Each question in the survey represents the facts or holding of a recent Supreme Court decision (see Appendices 1 and 2 for the actual wording of the surveys). Interestingly, the number of respondents answering "don't know" and "no answer" was quite small. This is in line with the notion that crime and criminal procedure are quite salient issues, and that the opinions respondents revealed in the survey were well-established and stable.

While other areas of criminal procedure, such as plea bargaining and jury trials, are also worth looking at, by examining the areas discussed in Chapter 2, I believe one can adequately answer the research question.

SUMMARY OF CHAPTERS

Chapter 2 will review the current state of the law for the issues that I have examined in this study, including search warrants, in relation to the search of the person, cars, and boats. The right to counsel is also studied. The review of the current state of the law should give the reader the necessary legal background to understand the two sides to each issue presented in the survey measures.

Chapter 3 examines basic differences in opinion between the mass public and legal elite for sixteen issues of criminal justice recently decided in the United States. The chapter also investigates differences within the mass public for different levels of knowledge and education. The results of factor analysis performed on the measures of criminal justice attitudes for both the surveys of the mass public and legal elite, as well as for respondents with different levels of knowledge and education, are examined in exploring differences and similarities in structure. Based on these results, scales are developed to improve the measurement of the dependent variables. The scales measure mass public and legal elite support for civil liberties, as well as their agreement with Supreme Court decisions. Chapter 3 resolves the question regarding what effects a legal education versus traditional education and political knowledge has upon one's opinion regarding issues of civil liberties in the area of criminal justice. The results reveal that though lawyers are more civil libertarian than nonlawyers, the differences are not as great as one might expect. In other words, the mass public is not as civil libertarian as members of the legal profession, yet its opinions do not seem to rise to the level of intolerance.

Chapter 4 examines possible explanations for differences in opinion. It also covers other basic differences in opinion between the mass public, legal elite, as well as opinions within the mass public, for different levels of education and knowledge. This chapter provides basic results for additional independent variables, including beliefs regarding the root causes of crime (e.g., lack of income equality, lack of economic opportunities for the poor and for members of minority groups, the media's emphasis on the rights of the accused and not on the rights of the victim), race and crime (i.e., blacks and the death penalty, blacks and the criminal court system), courts and crime (i.e., beliefs regarding harshness of the criminal justice system), respect for police, fear of crime, the worst crime one suffered, the role of the courts, confidence in the courts, sources of information, hours of television viewing, as well as various demographic variables (e.g., race, community type, gender, income, age, region, marital status). This chapter presents the basic demographic differences between the mass public and legal elite which can lead to differences in opinion regarding issues of civil liberties.

Chapter 5 reports the bivariate results based on the survey of the mass public. The means that all the categories of independent variables are estimated on the scales developed in Chapter 3. Multiple regression analysis is then used for the mass sample, as well as for the differing categories of knowledge and education within the mass public to examine multivariate and possible interaction effects. This chapter presents possible explanations for the differences in opinion caused by various levels of education, knowledge, and other demographic variables.

Chapter 6 reports the parallel bivariate and mulitivariate results for the survey of the legal elite. The chapter also reports differences in opinion within the legal profession caused by specialty, region, and other demographic variables.

In the concluding chapter, I recap the findings and discuss the future of criminal procedure. Questions asked are: Do reasons exist why the public's opinion, as opposed to the elite's or the Court's, should matter more in the area of criminal procedure than in other areas of the law? Is it worthwhile for the legal elite to fulfill its role as educators of society? Do the factors which lead the mass public to be less civil libertarian than lawyers lend themselves to change? Do United States Supreme Court decisions have a greater effect on the opinions of lawyers than the mass public? Has the Supreme Court's recent turn to the Right led lawyers and the more knowledgeable and educated to follow suit?

It is hoped that the analysis of the surveys which I have conducted will help educators, whether in the academy or the media, to understand what causes one to appreciate the importance of protecting civil liberties, even for those whom one may personally dislike.

In Chapter 2 an overview of recent United States Supreme Court decisions relevant to the questions included in the survey is presented. This provides basic information about the law regarding criminal justice procedures. This information provides the bases for considering why certain groups might be more or less civil libertarian than others depending upon the nature of the cases and points of law.

Current State of Law

INTRODUCTION: THE RIGHT TO PRIVACY VERSUS THE PREVENTION OF CRIME

The right of citizens to be free from government intrusion has long been a valued right in the United States. At the American founding itself, many were worried about governmental intrusion during criminal and other investigations. Twelve of the twenty-three rights set aside for individuals vis-à-vis their government within the Bill of Rights concern the area known as criminal procedure. The amendments that deal with criminal procedure are the fourth, fifth, sixth, and eighth amendments. Originally, these amendments were only applied to the federal government. However, in the 1960s, the Supreme Court began applying these same standards to the states as well, through the fourteenth amendment.

The fourth amendment deals with unreasonable searches and seizures; the fifth guarantees the right to a grand jury indictment, the privilege against self-incrimination at trial, as well as the guarantee against double jeopardy; the sixth guarantees a criminal defendant the right to counsel, a speedy and public trial with an impartial jury, and a right to confront opposing witnesses. A defendant also has protection against excessive bail and the right to a grand jury indictment in felony cases, though these last two rights have not been extended to state actions.

The extension of these rights, and their consequences throughout American culture, has led to a national debate concerning the value and need for these rights. How do Americans in the 1990s feel about government surveillance, searches, and other criminal justice procedures? To what extent do Americans hold different opinions and what explains these differences? What are the differences in opinion between the mass public and members of the more educated elite? And, specifically, what are the differences in opinion between lawyers and nonlawyers.

Of late, with the rise of antigovernment paramilitary groups and the terrorist acts they have perpetrated, the criminal procedure area of the Bill of Rights has again become salient. There has been much debate concerning the freedom from unwarranted government intrusion. For example, in recent public discourse, many believe that the federal government has been crossing the line between the need to enter private property under the guise of law enforcement and blatant governmental intrusion. This debate occurred in the mid-1990s during the Ruby Ridge and antiterrorism hearings on Capitol Hill. Conservatives and civil libertarians alike seem to believe that the government needs to respect private property and the privacy of the individual. However, in sharp contrast, the public also believes that the government needs to do more to protect its citizens from criminal activity. For example, if members of the public were asked whether or not the government can search a person's property from the air without a search warrant, the above-mentioned beliefs would be in conflict. For purposes of cracking down on crime, one might favor this procedure; however, to allow the government to conduct this activity would interfere with a person's privacy. Thus the public's desire for the government to put an end to crime, and its wish for the government to respect people's privacy can come into conflict.

This chapter provides some basic legal background, by reviewing some of the cases concerning the criminal procedures covered in the survey study. The chapter also attempts to clarify the balancing act that judges, as well as members of the public, must make when formulating opinions concerning issues of criminal justice. A general tension exists between the need to control crime by giving police greater discretion in apprehending criminals, and guaranteeing criminal defendants protections from unreasonable police intrusion.

The chapter is divided into four sections, which describe the four different types of criminal procedure cases that are described, and replicate the different types of issues asked about by the survey questions.

The first section describes cases that deal with search and seizure issues. These arise when the police attempt to garner enough evidence, so as to have probable cause to arrest a suspect. Specifically, the section discusses when the need for a search warrant is waived. The second group of cases deals with post-detainment situations, which arise after the police have obtained enough evidence to have the defendant arrested. This includes issues pertaining to the right to counsel. Generally, if the defendant confesses to a crime without being aware of the right to speak to a lawyer, or through outright coercion without a lawyer being present, the confession can be nullified. The third group of cases deals with moral dilemmas that arise within criminal procedure. The two issues examined in this section, and also in the survey, concern the police's use of trickery while fighting crime, as well as whether or not to allow a mentally ill individual to waive the right to counsel. The last set of cases deals with the death penalty for both murderers and rapists. These issues are distinguishable from the others because of their greater saliency. These four areas of criminal procedure were chosen, since they represent an important cross-section of cases that the court deals with in the area of criminal procedure. Therefore, the survey, which covers these issues, should provide evidence revealing the level of civil libertarian support, as well as support for United States Supreme Court decisions, among the mass public and legal elites.

SEARCH AND SEIZURE ISSUES

Searches of Public Property

When a defendant is arrested based upon evidence uncovered in a search, the defendant will usually request a suppression hearing, where there will be an attempt to prove that the search, which resulted in the discovery of the evidence which caused the arrest, was made in violation of the fourth amendment. The fourth amendment states: "The right of the people to be secure in their persons, houses, papers, and effects, against unreasonable searches and seizures, shall not be violated, and no warrants shall issue, but upon probable cause, supported by oath or affirmation, and particularly describing the place to be searched, and the persons or things to be searched." If the defendant is successful at proving the case against the state, the evidence obtained in the search will be deemed inadmissable at trial.

One of the defenses the government might raise is that due to the facts of the case, a warrant was not necessary. The case of *Katz v. U.S.*, decided in 1967, set the standard for when one is entitled to fourth amendment protection. The places covered by the fourth amendment both expanded and contracted in the 1960s. Until *Katz v. U.S.*, the Supreme Court generally limited the scope of the fourth amendment to the private property of the defendant. In other words, the Court used an objective test to determine privacy. In *Katz*, this was changed. The defendant in *Katz* was a bookie who conducted his business from a public telephone booth. Subjectively, Katz believed the telephone booth to be his private office. In other words, Katz had a subjective expectation of privacy, even though he did not own the telephone booth. In this landmark case, the Supreme Court ruled that the fourth amendment protects people rather than places. In other words, if a person does not attempt to claim as private items located within property owned by the defendant, fourth amendment protection will not be applicable to the items. However, if a person attempts to declare an area private, even if he does not own that particular area, and even if that particular area is located within public property, fourth amendment protection can be applicable. Further, due to the holding of *Katz*, it is possible for the police in fact actually to trespass upon a person's property, yet not violate the fourth amendment. This would occur when an individual has private property, yet a reasonable person would not believe there can exist a reasonable expectation of privacy.

Searches of Private Property

The fact pattern alluded to in the *Katz* case emerged in *U.S. v. Dunn* (1987). In *Dunn*, the Supreme Court ruled that federal agents did not violate the defendant's fourth amendment rights when they entered his 190-acre ranch, without a warrant, to search for drugs. Their reasoning was that the area searched was around sixty yards from the actual house. Since it was possible to peer at the searched area from the open fields within the defendant's property, the Court ruled that there could be no subjective right to privacy. In other words, the Court decided that even though the defendant had an actual subjective expectation of privacy, he did not have an expectation "that society is prepared to recognize as reasonable." In sum, ownership of the property in question does not determine whether or not one has a right to privacy.

In *Oliver v. U.S.* (1984), the Court ruled that open fields which are located beyond the curtilage of a home are not protected by the fourth amendment. The Court reasoned that an individual cannot have a reasonable expectation of privacy in regard to open fields. They stated that open fields should not be protected since there they "do not provide the setting for those intimate activities that the amendment is intended to shelter form government surveillance." This occurred despite that in *Oliver*, the defendant placed "no trespassing" signs around his farm and kept the gate to his farm locked at all times. Nonetheless, the Court ruled that no matter what actions might be taken by the owner of the property, no right to privacy exists.

The Court continued to contract the rights of property owners in *Dow Chemical Co. v. U.S.* (1986). In a narrow 5-4 decision, the Court ruled that it was not unconstitutional for the government to use a sophisticated aerial camera to photograph the defendant's private property. This was so, even though they could not have actually entered from the ground. The dissent argued, that as technology becomes more and more sophisticated, citizens may gradually lose all rights to privacy.

The right to privacy was further restricted in *California v. Ciraolo* (1986), in which the Court ruled that the police can search, without a warrant, any portion of the defendants property from the air, as long as the airplane is in public airspace, and the police can see the suspected criminal activity with the naked eye. The Court reasoned that even though the defendant built a ten-foot wall around his backyard, in an attempt to shield it from outsiders, the defendant's growing marijuana in his backyard was not a privacy right "society is prepared to honor." Again, the dissent disagreed strongly, arguing that as a result of the ruling, "families can expect to be free of official surveillance only when they retreat behind the walls of their homes."

The Court dealt with similar issues in *California v. Greenwood* (1988), where it ruled that the defendant has no right to privacy regarding trash placed outside of the defendant's property. The Court reasoned that the defendant did not have an objectively reasonable belief of privacy, since the trash is deemed abandoned. Also, even if a person has a subjective belief that the trash will not be touched or examined by others, it is not an objectively reasonable belief.

The dissent strongly disagreed with this assessment, arguing that "most of us would be incensed to discover a meddler—whether a neighbor, reporter, or detective—scrutinizing our sealed trash containers to discover some detail of our personal lives." The dissent reasoned that if the possibility of a snoop in one's garbage negates the right to privacy via the garbage, then "the possibility of a burglary (should) negate an expectation of privacy in the home."

Searches of Automobiles

Similar questions have arisen regarding automobiles. The rationale behind many of the decisions regarding automobiles, is, as the court in *California v. Carney* (1985) stated, that a person has a lesser expectation of privacy regarding an automobile than regarding a home. There are also practical reasons as to why lesser privacy rights should exist regarding an automobile. The Court has pointed out that the contents of an automobile, as well as the automobile itself, can be disposed of more quickly and easily, than the contents of a house or other stationary objects. Examples of the need to suspend ordinary rules of warrants date back to the 1925 case of *Carroll v. U.S.*, in which the Court decided that "exigent circumstances" negated the need for a warrant, since there was a fear that the car would be driven to an area not within the jurisdiction. Another case in which an exception to the general rule regarding warrants occurred was *New York v. Belton* (1981), in which the court ruled that the passenger compartment of the car may be searched "incident to the arrest" of either the passenger or the driver of the automobile.

The Court furthered its distinction between houses and cars in *Chambers v. Maroney* (1970), in which the Court validated a warrantless police search of an impounded automobile, seized in hot pursuit, from a suspected bank robber. The Court reasoned, that since the police would have been allowed to search the automobile immediately at the time they detained the suspect, the police should not have to wait for a warrant now that it was impounded.

These same broad powers, however, are not given to the police when they are dealing with homes or apartments. In *Vale v. Louisiana* (1971), the Court stated that the police may stand guard at the home of a suspected criminal, to assure that relatives or partners do not come to destroy evidence. However a "sweep" of the premises would not be permitted without a warrant.

In contrast, in the case of *Coolidge v. N.H.* (1971), the Court ruled that when the police could have obtained a warrant before stopping a vehicle, and did not, evidence obtained through a warrantless search, conducted while the vehicle is impounded, will not be admissible in court. The Court distinguished this case from the *Chambers* case, by noting that the facts of *Chambers* indicated that the police could not have procured a warrant before apprehending the suspect. This was not the case in *Coolidge*, where the police had been tracking the suspect for two weeks, and had more than ample time to obtain a warrant. The Court has also upheld exceptions to the warrant rule regarding searches of closed containers in the case of *U.S. v. Ross* (1982). The Court ruled that it is permissible for the police to conduct a warrantless search of a vehicle, and all closed containers that can reasonably be holding or concealing contraband, as long as there is probable cause to believe that contraband is in the vehicle, and there was probable cause to stop the vehicle. In other words, the police are allowed to search all packages within the automobile that can possibly contain an illegal substance. The dissent strongly disagreed with the majority's logic, pointing out, in their opinion, two major fallacies in the logic of the opinion. First, though a car can be easily moved, the police can impound the closed container or the car itself and wait until they have obtained a warrant to open the container. Hence, there is no need to open closed containers without a warrant. Second, the items within the closed container are not in "plain view" of the officer, and therefore should not be subject to a lower level of fourth amendment protection.

In *South Dakota v. Opperman* (1976) and *Colorado v. Bertine* (1987), the Supreme Court expanded the situations in which police may search closed containers in a vehicle when it is impounded. According to the holdings of these cases, police have authority to conduct a warrantless search of the entire vehicle, including the contents of closed containers located within the vehicle. In *Opperman*, the Court ruled that a search of all contents of a vehicle during a routine inventory search, once the car has been impounded, is justified, since, among other possible explanations, the police are protected in this way against claims concerning lost or stolen property. The dissent argued that with or without a warrant, such searches are unconstitutional. Their rationale in the 5-4 decision was that one would need "probable cause" to obtain a warrant, and there is no probable cause to search a vehicle merely to conduct an inventory.

In *Bertine*, the Court extended searches of impounded vehicles to the closed containers located within the vehicles. The logic of the Court was the same as it was in *Opperman*. These searches are needed to protect police from false claims of theft, and to protect the safety of police officers. Without such inventory searches, owners of impounded vehicles might claim to have had expensive items in the vehicle, and request repayment from the police department. In addition, the search is necessary due to the possibility of explosive material which might be stored in the vehicle. This decision was qualified by the case of *Florida v. Wells* (1990), in which the Court ruled that police cannot use an inventory search as a ruse "for a general rummaging in order to discover incriminating evidence." The judges stated that for an inventory search to be constitutional, there must be "standardized criteria" governing the search, without which such searches are unconstitutional.

In sum, a majority of justices on the Supreme Court have been willing to allow the police to search closed containers in a car during a routine traffic stop as long as an officer has a reasonable suspicion to believe that illegal items are located within the vehicle. The police do not need probable cause, but merely reasonable suspicion.

Frisks and Stops

The Supreme Court has long held (*Terry v. Ohio*, 1968) that it is permissible to "stop and frisk" an individual who seems suspicious. The stop and frisk can occur, despite the lack of probable cause for an actual arrest or search. The Court did state that the stop and "pat down" of the defendant had to be "reasonable" under the circumstances, though actual probable cause is not required. The rationale of the Court was that "where a police officer observes unusual conduct which leads him reasonably to conclude in light of his experiences, that criminal activity may be afoot and that the persons with whom he is dealing may be armed and dangerous . . . he is entitled for the protection of himself and others in the area to conduct a carefully limited search of the outer clothing of such persons in attempt to discover weapons which might be used to assault him." Generally, all stop and frisks by police officers who do not have probable cause for the frisk, and therefore do not and cannot obtain a warrant, are referred to as "Terry" stops.

In *Adams v. Williams* (1972), the Court extended the Terry stop to include stop and frisks based on tips by trusted informants, rather than suspicions based upon actual sightings by the officer. This case also extended the Terry stop to include vehicles. In addition, in *Pennsylvania v. Mimms* (1977), the Court ruled that the driver in the automobile subject to the Terry stop can be asked to leave the vehicle, and at that point is subject to the frisk. The dissent in *Adams* disagreed strongly, arguing that it was quite easy for a police officer to "invent" an informant, so as to have his "reasonable suspicion" for a Terry stop. Using this decision, they reasoned, police officers can now stop and frisk all suspects they wish.

Recently, the court has expanded its definition of what amount of suspicion is sufficient to warrant a Terry stop. For example, in *U.S. v. Sokolow* (1989), the Court ruled that if a person performs a number of acts which each on their own appear innocent, yet taken together appear potentially criminal, a Terry stop is permissible. In *Sokolow*, the potential defendant paid for a plane ticket in cash, completed a round trip between cities known for illicit drugs, had not checked in any of his luggage, had stayed forty-eight hours or less in each of the cities, and appeared nervous during the trip. The dissent noted that each of these events might have had an innocent cause on their own. Again, they argued that the Court was putting too much discretion in the hands of the police. Innocent citizens, according to the general rule laid down by the majority, could be stopped at the whim of police officers, since no "objective" justification need exist.

Drug Trafficking

The issue of what is a stop and what is an arrest is important, as mentioned, in determining whether or not there exists a necessity for probable cause. If the stop is for a lengthy time period and intrusive in nature, the stop will be deemed an arrest, and will necessitate probable cause. Generally, the courts have ruled that the length of time permissible for a stop must be reasonable, in light of the reason for the stop.

However, in the case of *U.S. v. Sharpe* (1985), in which a police officer forced the defendant to wait for around twenty minutes until his partner arrived after they were separated during a high-speed chase, the Court stated that the nature of the stop must be reasonable in light of "the law enforcement needs of the officers who are performing the search." In other words, the Court's decision in *Sharpe* sets a new precedent for the meaning of "reasonableness." The reasonableness of the duration and intrusiveness of the stop is set by its reasonableness to the police, as opposed to its reasonableness to the suspect.

An example of a case in which this logic played out was in an area of the law which has received attention in the media and on the Court docket: drug trafficking. In the case of *U.S. v. Montoya de Hernandez* (1985), the Court ruled that it was permissible to detain a suspected drug smuggler for twenty-seven hours, even though agents had not yet found drugs in her rectum, nor had they officially arrested her. In addition, the Court ruled that it was constitutional for the defendant to be given a choice of undergoing an X-ray examination or being detained until producing a bowel movement. All this was ruled constitutional, and included within the Terry stop, even though the agents involved did not seek a court order until twenty-four hours after the scenario had begun, at which point the Court gave permission for the agents to conduct a rectal examination to search for the drugs. The rationale of the Court was that the "defendant's detention was long, uncomfortable, indeed, humiliating; but both its length and its discomfort resulted only from the method by which she chose to smuggle illicit drugs into this country." Further, the Court seemed to shift the burden of proof to the defendant, by declaring that "the detention of a suspected alimentary canal smuggler at the border is analogous to the detention of a suspected tuberculosis carrier at the border: both are detained until their bodily processes dispel the suspicion that they will introduce a harmful agent into this country."

The dissent in the case categorized the Court's decision as a "disgusting and saddening episode" in the history of the Court. They argued that "the law of nature" does not support requiring "people to excrete on command." Their logic was that it is not unrealistic "to predict that an innocent traveler, locked away in incommunicado detention in unfamiliar surroundings in a foreign land, might well be so frightened and exhausted as to be unable so to cooperate with the authorities." In sum, the majority in *Montoya de Hernandez* took the opinion that the law should hold the needs of the police in highest regard, while the dissent wanted the Court to highlight the needs of the suspect.

Ships

Another salient issue of late, involving warrantless searches, has been that of illegal immigration and the protection of U.S. borders. The Court has long held that different rules regarding search warrants exist at the nations borders. For example in *Almeida-Sanchez v. U.S.* (1973), the Court stated that "travelers may be stopped in crossing an international boundary because of national self protection reasonably requiring one entering the country to identify himself as entitled to come in, and his belongings as effects which may be lawfully brought in." In other words, searches of persons and vehicles entering the United States may be searched, even with absolutely no reason for suspicion of wrongdoing.

In the case of *U.S. v. Villamonte-Marquez* (1983), the Supreme Court ruled that the authorities may board any vessel with "ready access to the open sea" to inspect any documents on board. This can occur, even though there is no probable cause to believe that contraband is aboard the ship. No warrant is necessary for this type of search. The Court's rationale is that there is a national interest in protecting our nation's borders: therefore, the officers need not have any suspicion of wrongdoing. The court cited *U.S. v. Martinez-Fuerte* (1976), wherein the Court decided that fixed checkpoints set up within the United States border are legal, as long as all automobiles are stopped. In addition, the court ruled that directing a vehicle to a second location, where the occupants would be further questioned, may be made "largely on the basis of apparent Mexican ancestry."

The court has expanded the realm of cases that fall under these exceptions to the warrant requirement to include nonborder cases as well. In the case of *Michigan Department of Police v. Sitz* (1990), the Court ruled that the police may randomly stop all drivers at sobriety checkpoints, to check for drunk drivers. The Court reasoned that the intrusion to the drivers was slight, compared to the societal interest in keeping the roads clear of drunken drivers. The dissenting judges disagreed with the logic of the majority on several points. First, they disagreed with the majority's assertion that stopping motorists late at night at sobriety checkpoints is not a great intrusion; further, they believed that less intrusive means were available for the police in apprehending drunk drivers, such as observing inexplicable swerves, or other erratic driving.

In contrast, the Court in *Delaware v. Prouse* (1979) held that the police may not stop cars at random to check for license and registration. If such a stop were to occur, all evidence obtained during the course of the stop would be excluded from evidence. However, even in said circumstance, the Court implied that such a stop would be constitutionally permissible if all cars, as opposed to every third or fourth, would be stopped. Their reasoning was that this would take away undue police discretion. The dissent argued that such random stops in which every few cars are stopped for license and registration should be permitted, since the state has a vested interest in disallowing unlicensed drivers on their roads. This is an extremely important interest, they contended, since unlicenced drivers were more likely than licensed drivers to be involved in driving accidents.

In sum, the Supreme Court gives greater discretion to the police at the border, though it would also allow police to stop all cars at fixed checkpoints to check for drunk drivers, and possibly license and registration, as well. The only stop the Court has disallowed is the stopping of every few cars on non-border roads, since that would give the police too much discretion.

Dogs Sniffing for Drugs—Plain Odor

Another area in which the Court has dealt with the need for a warrantless search is the area of "plain odor." In *U.S. v. Place* (1983), the Court extended the notion of "plain view" to "plain odor." As mentioned earlier, the plain view doctrine states that when the police standing in public property see contraband within an individual's private property, they can enter the dwelling to seize the contraband. In *Place*, the Supreme Court held that dogs can be used to "sniff test" luggage in order to discern whether or not drugs are in the luggage.

The interesting question this case highlights is the fact that the individual was not being subjected to a Terry stop, rather, the luggage was the subject of the stop. In *Place*, the individual refused to have his bags sniffed by police dogs. After the refusal, the police seized the bags, and subsequently conducted the sniff test and found the contraband. The philosophy of the Court, stated rather broadly, is that "when an officer's observations lead him reasonably to believe that a traveler is carrying luggage that contains narcotics, the principles of Terry and its progeny would permit the officer to detain the luggage briefly to investigate the circumstances that aroused his suspicion, provided that the investigative detention is properly limited in scope." Concurring judges in *Place* disagreed with the notion of setting new boundaries to Terry stops, arguing that the police should not have the authority seize items not in the defendants possession, during a Terry stop, without the presence of probable cause.

POST-DETAINMENT SITUATIONS

Charging the Defendant

After a suspect has been detained by police officers, who had conducted a warrantless search, an immediate postarrest hearing must take place. A question has been raised regarding the amount of time the police may detain a criminal suspect without charging the accused with a specific crime. In the case of *County of Riverside v. McLaughlin* (1991), the Supreme Court ruled that barring unusual circumstances a determination must be made within 48 hours to determine whether or not there is the necessary probable cause to hold the suspect in custody. However, the Court ruled that there is no absolute 48 hour rule. In other words, it is constitutionally permissible to hold a defendant more than 48-hours as long as the state can prove that a more immediate hearing was not possible.

Impeaching Witnesses

Generally, evidence obtained illegally cannot be used by the prosecution in making its case against the defendant. However, there are circumstances in which the Court has made exceptions to the general rule.

In *Harris v. New York* (1971), the Supreme Court allowed illegally obtained evidence to impeach statements made by the defendant during his direct testimony. In *U.S. v. Havens* (1980), this logic was extended to statements made by the defendant during cross-examination. The rationale of the Court's decision is that "truth is the fundamental goal of our legal system." The Court further explains that "when defendants testify, they must testify truthfully or suffer the consequences." The dissent in *Havens* disagreed with the majority, on the grounds that this would force many defendants into giving up their right to testify on their own behalf. Their reasoning as to why illegally obtained evidence should not be allowed to impeach the defendant during cross-examination was that this would pass "control of the exception (for admitting illegally obtained evidence) to the government, since the prosecutor can lay the predicate for admitting otherwise suppressible evidence with his own questioning." This would, of course, allow "even the moderately talented prosecutor to 'work in'" the illegally obtained evidence on cross examination.

However, in a narrow 5-4 decision, in *James v. Illinois* (1990), the Supreme Court ruled that illegally obtained evidence could not be used in an attempt to impeach the testimony of any witness other than the defendant. They reasoned that if the defendant's witnesses could be impeached by illegally obtained evidence, his ability to present his defense would be in jeopardy. Naturally, there would be a chilling effect on the defendant calling any witnesses, since they could be impeached by any and all evidence, obtained through legal or illegal means. The dissent strongly argued that this Court decision would lead to false testimony being introduced. The dissent stated that the opinion of the Court will "grant the defense side in a criminal case broad immunity to introduce whatever false testimony it can produce from the mouth of a friendly witness."

Right to Counsel

In *Miranda v. Arizona* (1966), the Court established numerous rights for defendants who have been taken into custody. However, the case also stated that "an express statement that the individual is willing to make a statement and does not want an attorney followed closely by a statement could constitute a waiver." What constituted such a waiver, whether express or implied, has been the subject of numerous subsequent Court cases.

In *Brewer v. Williams* (1977), the Supreme Court ruled that once a defendant has asked to speak to a lawyer, a voluntary admission without an unequivocal renunciation of the right to speak to a lawyer will be deemed inadmissible. In other words, a voluntary admission of a crime which occurs after a suspect asks for a lawyer and the lawyer is not present is inadmissable in court. In addition, according to the holding of *Brewer*, the burden of proof is on the prosecution to show that the defendant understood that he or she has a right to remain silent and intended to abandon this right. *Miranda* stated that "if the interrogation continues without the presence of an attorney and a statement is taken, a heavy burden rests on the government to demonstrate that the defendant knowingly and intelligently waived his privilege against self-incrimination and his right to retained or appointed counsel."

The *Miranda* decision also held that "a valid waiver will not be presumed simply from the silence of the accused after warnings are given or simply from the fact that a confession was in fact obtained." Interestingly, however, the courts have also ruled that the waiver need not be verbal. For example, some courts have stated that a nod of the head by a suspect can constitute both an understanding and a waiver of one's right to counsel.

Another problem in interpreting whether or not one has waived one's Miranda rights occurs when one sends conflicting messages through actions and words. For example, in the case of *North Carolina v. Butler* (1979), the suspect stated that he was waiving his right to counsel, but refused to sign a waiver. In this case the Court ruled that this verbal waiver was enough proof that the suspect was waiving his right to counsel. As the Court noted, at times a waiver "can be inferred from the actions and words of the person interrogated." The dissent strongly objected to the majority allowing such a waiver. They argued that without an unequivocal waiver, courts will find a defendant's waiver of his Miranda rights when there is none.

Another issue that has arisen in post-*Miranda* cases is the question of when the right to counsel takes hold. In *Miranda*, the Court stated that this right to counsel only takes hold during custodial interrogation. Specifically, the Court stated that "by custodial we mean questioning initiated by law enforcement officers after a person has been taken into custody or otherwise deprived of his freedom of action in any significant way." The Supreme Court clarified what is meant by a custodial interrogation in the case of *Beckwith v. U.S.* (1976). In *Beckwith*, the Court ruled that the mere fact an investigation has already "focused" on a suspect does not cause the situation to rise to the level of one being in "custody," and does not trigger the need for the Miranda warnings to be read to the defendant.

A case in which these considerations come into conflict was *Illinois v. Perkins* (1990). In *Perkins*, the government placed undercover agents within the defendant's cell prior to his being indicted, and these agents elicited an admission from the defendant who, when admitting to the crime, was unaware that the people he was speaking with were government agents. Therefore, unlike the *Brewer* case, there was no possibility of governmental intimidation, and there was no "custodial interrogation."

In the more recently decided case of *Stansbury v. California* (1994), the Court explained that when examining whether or not a custodial situation exists, the Court should look into the mind of the defendant, as opposed to the officer; and "an officer's subjective and undisclosed view concerning whether the person being interrogated is a suspect is irrelevant to the assessment whether the person is in custody." The Court further explained that "an officer's views concerning the nature of an interrogation, or beliefs concerning the potential culpability of the individual being questioned, may be one among many factors that bear upon the assessment whether that individual was in custody, but only if the officer's views or beliefs were somehow manifested to the individual under interrogation and would have affected how a reasonable person in that position would perceive his or her freedom to leave."

Along these lines, the court in *Oregon v. Mathiason* (1977) stated that if a defendant gives a voluntary confession, after coming voluntarily to the police station, he is normally not in custody, and need not be given the Miranda rights. In sum, whether or not the defendant is in custody and needs be read his Miranda rights turns on whether or not the defendant reasonably believes himself to be in custody. What the officers believe subjectively, but nonverbally, is irrelevant. Thus, the courts take the mind-set of the defendant quite seriously in determining whether or not a custodial interrogation has triggered the need for Miranda warnings.

MORAL ISSUES

Mental Illness

As mentioned in the previous section, whether or not a waiver of one's Miranda warnings has taken place has become the source of much debate in the courts. An interesting dilemma arose in a recent case where the waiver of Miranda rights was not caused by police coercion, rather, the waiver was caused by the irrational behavior of the defendant.

In *Colorado v. Connelly* (1986), the Court ruled that a mentally ill defendant who, due to his illness, confesses to a crime after waiving the Miranda rights, cannot use the illness as a ground to suppress the confession. In other words, police coercion rather than the mental state of the defendant is what determines whether or not a valid waiver of constitutionally valid rights occurred. The Court's rationale was that "Miranda protects defendants against government coercion leading them to surrender rights protected by the fifth amendment; it goes no further than that." Specifically, the Court stated that the defendant's "perception of coercion flowing from the 'voice of god,' however important or significant such a perception may be in other disciplines, is a matter to which the United States Constitution does not speak." The logic of the Court was that "coercive police activity is a necessary predicate to the finding that a confession is not 'voluntary' within the meaning of the due process clause of the fourteenth amendment."

In a blistering opinion, the dissent argued that if one were to look at the "the totality of the circumstances," one would discern that neither the confession nor the waiver of the Miranda rights were reliable "beyond a reasonable doubt."

This concept came under public scrutiny during the trial of the "Long Island gunman," Colin Ferguson, in which, due to the current logic of the Supreme Court, Ferguson was allowed to waive his right to counsel. This was the case, even though he may not have been sane enough to understand the implications of his action.

In sum, under current Supreme Court precedent, the Court will not take into consideration any wrongdoing, in convincing the defendant to confess and waive Miranda rights, by members of the public who are not police officers or government agents. The Court will also not take into consideration any outside factors, other than actual police coercion, that might have caused the defendant to waive the right to counsel. Hence, mental illness or any other defendant disability that impairs a defendant's capacity to make a rational decision, absence any police coercion, is no defense. Only "police coercion" is a valid defense in arguing that a confession is not voluntary.

Police Trickery

As the Supreme Court has more and more been deciding cases in favor law enforcement, the holdings of some of the Court's recent decisions suggest that it has been sanctioning actual police trickery.

Over time, the Supreme Court has allowed the police to use various forms of trickery to elicit an admission or to obtain evidence to prove a defendant's guilt. The case which shocked many Court observers, as well as a minority of the Supreme Court, was *Moran v. Burbine* (1986), in which the Court ruled that a defendant's admission of a crime was admissible even though the officers did not inform the defendant that his sister had retained a lawyer on his behalf, and was trying to reach him. In a quite sweeping and inclusive statement, the Court argued that "events occurring outside of the presence of the suspect and entirely unknown to him surely can have no bearing on the capacity to comprehend and knowingly relinquish a constitutional right." Regarding the importance of the police dealing in an honest manner with the defendant, the Court argued that the information "would have been useful to the defendant; perhaps even it might have affected his decision to confess. But we have never read the Constitution to require that the police supply a suspect with a flow of information to help him calibrate his self interest in deciding whether to speak or stand by his rights." Furthermore, the Court seemingly condoned actual police trickery by stating that "even deliberate deception of the attorney could not possibly affect a suspect's decision to waive his Miranda rights unless he (the defendant) were at least aware of the incident." The only sort of deception which could pose constitutional problems for the police would occur if "it deprives a defendant of knowledge essential to his ability to understand the nature of his rights and the consequences of abandoning them."

The dissent had an entirely different view of what *Miranda* required. Rather than looking at *Miranda* as a series of technical requirements, they viewed *Miranda* as a new way for the police to conduct their affairs. They argued that "Miranda clearly condemns threats or trickery that cause a suspect to make an unwise waiver of his rights even though he fully understands those rights." The two groups within the Court also apparently disagreed on whether society had a greater interest in convicting criminal defendants or protecting their constitutional rights. The dissent pointed out the dangers of trying to justify the minimization of constitutional guarantees. They argued that "the cost of suppressing evidence of guilt will always make the value of a procedural safeguard appear 'minimal,' 'marginal,' or 'incremental.'" They note that "the individual interest in procedural safeguards that minimize the risk of error is easily discounted when the fact of guilt appears certain beyond doubt."

Another case in which the Supreme Court seemed to condone police trickery was in *California v. Acevedo* (1991), in which it ruled that the police may wait to conduct a search of a container, which they have probable cause to believe contains contraband, until it is brought into an automobile. As mentioned earlier, such searches of an automobile do not require the police to obtain a search warrant, as opposed to before it enters the automobile, at which time a warrant would be required. In other words, the police did not have a right to search the container until the defendant placed the container in the trunk.

The dissent pointed out the contradictions in this logic by noting that "surely it is anomalous to prohibit a search of a briefcase while the owner is carrying it exposed on a public street yet to permit a search once the owner has placed the briefcase in the locked trunk of his car. One's privacy interest in one's luggage can certainly not be diminished by one's removing it from a public thoroughfare and placing it—out of sight—in a privately owned vehicle." Interestingly, twelve years prior to the *Acevedo* decision, in the case of *Arkansas v. Sanders* (1979), the majority of the Court believed that the police could not search a closed container merely because it had been placed in the trunk of an automobile. They ruled that the police may not search the trunk, and examine the container, unless they had obtained a warrant, or believed there existed exigent circumstances that mandated an immediate search. Though the fact patterns of the two cases are different so that the Court can argue that they have not actually overturned a past decision, a comparison of the holdings in the *Acevedo* and *Sanders* decisions lends credence to the notion that the Court has been moving further to the side of law enforcement.

In sum, it seems that the Supreme Court has been sympathizing to a greater degree with law enforcement, both in the area of right to counsel and search and seizure. This sympathy seems to extend even to situations many would consider morally troubling.

DEATH PENALTY—RAPE, MURDER

Arguably, the most politically charged criminal justice issue has been the death penalty. Polls indicate that an overwhelmingly majority of the public favors the death penalty in cases of murder. In *Gregg v. Georgia* (1976), the Court ruled the death penalty was not disproportionate punishment to the crime of murder. This built upon the Court's decision in the case of *Furman v. Georgia* (1972), in which the court ruled that the death penalty was unconstitutional unless clearer guidelines were established for its imposition. The Court's reasoning in *Gregg* was that "the imposition of the death penalty for the crime of murder has a long history of acceptance both in the United States and England." In addition, the Court also took note of the change in public opinion regarding the death penalty. They stated that it "was now evident that a large proportion of American society continues to regard it as an appropriate and necessary criminal sanction." In addition, they argued that the death penalty serves societal functions as well. The Court argued that the death penalty serves "two principal social purposes: retribution and deterrence of capital crimes by prospective offenders."

In contrast to its decisions regarding the death penalty for murder, in *Coker v. Georgia* (1977), the Court ruled that the death penalty is a disproportionate penalty for the crime of rape. The Court stated:

> Rape is without doubt deserving of serious punishment; but in terms of moral depravity and of the injury to the person and to the public, it does not compare with murder, which does involve the unjustified taking of human life. Although it may be accompanied by another crime, rape by definition does not include the death or even the serious injury to another person. The murderer kills; the rapist if no more than that, does not. Life is over for the victim of the murderer; for the rape victim, life may not be nearly so happy as it was, but it is not over and normally is not beyond repair. We have the abiding conviction that the death penalty which is "unique in its severity and irrevocability," is an excessive penalty for the rapist who, as such, does not take human life.

One commentator, Solomon Radin (1978), has noted that this case was "the first modern decision in which the Supreme Court has relied on disproportionality to invalidate a punishment under the cruel and unusual clause." Furthermore, two dissenters in *Coker* state that this decision "casts serious doubt upon the constitutional validity of statutes imposing the death penalty for a variety of conduct which though dangerous, may not necessarily result in any immediate death, e.g., treason, airplane hijacking, and kidnaping." Thus, the Court at present seems willing to sanction the death penalty for acts of murder, or acts leading to murder.

In sum, this chapter should give the reader the necessary legal background. In the next chapter, I report the basic results of the surveys of the mass public and the legal elite.

It is important to note that the public does not have the benefit of a legal background. It relies on whatever information it has, and values, perceptions, and shortcuts/heuristics that are readily available to it (see Sniderman, Brody, and Tetlock, 1991). As mentioned earlier, this necessitates and makes possible an important opportunity for those who do have intricate knowledge—members of the legal profession—to help pass along this knowledge to the rest of the population. Questions of how much in agreement with the Supreme Court and how protective of civil liberties the public is, are examined in the next chapter. The opinions of the public are compared to the holdings of the Court and also with the portions of the elite in the field—members of the legal profession.

Chapter 3

Differences Between Public and Legal Elite in Opinions Toward Criminal Justice Procedures

In this book I examine mass-elite opinion differences toward criminal procedures. Specifically, I compare the opinions of lawyers and ordinary citizens. Past research has shown that educated and more knowledgeable citizens are more tolerant of groups whose opinions or actions might cause others in society, to not only ostracize the members of the group, but deny them basic civil liberties (McClosky and Brill, 1983; Delli Carpini and Keeter, 1996). One can assume that, as with tolerance, the more educated and knowledgeable, as well as members of the legal profession, would be more willing than others to assure members of the public, including criminal defendants, constitutional protections. Part of the explanation for this is that the better informed know about and are thus more likely to value these protections that have been guaranteed, to various degrees, by the courts. However, would this be the case even if the Supreme Court ruled *against* expanding the rights of the defendant? In this case, the more educated and knowledgeable would also be more likely than others to be aware of any new Court rulings (see Zaller, 1992).

Many lawyers in particular acquire their knowledge of the law by reading Supreme Court decisions. It is possible that in recent years as the Court has moved not only against expanding personal liberty, but also in favor of limiting the area wherein one is free of police intrusion, the more educated and knowledgeable, as well as members of the legal profession, have followed suit. Moreover, it would be reasonable to assume that lawyers recently out of law school, whose first taste of the law has been reading the most recent decisions of the Court, might be the cohort least inclined to take an expansionist view regarding civil liberties. The implications of this possibility are obvious. Consistent with this, past research has shown that believing in ideas related to rights and liberties in the abstract might be different from supporting the implementation of particular legal protections (Schuman, Steeh, and Bobo, 1985). While the more knowledgeable and better educated might be supportive of protecting the rights of individuals as a general idea, it is possible that when it comes to specific situational contexts their support might wane (see Stouffer, 1955; Prothro and Grigg, 1960; Page and Shapiro, 1992, Ch. 3).

Using the data from my surveys of the mass public and legal elite that I designed and conducted for this study, I examine attitudes toward the intrusiveness of government in the areas of surveillance, searches, and criminal rights. In this chapter, I examine the responses to fourteen questions that measure support for recent Supreme Court decisions concerning personal rights in the area of criminal procedure. The survey explores opinions concerning the root causes of crime, as well as general attitudes toward procedural safeguards for the accused. In addition, the survey provides measures of other variables that affect attitudes toward surveillance and rights of the accused, which will be examined in greater detail in Chapter 4. Later, the analysis in Chapters 5 and 6 will focus on the differences in one's support for civil liberties that are education, knowledge, and other demographic variables. The data make it possible to discern what drives individuals to be more or less civil libertarian toward criminal procedures. These data may also shed light as to what extent the Supreme Court opinions have accorded with that of the mass public, the legal elite, or neither, in the context of the Court's recent turn to the Right.

The results presented in this chapter indicate that opinions of lawyers are more civil libertarian than those of the mass public. However, in those instances in which the Supreme Court has ruled against the civil libertarian alternative, a majority of lawyers have followed the lead of the Court. In addition, the reason for the differences in opinion regarding issues of civil liberties, as examined in later chapters, might be traced to differences in opinion regarding the root causes of crime, which may influence the people's opinions regarding the importance of civil liberties to change as well.

PATTERNS OF SUPPORT FOR CRIMINAL PROCEDURES

In their landmark study on public opinion and civil liberties, McClosky and Brill (1983) found the mass public to be more supportive of civil liberties in the abstract than in specific instances (see also Schuman, Steeh, and Bobo, 1985). They also found the public less supportive of less salient issues, and less supportive of civil libertarian norms, than the legal elite, in nearly all cases, ranging from issues dealing with free speech to the rights of criminal defendants. This is consistent with most studies on general educational effects regarding one's opinions concerning issues of civil liberties (Stouffer, 1955; Nunn, Crockett, and Williams, 1978; Hyman and Wright, 1979). However, as the Court has moved to the Right in recent years, and as all in society have been affected by higher crime rates, and a perception of even higher crime rates, it is possible that lawyers have moved toward opinions less protective of civil libertarian norms. To examine this, this survey includes a cross-section of lawyers, in contrast to the McClosky and Brill survey (p. 469), which defined legal elite as "Criminal attorneys, district attorneys, public defenders/legal aid attorneys, civil rights attorneys, judges, and sheriffs or policemen." It is possible that McClosky and Brill found lawyers to be more civil libertarian since the specialty of the lawyers surveyed might have been related to their opinions, so that because of their prior opinions chose a particular specialty. Most important, their survey, which was conducted in the 1970s, is dated; as the courts moved to the right, this might have caused those who follow the Court opinions closely, namely legal elite, to alter their opinions as well.

The Survey

The first part of the survey dealt with basic opinions concerning specific cases in the area of civil liberties. These questions were included to gauge the public's opinion regarding issues of criminal justice. In addition, all of these questions dealt with issues that were recently decided by the United States Supreme Court. Therefore, one might also discern possible effects of Supreme Court decisions. Half of the questions dealt with search and seizure issues, which arise before a suspected criminal has been officially charged with a crime. The other questions dealt with possible situations after a suspect has been charged, bearing on "the rights of the accused." An example of a question is: "Would one allow authorities to search a suspect's private body parts for drugs?"

A number of important research questions can be addressed based on this portion of the survey. First, are individuals with more education and knowledge, especially members of the legal profession, more civil libertarian than those with less knowledge and education? Second, are they more likely to share the opinions similar to those of the Supreme Court, regardless of the ideological direction of the Supreme Court's decisions? Or, does the nature of any issue at hand cause one to be more or less civil libertarian, or more or less supportive of recent Court decisions?

Political Knowledge and Education

As noted, one might expect the more knowledgeable and more educated to be more civil libertarian when it comes to criminal procedure. However, as the Court has turned to the right it is possible that the more educated and knowledgeable might follow suit. In addition, do the more educated and knowledgeable support civil libertarian concepts in the abstract, while being less supportive when presented with particular situations (Schuman, Steeh, and Bobo, 1985)? Some have observed this pattern regarding issues of racial justice (Schuman, Steeh, and Bobo, 1985).

To measure the respondents' level of political knowledge, they were asked five questions dealing with general political knowledge and four questions dealing with legal knowledge (see Appendix 1 for question wording). There was little difference between the effects on opinions of one's knowledge concerning political issues and the knowledge concerning legal issues. Therefore, the questions concerning general knowledge were used in the analysis, since they have proven to be both valid and reliable in measuring one's exposure to a broad range of political information (Delli Carpini and Keeter, 1991, 1996).

Political Knowledge and Education as Dependent Variables

Table 3.1 reports the aggregate responses to the questions in the surveys that derived from past Supreme Court decisions and also the direction of the Supreme Court's holding for the case upon which the question is based. The survey opened with questions that dealt with the death penalty for murderers and rapists, and continued with fourteen additional questions that dealt with issues of criminal procedure. Table 3.1 begins with the comparisons of mass public, legal elite, and United States Supreme Court opinion regarding the fourteen issues of criminal justice that replicated past court decisions, followed by the death penalty questions. The court cases bearing on these were described in Chapter 2. Table 3.2 does the same for segments of the mass public, with different levels of education and knowledge. (All tables are at the end of this chapter.)

Table 3.2 presents data on the mass public support for criminal procedures for different levels of knowledge and education. For knowledge, those who answered all five questions correctly (Knowledge=high) were compared with those who answered three or four questions correctly (Knowledge=middle) versus those who answered two or fewer correctly (Knowledge=low). For education, those who had at least some college (Education=high) were compared with those who had only a high school diploma (Education=middle) versus those who had not finished high school (Education=low).

The results presented in Table 3.2 also shed light on to what extent individuals with more knowledge and education, who have not received a formal legal education, are more civil libertarian than those with less knowledge and education. In particular we can ask: does being a member of the "attentive public" cause one to be more civil libertarian, despite the recent move to the Right by the Supreme Court?

SEARCH AND SEIZURE ISSUES

Searches of Private Property

As noted in Chapter 2, a politically complicated and controversial political question, of late, has been the issue of government intrusion onto private property. Both civil libertarians and certain types of conservatives have come to question the extent and necessity of such intrusion. The Supreme Court, however, has been granting the government more leeway in its warrantless searches of private property.

As reported in Table 3.1, when respondents were asked whether they would "allow the police to view a person's property, which can be viewed from the air, without a search warrant," lawyers , by a margin of 11 percentage points, were more likely than the mass public to allow this to occur (63% vs. 51%; p = .0003). Table 3.2 indicates that within the mass public, the educated and more politically knowledgeable were less civil libertarian than those respondents with less education and knowledge. There was little difference among (and not statistically significant) the different education categories in their support of such searches (53% support search [high] vs. 52% [middle] vs. 51% [low], p = .966). Interestingly, knowledge was a more important factor. Of those with high levels of knowledge, 57% supported the search vs. 52% with middle levels of knowledge vs. 47% with low levels of knowledge (p = .104). This followed the same pattern set by the mass public and legal elite: individuals with higher levels of knowledge are more supportive of the aerial search, and thus more protective of the privacy of one's property.

This is consistent with the fact that the Supreme Court has been moving to the right on this issue, and has ruled that the police can use a sophisticated aerial camera to photograph the defendant's private property (*Dunn* [1987], see Ch. 2). It is probable that individuals with more knowledge would be more aware of Court decisions than others, and therefore more prone to have their opinions guided by Court decisions, even against civil libertarian ideals. Another possible explanation is that the logic of why this search is permissible is simply clearer to individuals and judges with more education and knowledge. They believe that this type of search is both legally sensible and correct. Possible explanations as to why knowledge has a greater effect than education will be examined later.

A very commonplace question, concerning the right to private property, recently came before the court. It was asked to decide whether or not the police may search one's garbage without a search warrant (*California v. Greenwood* [1988], see Ch. 2). This question drew quite differing comments from the respondents in the survey, which ranged from "how dare they," to "who cares."

Table 3.1 reports that when asked whether or not they would "allow searches of a citizen's trash, placed outside of the person's property, without a search warrant," lawyers were more likely than the mass public to approve of such behavior—64% of lawyers as opposed to 49% of the mass public approved of such searches (p = .006). Table 3.2 indicates that within the mass public there was greater difference according to education, than for different levels of knowledge. Individuals with a high level of education were 15 percentage points less likely to support a search of one's trash than were those with low levels of education (46% support search [high] vs. 50% [middle] vs. 61% [low], p = .022). For those with differing levels of knowledge there was no significant difference.

Again, the Supreme Court has taken a position against a full civil libertarian norm in this situation. In the case of *California v. Greenwood*, the Court ruled that a warrantless search of trash placed outside of one's property is permissible. This may help explain why neither a legal education nor knowledge led to greater support for the civil libertarian alternative. It should be noted that while education may be highly correlated with higher levels of political knowledge, it does not, per se, necessarily lead to knowledge about the courts. Therefore, it is possible that the Supreme Court's recent move to the Right would have its greatest effect on those individuals with higher levels of knowledge, namely lawyers, while individuals who are more educated, though not as knowledgeable, will stick to their civil libertarian ideals. This seems to have occurred in the cases of both air and trash searches.

Searches of Automobiles

Another area of controversy has been the automobile. Though one would not expect the same level of privacy in a car, as one would in one's home, some degree of privacy and protection from police intrusion is expected. However, the recent proliferation of drugs, illegal weapons, and other contraband, many times transported in automobiles, has caused police officers to become quite vigilant of any suspected wrongdoing by both driver and passenger.

There were large differences, between the mass public and legal elite, in their responses to the question which asked whether or not the respondent would "allow the police to search any closed containers in a car, during a routine traffic, without any strong belief that illegal items are inside the container"— 44% of the public, but only 10% of lawyers favored such a search (p=.000). Among the public, there were more pronounced differences associated with the different levels of knowledge, than for those with different levels of education. Those with high levels of knowledge were 10 percentage points more likely than those with low levels of knowledge to take the civil libertarian viewpoint (40% support search [high] vs. 44% [middle] vs. 50% [low], p=.058), while the difference was only 6 percentage points for the same categories of education (42% support search [high] vs. 47% [middle] vs. 48% [low], p=.353).

As described in Chapter 2, unlike the Supreme Court decisions in the right to privacy cases dealing with land rights, where the Court has greatly cut back on its support for civil liberties, the Supreme Court has taken a more middle-ground approach to civil liberties regarding automobiles. For example, the Court has not ruled that police can search closed containers in a car during a routine traffic stop. This might help explain why lawyers, to such a great degree (34 percentage points), were more supportive of the civil libertarian alternative, than were members of the mass public (44% support search [lawyers] vs. 10% [mass public], p=.000). This was a circumstance where the Court's support of civil libertarian principles helped reinforce the tendency toward supporting civil liberties brought about by a legal education. This also helps explain the greater levels of support for civil liberties among the more knowledgeable, than among the more educated (education: 42% support search [high] vs. 47% [middle] vs. 48% [low]; knowledge: 40% [high] vs. 44% [middle] vs. 50% [low]). In this instance, the more educated obtain cues to support civil liberties from their education, while the more knowledgeable obtain cues as well from their knowledge about and support of Supreme Court decisions.

Frisks and Stops

Case law has long established that, at times, police officers must make split-second decisions on their beat without consulting a magistrate. Some have argued that with rising crime rates, police should be given more discretion than before, to stop and frisk individuals. Two questions in the survey dealt with this topic: the first with granting police power to stop suspects based on probable cause; the second with police stopping a suspect even when probable cause is lacking.

A large majority of both the public and lawyer samples favored "allowing the authorities to frisk a suspect if there is probable cause to believe there is incriminating evidence,"—81% of the mass sample vs. 79% of lawyers would allow the frisk (p=.355). Though respondents at all levels of knowledge and education supported the right of the police to stop and frisk a suspect, if probable cause existed, the more knowledgeable were possibly less civil libertarian than the less knowledgeable (84% support frisk [high] vs. 82% [middle] vs. 79% [low], p=.465). This pattern was not suggested for education, which made even less difference for this question (82% support frisk [high and low] vs. 84% [middle], p=.457).

It is long-settled Court doctrine (*Terry v. Ohio* [1968]), that police may conduct a stop and frisk, if they have probable case to suspect the person subject to the frisk is in the act of, or has committed, some sort of criminal activity. This might help explain the strong support of this procedure within both the mass public and legal elite. The notion of an officer stopping and frisking a suspect has become so much a part of our mainstream norms, that all in society have accepted this act to be justified. Again, it is possible that the more knowledgeable are more supportive of the frisk, since they are aware of and persuaded by the Supreme Court decisions.

Recently, the Court has dealt with cases which were not as clear cut as *Terry*. What happens when objective facts do not exist to justify a Terry stop (see Ch. 2). Is a warrantless stop and frisk still justified? One must remember that the nation has become more and more cynical of the court system, while still displaying a great deal of confidence in police officers (see results of GSS [General Social Science] surveys and the surveys for this study). In addition, the police officer is on the scene, while the magistrate will only listen to testimony. Thus, some may argue that the police officer is in the best position to make the call.

A majority of both samples favored the idea of "allowing the police to stop a suspect who appears to be acting suspiciously: for example, pacing in front of a building at night." Lawyers, however, were significantly less supportive—82% of the mass public vs. 64% of lawyers favored such police action (p=.000).

Among the public there was little difference by knowledge and education. Individuals with higher levels of education were very highly but slightly less likely than others to support the notion of police stopping individuals without probable cause (80% support search [high] vs. 85% [middle] vs. 84% [low], p=.264). A similar pattern held for different categories of knowledge, with the more knowledgeable slightly less likely to support such searches (80% support search [high] vs. 83% [middle and low], p=.894).

In 1989 the Supreme Court ruled that a police officer can perform a stop and frisk of an alleged suspect, even if there is no probable cause to believe criminal activity is afoot, and even if the suspect did not perform any acts that appear criminal to an objective individual. In *U.S. v. Sokolow*, the Court ruled that the police officer is given the discretion to judge "the totality of the circumstances," and can stop an individual at the officer's own discretion. This helps explain why the educated and more knowledgeable are not more civil libertarian than the mass public. It is possible that members of the legal profession did not move over to the right on this issue, because the question wording might conjure up images of racism practiced by many police departments, who occasionally stop people for being suspicious merely because they are black. Lawyers, one sees from other questions, are extremely sensitive to issues of racial injustice.

Drug Trafficking

Drug trafficking has become a major problem in America. In addition, many people argue, not only has American society been harmed by drugs per se, but also that drugs have helped spur rising crime rates, through their debilitating effect on the American society. How much power and authority, then, do the public and lawyers give the police and border patrol in fighting drug trafficking?

The public was more likely than the lawyers to "allow authorities to search a suspect's private body parts for drugs" (56% vs. 44%, p=.006). Within the mass public, there were much greater differences among education categories than those attributable to knowledge. The least educated were much more likely to support the searches of the suspect's body part for drugs, than individuals with higher levels of education (56% support search [high] vs. 50% [middle] vs. 74% [low], p=.000). The least knowledgeable were also more likely to support the search, but the differences were much less pronounced (55% support search [high] vs. 56% [middle] vs. 61 [low], p=.364).

As described in Chapter 2, in a much publicized case (*Montoya de Hernandez* [1985]), the Supreme Court ruled that the police can detain a suspect until the suspect agrees to an X-ray examination or produces a bowel movement. In addition, the authorities can conduct a rectal examination on the defendant, with the burden of proof on the defendant to prove that an examination is not necessary. Again, the Court's endorsement of this procedure might have caused the lack of differences in opinion due to knowledge. Regarding the legal elite's disagreement with the Supreme Court, it is possible that blistering dissent, as well as the great controversy surrounding the decision, offered the lawyers a second legitimate opinion to follow. That is, a united Supreme Court, and an elite consensus, did not exist. In fact, as noted in Chapter 2, the dissent called this "a disgusting and sad episode" in the history of the Court. Those knowledgeable and exposed to new information among the public might know of Court decisions but not follow them to such an extent as to know of a dissenting opinion, however strongly worded the dissent might have been.

Ships

Within the area of warrantless searches, this study includes ship searches. Their issue has been prominent because of the need to stop illegal immigration and the inflow of drugs. Some argue that heightened security is needed at the nations borders and that exceptions, therefore, need be made to the general warrant requirement. In addition, many argue that United States officials should be allowed to board vessels which have access to the high seas, so as to protect American security interests.

Large mass-elite differences occurred for the question whether or not one would "allow the police to board any ship or boat to inspect any documents on board, when the ship is on the open seas." The mass public was much more likely than lawyers to support such a policy by a margin of 31 percent (67% vs. 36%; p=.000). Among the public, there was very little difference based upon different levels of knowledge and education. The individuals with greater levels of education were only slightly more civil libertarian (68% support search [high] vs. 65% [middle] vs. 73% [low], p=.268), as were members of the public with greater levels of knowledge (67% support search [high] vs. 69% [middle] vs. 70% [low], p=.831).

The Supreme Court (*Villamonte-Marquez*, [1983]) has ruled that authorities may search ships, with access to the open seas, to inspect any documents on board, even though they have not procured a search warrant. It is probable, once again, that the lack of differences among individuals with varying levels of knowledge and education was attributable to the Court's support for the warrantless search. The more knowledgeable, who would ordinarily have opinions of the civil libertarian nature, do not have such opinions since the Court, which sets the tone of elite discourse in the field of law, does not have a highly civil libertarian holding on this particular issue. A possible explanation for the lawyers bucking elite opinion might be personal. It is possible that lawyers own more ships, or have associates with ships, than other less financially secure members of the public, and are therefore more supportive of the right to privacy for those who sail.

Dogs Sniffing for Drugs—Plain Odor

The final question that I will examine dealing with searches also has do with the drug problem. Many people would turn over great authority to the police to fight the importation of drugs. However, would the public turn over the authority to carry out the search for drugs, so to speak, to nonhumans?

Respondents were asked whether or not they would "allow authorities to use dogs to sniff for drugs in all luggage entering the United States." An overwhelming majority of both the public and lawyers approved of this—91% of the public and 86% of the legal professionals favored this idea (p=.002). Among the public, those with more education were slightly less likely to approve the sniff search (92% allow sniff [high] vs. 90% [middle] vs. 96% [low], p=.201), while individuals with more knowledge were slightly more likely to support the sniff search (94% support [high and middle] vs. 87% [low], p=.002).

In the case of *U.S. v. Place* (1983), the United States Supreme Court ruled that the doctrine of plain view, allowing the police to obtain and detain any evidence within their plain view, also allows the police to do the same regarding evidence that can be detected through the plain odor of contraband sniffed by dogs. From the results of both surveys it would seem that this doctrine, that of allowing dogs to sniff for drugs in luggage, has become a settled issue of law for Americans: all elements of the public, from those who are least to the most educated and knowledgeable clearly support it.

POST-DETAINMENT SITUATIONS

Charging the Defendant

After the defendant has been arrested, it is established law that the charging of the defendant must take place within a reasonable time. The question is, though, what is "reasonable." As crime has, in the minds of many, been on the rise (see GSS data; Frankel, 1997), much of the public might give the authorities more leeway regarding what is a reasonable amount of time, rather than take the chance of having a criminal on the loose. What would the public call too long? The United States Supreme Court has decided (*County of Riverside*, 1991), barring unusual circumstances, a defendant may not be held for more than forty-eight hours without being charged with a specific crime (see Ch. 2).

In response to the survey, the public, though less than a majority, was more likely than lawyers to "allow the government to detain a suspected criminal for more than 48 hours without being charged with a specific crime" (30% vs. 12%, p=.000). While a majority within all categories of education and knowledge opposed the idea of detaining a suspect for more than 48 hours without an official charge, there were still significant differences. Those with higher levels of knowledge were 15 percentage points less likely to allow a longer detention (24% support [high] vs. 30% [middle] vs. 39% [low], p=.002), while those with high levels of education compared to low were seventeen percentage points less likely to support the detention (26% [high] vs. 33% [middle] vs. 43% [low], p=.002).

The Supreme Court's support for the civil libertarian position would help explain why the educated and more knowledgeable individuals would be more opposed to lengthy detention of criminal suspects. Again, the difference due to knowledge and education occurs because the attentive public has opinions different from those less educated and knowledgeable, since it has, in effect, been guided by the Court and legal elite.

Impeaching Witnesses with Tainted Evidence

Another controversial area of criminal procedure has been the discarding of evidence due to technicalities. Some have argued that if the technical rules imposed on the system since the 1960s would disappear, so would crime. Many have been displeased when important evidence has been thrown out in court because it was obtained in an unconstitutional manner.

By a margin of 6 percentage points, lawyers were more likely to "allow evidence which was illegally obtained to be used to contradict witnesses for the defendant"—33% of lawyers vs. 27% of the public (p=.042). A large majority of the public and lawyers opposed the admission of evidence that was illegally obtained. The opposition was strongest among the more educated and knowledgeable. The better educated were 13 percentage points less likely than the less well educated to allow to "allow evidence which was illegally obtained to be used to contradict witnesses for the defendant" (24% allow [high] vs. 28% [middle] vs. 37% [low], p=.024). The more knowledgeable were eight percentage points less likely to allow to allow the illegally obtained material into evidence than the less knowledgeable (24% allow into evidence [high] vs. 27% [middle] vs. 31% [low], p=.175).

In *James v. Illinois* (1990), the Supreme Court ruled that illegally obtained evidence cannot be used to impeach any witnesses of the defendant, arguing that permitting such evidence would affect the defendant's ability to argue her case (see Ch. 2). Again, this would help explain why members of the public with greater education and knowledge take a more civil libertarian position here. However, the Court has been signaling its desire to allow, under certain circumstances, evidence that was illegally obtained. If this does occur, it would be quite interesting to see whether or not opinions of the more knowledgeable would change accordingly. In fact, it is possible that lawyers are already taking cues from the Court regarding a possible shift in Court opinion, and this may be the cause for the low levels of support among lawyers for the civil libertarian alternative. It is also possible that though lawyers are generally more civil libertarian, this might be an exception to the general rule.

Right to Counsel

The public has been critical and cynical toward the legal profession. One stereotype is that a criminal lawyer has no interest in finding the truth but, rather, is only interested in getting clients set free. Two survey questions were asked regarding the right to counsel. The first involved an admission of a crime to undercover agents; the second involved the allowance of a voluntary confession by a suspect without a lawyer present.

A majority of the public and lawyers opposed the idea of "allowing the authorities to use undercover police to obtain an admission from a suspect when his/her lawyer is not present"—36% of the mass public favored such an action, compared to 25% of lawyers who would allow the admission into court. There were small differences among the public based upon the level education and knowledge. Those with greater education were 7 percentage points less likely to allow such an admission into evidence (35% allow admission [high] vs. 37% [middle] vs. 42% [low], p=.384), while there was only a three percentage point difference between the different levels of knowledge (34% allow admission [high] vs. 37% [middle and low], p=.584).

In the case of *Illinois v. Perkins* (1990), the Court ruled that it is permissible to use undercover agents to elicit an admission from a defendant. Their reasoning was that the defendant did not know he was speaking to police officers, so a custodial interrogation could not have occurred. Interestingly, this was a case in which the Court and the public were totally out of line with each other. A possible explanation for the difference in opinion between the Court and lawyers is that the lawyers might have taken offense that the police were permitted to bypass them, by tricking the suspects into confessions without a lawyer being present. The mass public was less likely to appreciate the technicality of the existence of a custodial interrogation; rather, they were more likely to see it as plain and simple police trickery.

A quite different problem emerges when no police trickery is involved and a defendant decides, on his or her own, with no police involvement, to waive right to counsel. This may be the type of situation that causes many in society to have a dim view of the legal profession. Simply put, if a person admits to a crime, who cares if a lawyer is not present?

As opposed to the previous right to counsel case involving undercover agents, a majority of the public would "allow a voluntary admission of a crime even when the suspect asks for a lawyer and the lawyer is not present"—52% of the mass public vs. 29% of lawyers would allow such an admission into court (p=.000). Among the public there was little difference in opinion based upon education or knowledge. Interestingly, individuals with higher levels of education and knowledge were slightly more likely to allow the admission into evidence. There was an 8 percentage point difference among different levels of education (52% allow admission [high] vs. 55% [middle] vs. 47% [low], p=.407). There was a smaller and insignificant difference for the different levels of knowledge (53% allow admission [high] vs. 54% [middle] vs. 50% [low], p=.611).

The United States Supreme Court has long held that once a suspect has asked for a lawyer, all questioning must cease until the suspect gives a voluntary and intelligent waiver of his or her rights. A mere confession, without a knowing and intelligent waiver, will cause the admission to be deemed inadmissable. As with the other right to counsel case that dealt with undercover agents, there seem to be influences at work, other than the decision of the Court. For the lawyers, allowing the police go around them and question the defendant was unacceptable. For the mass public, it contradicted sensibility that an uncoerced admission by a criminal defendant, even one accused of a very violent crime, would get thrown out of court on a technicality.

MORAL ISSUES

Mental Illness

As evidenced by the results of the survey, that an overwhelming majority of the public believe that the courts in their area are too lenient, much of the public appears to want the courts to give more power and authority to the side of law enforcement. The question now becomes: how much exactly? Would the public approve of the police and courts using *any* means possible? Would the public approve of the courts violating what might be also perceived as be fundamental rules of fairness?

A majority of both the lawyer and mass samples opposed "allowing a suspect who is mentally ill to waive the right to counsel." Only 18% of the public and 8% of lawyers favored this (p=.0000). Within the public, while a majority of all categories of education and knowledge disapproved of a mentally ill individual waiving his right to counsel, there were some clear differences. Those with low levels of education were much more likely to believe that the waiver should be allowed (14% allow waiver [high] vs. 16% [middle] vs. 30% [low], p=.000), and the least knowledgeable were also more than twice as likely to allow the waiver than the less knowledgeable (11% allow waiver vs. 16% [middle] vs. 26% [low], p=.000).

In a quite controversial decision (*Colorado v. Connelly*, 1986), the Court ruled that the defendant's mental state is irrelevant but, rather, what is important is police coercion: absent police coercion, a waiver of the right to counsel stands. Clearly from the survey, neither the mass public nor the legal elite agree with the Court's logic. In contrast to other cases in which the Court ruled against the civil libertarian alternative, the more educated and knowledgeable were much more civil libertarian than the Court and the least sophisticated and attentive segment of the public. There are at least a few possible explanations. First, the attentive public rejected the logic of the Court decision and agreed with the logic of the blistering dissent, which argued that the Court should look at the "totality of the circumstances." Second, it is possible that the less educated and knowledgeable do not fully understand the complications of mental illness, and therefore see nothing wrong with allowing the waiver. In addition, as with the other right to counsel cases, lawyers might have seen this as a way to get around the necessity of providing a lawyer to suspects.

Police Trickery

Police trickery can come in many forms. Some forms of this can cause innocent people to suffer, while at other times the police bend the rules to catch guilty persons. Their justification is that, due to rules set by courts, this is needed to stay in close touch with what goes on in the streets. Thus, wouldn't the public allow outright police trickery, in order to help catch alleged criminals?

When respondents were asked whether or not they would "allow the police who are investigating a crime to use methods such as flashing papers, which look like search warrants," an overwhelming majority of both the public and lawyers refused to allow the police this option. Fully 95% of lawyers and 90% of the mass sample opposed this form of action ($p=.001$). Among the public, there were some differences based upon education and knowledge. Individuals in the middle level of education category were most likely to allow the usage of fake papers (9% allow usage [high] vs. 14% [middle] vs. 9% [low], $p=.065$), and those with high levels of knowledge were least likely to allow the police to use such trickery (5% allow usage [high] vs. 12% [middle] vs. 14% [low], $p=.014$).

The Court has never declared such outlandish police behavior permissible. However over the course of the last decade, the Court has allowed the police to use various questionable tactics such as allowing the police to not inform a defendant that his lawyer is available. In addition, the Court agreed that the police can postpone a seizure until the defendant has moved his belongings to his car from his home. This would be done in order to take advantage of the lower threshold of suspicion needed to conduct searches of automobiles than homes. A list and explanation of these cases appears in Chapter 2. Although, at the present time, using papers to avoid obtaining a warrant is still regarded throughout American society to be a violation of the accepted norms, one can only wonder what would happen if the Court continued to turn the other way and at times condone various acts of police trickery, which would seem to be in violation of the United States Constitution.

DEATH PENALTY FOR MURDER/RAPE

The constitutionality of the death penalty has been a quite salient issue. Individuals who believe that the death penalty should be legal argue that it is not "cruel and unusual punishment" and is a deterrent to murder. Individuals who believe the death penalty should be illegal argue that the death penalty is cruel and unusual and is not a deterrent.

Responding to the question concerning the death penalty for murder, lawyers were less likely to favor the death penalty, than was the public as a whole, by a margin of 23 percentage points (57% vs. 80%, p=.000). Within the public, there was widespread support for the death penalty, with few differences based upon knowledge and education. Five percentage points separated respondents according to knowledge (77% support death penalty [high] vs. 82% [middle] vs. 80% [low], p=.371), while there was an 8 percentage point spread for education (76% support death penalty [high] vs. 84% [middle and low], p=.021).

The Supreme Court in 1976 (*Gregg*), ruled the death penalty constitutional in instances where the defendant was convicted of murder. From the survey data, it seems that the uniform acceptance of the death penalty has permeated all levels of the American public. Helping this occur, most probably, has been the extreme salience of the death penalty, as well as the salience of the issues associated with it: crime and murder. Since crime and murder are given such great attention on the nightly news (see Frankel, 1997), all cohorts within the mass public have been greatly exposed to these issues through common news media.

Though the public clearly supports the death penalty for individuals convicted of murder, there has been little attention given to public opinion concerning the death penalty for other crimes. In particular, to what extent is there support for the death penalty for persons convicted of rape?

The answer is much less. But the same general pattern, as that of the death penalty for murder, held for the support for death penalty for rapists. By a margin of 21 percentage points, lawyers were less likely to favor the death penalty (21% vs. 42%, p=.000). Among the public, there was not much difference based upon the respondents level of education (43% support death penalty [high] vs. 41% [middle and low], p=.697). There were significant differences, however, based upon one's level of knowledge: individuals with lower levels of knowledge were much more supportive of the death penalty than others (33% support death penalty [high] vs. 43% [middle] vs. 48% [low], p=.005).

In *Coker v. Georgia* (1977), the Supreme Court ruled that the death penalty is a disproportionate for the act of rape. This confirmation by the Court has almost certainly contributed to the opposition of lawyers, and of individuals who are more knowledgeable and attentive. Clearly, in contrast to murder, the death penalty has not become an accepted punishment for rape in elite discourse, and consequently more broadly society as a whole.

THE PUBLIC VERSUS LEGAL ELITE

To sum up, mass public support for increased government investigative power ranged from 11% in the case of police using fake papers instead of warrants to expedite an investigation, to 91% allowing dogs to sniff for drugs in luggage entering the United States. A similar range occurred for members of the legal profession, with 5% supporting the use of fake papers and 86% supporting the use of dogs to check for drugs.

Among the differences in opinion between the mass public and lawyers were a mass public more likely than the legal elite to allow the police to search a suspect's body parts for drugs and to board ships to search for ownership documents. It is possible that this occurred since much of the public could not picture itself in such situations, in contrast to their vulnerability to air and trash searches. In the latter cases members of the public were more likely, than the legal elite, to take civil libertarian positions. Lawyers were also more likely to take civil libertarian positions, when there seemed an attempt by the Court to circumvent the need for lawyers.

In all, however, there were significant differences between the opinions of the public and lawyers. In all but three instances, the legal elite were more civil libertarian than members of the mass public, and the differences between the two groups were statistically significant in all but one circumstance (allowing police to frisk a suspect if good belief of incriminating evidence). The three instances in which the public was more civil libertarian than the lawyers (searching one's property from the air without a search warrant, searching one's trash, and allowing evidence illegally obtained to be used to contradict defendant's witnesses), were those in which the Court had ruled against civil libertarian norms (air and trash searches), or has been leaning in that direction (contradicting defendant's witnesses).

Public Opinion and the Supreme Court

The results suggest that aggregate public opinion is generally in line with Supreme Court rulings. The opinion of the Court and the majority opinions of the public and lawyers are in the same direction in ten of the fourteen cases. There are two instances in which there is great disagreement between the public and lawyers and the decisions of the Court, and another two in which there is slight disagreement. The two cases of great disagreement are the same in both surveys of the public and lawyers, while the two cases of slight disagreement differ. There is substantial disagreement for allowing a suspect who is mentally ill to waive the right to counsel and allowing undercover police to obtain an admission when the suspect's lawyer is not present. While the Court has ruled in favor of allowing a mentally ill individual to waive the right to counsel, only 17% of the mass public and 8% of lawyers support the waiver. Also, the Court would allow undercover police to obtain an admission when a suspect's lawyer is not present, whereas only 36% of the mass public, and 25% of lawyers favor this procedure. It seems that the public and the Court use different logic in reaching their conclusions. A majority of respondents to both surveys seem to believe that as long as there exists an aura of "unfairness," the admission should not be admissible, while the Court focuses apparently upon whether or not an "intimidating environment" existed.

The public and the Court disagree slightly on allowing searches of trash and allowing the admission of a suspect without a lawyer being present—52% of the public would allow a voluntary admission of a crime after a suspect has asked for a lawyer and the lawyer is not present, but the Supreme Court would not allow this admission into evidence. Also, the Supreme Court would allow searches of trash placed outside of one's property without a warrant, while the public, by a narrow margin (51%-49%), is opposed to the search. The lawyers and the Court disagree on allowing police to board ships to inspect documents, and on allowing police to search a suspect's private body parts for drugs. Only 36% of lawyers favor allowing police to board a ship to inspect documents, while the Supreme Court would allow this warrantless inspection. Also, the Court would allow searches of one's private body parts for drugs, while a majority of lawyers (56%) oppose this.

Knowledge and Education

To report the number of cases in which the more knowledgeable and educated were more or less in agreement with Court decisions and civil libertarian norms, than the less knowledgeable and educated, would be misleading. This is so, since the percentage separating the different levels of knowledge and education was usually quite small. Only through a case-by-case examination can a true picture emerge.

The results in Table 3.2 indicate that the more knowledgeable (9 of 14) and educated (10 of 14) are somewhat more likely than those less knowledgeable and educated to be supportive of civil libertarian positions on criminal procedures. Though the number of cases in which the more knowledgeable and educated are more civil libertarian seems large, the table indicates that the percentage that separates different categories of knowledge and education is much smaller than the percentage that separate the mass public and legal elite.

The cases in which more knowledge and more education are associated with less support of civil liberties were those in which the Supreme Court had ruled against the civil libertarian position, and also cases that dealt with the right to counsel.

The correspondence of opinion with Court decisions is more closely related to knowledge than education. In general those with high levels of knowledge have opinions more in accord with the Court, with the exception of cases involving the right to counsel alone. This pattern does not occur for education. For example, while the Court has ruled that authorities can search one's property from the air without a search warrant, 57% of those with high knowledge vs. 52% with middle knowledge vs. 47% with low knowledge favor such a search (p=.104). The same pattern only vaguely holds for education, and the differences are insignificant (53% vs. 52% vs. 51%). The more knowledgeable were also less civil libertarian in the case of searching one's trash without a warrant, which corresponds with the court ruling that the authorities may search trash placed outside one's property without a warrant. The survey indicates that this procedure is favored by 50% of those with high and middle knowledge vs. 47% with low knowledge. Education alone, however, is associated with clear differences in taking up the civil libertarian position—46% of the best educated favor the intrusive search vs. 50% of the middle category and 61% in the low education group. Also, the more knowledgeable are only slightly less likely than others to favor searching body parts for drugs, while the more educated are less likely to do so by almost 20 percentage points (education: 56% support search [high] vs. 50% [middle] vs. 74% [low], p=.000; knowledge: 55% support search [high] vs. 56% [middle] vs. 61 [low], p=.364). The Court has ruled such searches permissible.

The Court's decision in right to counsel cases did not seem to affect those high in knowledge and education. Few in any category of education and knowledge would allow a mentally ill individual to waive the right to counsel, with the more knowledgeable and better educated least likely to favor such waivers, even though the Court has allowed them. The Court also allows undercover agents to obtain admissions from suspects, while a majority in all categories of knowledge and education disapprove of the procedure. However, it is possible that the Court's decision caused the more knowledgeable to be as supportive of the procedure as those with less knowledge. Respondents were also asked whether or not they would allow a confession without a lawyer after the suspect had asked for a lawyer. While the Court has ruled this impermissible, the most knowledgeable and educated were actually more supportive of the procedure. This suggests that they might be using different reasoning in right to counsel cases. In contrast, according to the Court's approach, since the waiver of a mentally ill individual is voluntary, it should be allowed. The same logic led the Court to allow an admission to undercover agents: there is no police intimidation since the suspect does not know that the agents are police officers. Clearly survey respondents did not treat the issue in the same way. Allowing a mentally ill person to waive the right to counsel may have been perceived as inherently wrong and using undercover agents seemed like police trickery. In addition, while the Court disallowed a voluntary admission without a requested lawyer, citizens might conclude that if the person admitted to committing a crime without physical coercion, the result was a voluntarily confession.

In general, the better educated and knowledgeable members of the mass public were more civil libertarian. However, the differences were not nearly as large as those between the public as a whole and the legal elite.

STRUCTURE OF OPINIONS TOWARD CRIMINAL JUSTICE

To assess further the respondents' overall level of support for privacy and rights regarding criminal procedure, principal components and principal axis factor analyses were performed to see if the various survey responses reduced to a small number of underlying attitudes toward these matters (see Table 3.3).

The responses to questions dealing with police using fake papers during a criminal investigation and concerning a suspect with a mental illness waiving the right to counsel clearly had to be separated from the rest since they did not load on the first factor in the principal components analysis, nor did they load with other variables on separate factors. In these cases the respondents' reasoning was apparently driven by a different set of principles for the questions that dealt with mental illness and police trickery than for the other questions concerning other aspects of criminal procedure. The responses to these remaining twelve questions loaded on a single principle components factor. Based on this result, a single scale was created, in which for each question a respondent answered in a civil libertarian direction, one point was added.

There was evidence, however, based on eigenvalues greater than 1.0, that a 2-factor solution was technically more appropriate than a single factor. Table 3.4 displays the results of the factor analysis that included the twelve variables. Clearly eight of the variables load on a factor, while the remaining four variables load on a second factor. The eight questions deal with issues of search and seizure during a police investigation occurring before a defendant has been taken into police custody, while the four other questions deal with rights of a criminal defendant already accused of a crime. Based upon this, two additional simple scales were created, one for the eight search and seizure items and another for the remaining four criminal rights items. Thus, three criminal procedure scales were created for the analysis, in addition to the full public opinion scale that is presented in Chapters 4 and 6.

SUMMARY

The survey results indicate that the legal elite are more civil libertarian than the mass public in all but three of the recent Court cases that were included in the survey. Interestingly, the three cases in which the legal elite were less supportive of civil libertarian norms were those in which the Supreme Court has either ruled in favor of law enforcement or has been leaning toward that direction. As mentioned earlier, the Supreme Court has ruled that it is legal to search trash placed outside of one's property, as well as to search one's property from the air without a warrant. In these two cases, the legal elite are clearly on the side of law enforcement, while the mass public were about evenly split. In addition, the Court has been leaning toward admitting illegal evidence to contradict the defense's witnesses, which suggests why lawyers were more likely than the mass public to admit the evidence.

Further, it seems that the Court's decisions have had an effect on the opinions of more knowledgeable and attentive citizens. When the Court has decided against particular civil libertarian alternatives, the most knowledgeable have been less civil libertarian than they were in cases in which the Court has been more protective of civil liberties. Another explanation is that the correlation is spurious and the Court decisions have no direct effect on the educated and knowledgeable. According to this theory, the effect is caused by the influence of greater amounts of knowledge, education, and insight that judges share with others because of their education and knowledge.

From the results presented in this chapter, it would seem that if the Court moves to decide cases in favor of the civil libertarian alternatives, lawyers as well as members of the attentive public tend to adopt opinions closer to the civil libertarian alternative. In turn, the outlook of the entire society may change, and the importance of civil liberties may diffuse more fully to the mass public.

It must be noted, however, that while education and knowledge are related in some cases to additional support for Court decisions, and in some cases to greater support for protecting privacy and rights, these effects on average are not large. Other influences are clearly at work that affect opinions toward criminal justice procedures. These will be examined in the Chapter 4.

Table 3.1
Public and Supreme Court Support for Criminal Procedures
(percent allowing each procedure)

Supreme Court Case	Mass Public % (N)	Lawyers % (N)	Supreme Court
(Dunn)			
1. Allow person's property viewed from air without search warrant	51% (795)	63% (404)	Favored
	chi-square=12.945, df=1, p=.0003		
(Greenwood)			
2. Allow searches without warrant of trash outside of persons property	49% (802)	64% (410)	Favored
	chi-square=24.658, df=1, p=.006		
(Ross)			
3. Allow search of closed container in car without strong belief that illegal items are inside container	44% (804)	10% (409)	Opposed
	chi-square=145.336, df=1, p=.000		
(Terry)			
4. Allow police to frisk suspect if good belief of incriminating evidence	81% (804)	79% (405)	Favored
	chi-square=.854, df=1, p=.355		
(Sokolow)			
5. Allow police to stop individual who appears suspicious	82% (808)	64% (406)	Favored
	chi-square=46.500, df=1, p=.000		
(Montoya de Hernandez)			
6. Allow police to search suspect's private body parts for drugs	56% (793)	44% (396)	Favored
	chi-square=16.033, df=1, p=.000		

Supreme Court Case	Mass Public % (N)	Lawyers % (N)	Supreme Court
(Villamonte-Marquez) 7. Allow police to board ship on high seas to inspect documents	67% (795) chi-square=107.279, df=1, p=.000	36% (399)	Favored
(Place) 8. Allow dogs to sniff for drugs in luggage entering United States	91% (793) chi-square=9.537, df=1, p=.002	86% (409)	Favored
(County of Riverside) 9. Allow detention of suspect for 48 hours even when not charged with specific crime	30% (793) chi-square=48.579, df=1, p=.000	12% (405)	Opposed
(James) 10. Allow evidence illegally obtained to be used in contradicting defendant's witnesses	27% (800) chi-square=4.150, df=1, p=.042	33% (406)	Opposed
(Perkins) 11. Allow undercover police to obtain admission when suspect's lawyer is not present	36% (793) chi-square=14.417, df=1, p=.000	25% (407)	Favored
(Brewer) 12. Allow a voluntary admission of a crime after suspect has asked for lawyer and lawyer is not present	52% (803) chi-square=60.722, df=1, p=.000	29% (407)	Opposed
(Connelly) 13. Allow a suspect who is mentally ill to waive right to counsel	18% (791) chi-square=16.885, df=1, p=.0004	8% (404)	Favored
(Moran) 14. Allow police to use fake papers instead of obtaining a search warrant	11% (807) chi-square=10.359, df=1, p=.001	5% (404)	Opposed
(Gregg) 15. Allow death penalty for murder	80% (790) chi-square=68.497, df=1, P=.000	57% (406)	Favored
(Coker) 16. Allow death penalty for rape	42% (764) chi-square=52.305, df=1, p=.000	21% (403)	Opposed

Table 3.2
**Public Support for Criminal Procedures by Different Levels of Knowledge
and Education (percent of N, listed in parentheses, allowing each procedure)**

	Education			Knowledge		
	High	Middle	Low	High	Middle	Low
Search property from air	53%	52%	51%	57%	52%	47%
	(413)	(272)	(110)	(235)	(329)	(231)
	chi-square=.069			chi-square=4.532		
	df=2, p=.966			df=2, p=.104		
Search trash off property	46%	50%	61%	50%	50%	47%
	(417)	(273)	(112)	(241)	(329)	(232)
	chi-square=7.635			chi-square=1.059		
	df=2, p=.022			df=2, p=.589		
Search closed container in car	42%	47%	48%	40%	44%	50%
	(421)	(273)	(110)	(242)	(330)	(232)
	chi-square=2.082			chi-square=5.690		
	df=2, p=.353			df=2, p=.058		
Frisk suspect if probable cause	82%	84%	82%	84%	82%	79%
	(419)	(274)	(111)	(239)	(333)	(232)
	chi-square=1.566			chi-square=1.533		
	df=2, p=.457			df=2, p=.465		
Stopping suspicious person	80%	85%	84%	80%	83%	83%
	(422)	(275)	(111)	(243)	(333)	(232)
	chi-square=2.666			chi-square=.894		
	df=2, p=.264			df=2, p=.640		
Search body parts for drugs	56%	50%	74%	55%	56%	61%
	(410)	(271)	(112)	(236)	(326)	(231)
	chi-square=18.534			chi-square=2.019		
	df=2, p=.000			df=2, p=.364		
Search ship for documents	68%	65%	73%	67%	69%	70%
	(416)	(270)	(109)	(239)	(326)	(230)
	chi-square=2.631			chi-square=.370		
	df=2, p=.268			df=2, p=.831		
Dogs sniff for drugs	92%	90%	96%	94%	94%	87%
	(420)	(273)	(112)	(242)	(332)	(232)
	chi-square=3.206			chi-square=12.289		
	df=2, p=.201			df=2, p=.002		

	Education			Knowledge		
	High	Middle	Low	High	Middle	Low
Detain suspect 48 hrs before charge	26%	33%	43%	24%	30%	39%
	(413)	(272)	(108)	(239)	(326)	(228)
	chi-square=12.378			chi-square=12.028		
	df=2, p=.002			df=2, p=.002		
Illegal evidence contradicts defendant's witnesses	24%	28%	37%	23%	27%	31%
	(416)	(273)	(111)	(240)	(331)	(229)
	chi-square=7.481			chi-square=3.490		
	df=2, p=.024			df=2, p=.175		
Undercover agents obtain admission	35%	37%	42%	34%	37%	37%
	(417)	(268)	(108)	(236)	(330)	(227)
	chi-square=1.915			chi-square=1.076		
	df=2, p=.384			df=2, p=.584		
Admission w/o lawyer after request	52%	55%	47%	53%	54%	50%
	(421)	(272)	(110)	(243)	(330)	(230)
	chi-square=1.798			chi-square=.986		
	df=2, p=.407			df=2, p=.611		
Allow mentally ill to waive counsel	14%	16%	30%	11%	16%	26%
	(413)	(268)	(110)	(236)	(324)	(231)
	chi-square=15.237			chi-square=18.110		
	df=2, p=.000			df=2, p=.000		
Use fake papers instead of warrant	9%	14%	9%	5%	12%	14%
	(423)	(273)	(111)	(243)	(334)	(230)
	chi-square=5.475			chi-square=8.528		
	df=2, p=.065			df=2, p=.014		
Death penalty for murder	76%	84%	84%	77%	82%	80%
	(412)	(269)	(109)	(233)	(329)	(228)
	chi-square=7.723			chi-square=1.982		
	df=2, p=.021			df=2, p=.371		
Death penalty for rape	43%	41%	41%	33%	43%	48%
	(402)	(255)	(107)	(225)	(320)	(219)
	chi-square=.218			chi-square=10.787		
	df=2, p=.697			df=2, p=.005		

Table 3.3
One-Factor Principal Components Analysis for the Mass Public's Attitudes
Toward Criminal Procedures (N=811)

Search property from air	.56207
Dogs sniff for drugs	.38574
Search trash off property	.50846
Search body parts for drugs	.51928
Search closed container in car	.63722
Search ship for documents	.51834
Stopping suspicious person	.51829
Frisk suspect if probable cause	.47951
Detain suspect 48 hrs before charge	.45341
Undercover agents obtain admission	.54725
Admission w/o lawyer after request	.46772
Evidence illegally obtained contradicts defendant's witnesses	.50940
Police using fake papers instead of warrant	.18425
Allow mentally ill person to waive counsel	.18525

Table 3.4
Rotated Two-Factor Solution for the Mass Public's Attitudes
Toward Criminal Procedures

	Search and Seizure Factor 1	Rights of the Accused Factor 2
Search property from air	.55435	-.01015
Dogs sniff for drugs	.39389	-.04838
Search trash off property	.45898	.01015
Search body parts for drugs	.47895	-.01290
Search closed container in car	.44563	.17963
Search ship for documents	.39872	.07459
Stopping suspicious person	.48060	-.00463
Frisk suspect if probable cause	.42386	.01110
Detain suspect 48 hrs before charge	-.03333	.49475
Undercover agents obtain admission	.01827	.56397
Admission w/o lawyer after request	-.00676	.49962
Evidence illegally obtained contradicts defendants witnesses	.08919	.39856

Correlation between factors=.63

Note: Oblique/oblimin rotation from principal axis factoring; excludes items dealing with police using fake papers and a mentally ill individual waiving the right to counsel; factor pattern matrix, N=811.

Chapter 4

Other Differences of Interest
Between the Public and Legal Elite

In Chapter 3, the basic distributions of opinions toward criminal justice procedures were examined. The responses to the sixteen questions concerning past United States Supreme Court decisions were displayed and examined. The questions were asked of both the mass public and legal elite, and the public was asked questions that measured their level of both political and legal knowledge. It was thus possible to discern basic differences in the level of support for civil libertarian positions between the public and lawyers, as well as within the mass public. The results indicated that with a few exceptions members of the legal profession were more civil libertarian than nonlawyers. However, differences among the mass public based upon level of education and knowledge were not that great. Therefore, it would seem that it is mainly the members of the legal profession who might educate the more educated and knowledgeable members of the attentive public in the facts and law related to the importance of civil liberties. As mentioned, this can be accomplished through their role as experts on the nightly news, guest editorial writers in newspapers, as well as through other means of exposure lawyers now receive. In turn, the attentive public can then educate the less educated and knowledgeable members of the mass public (see Ch. 7). However, in order for this to be plausible to find out what is the cause of the mass public's lesser support for civil liberties, and the ability to educate the public in the importance of these norms, one must discern the causes for the lack of support for civil liberties among members of the mass public. In this chapter, I will present the basic results for some of the independent variables (e.g., age, race, gender, income), for the mass public and legal elite, as well as for different groups within the mass public based upon their level of education and knowledge.

OTHER VARIABLES INFLUENCING PUBLIC OPINION

The second part of the survey dealt with variables that potentially affect opinions on criminal procedures. General questions were asked concerning one's attitude toward warrants, police officers, and other related issues. Respondents were also asked about the root causes of crime; that is, they were asked whether or not they thought that poverty causes crime, lack of opportunity causes crime, and whether or not spending on social programs instead of building more prisons causes crime. Respondents were also asked for their opinions concerning race and crime, courts and crime, policing and crime, fear of crime, personal experience with crime, and sources of information concerning crime. Background questions such as party ID, race, gender, income, and others of interest were also included (see Appendices 1 and 2 for exact question wordings). Since education and knowledge were not found to be as important as one might expect in predicting one's opinion, the need to examine other demographic variables is quite apparent. The relationship of these variables to education and knowledge will be examined as they bear on civil libertarian opinion and support for Supreme Court decisions.

ROOT CAUSES OF CRIME

This section of the survey was included especially to discern whether or not one's views regarding the root causes of crime might affect one's civil libertarian opinions. For example, it is possible that one who believes poverty causes crime might be more civil libertarian than an individual who feels that poverty is not a major explanation. An individual who feels poverty and lack of opportunity contribute to crime might have more compassion for suspected criminals and consequently wish to give little leeway to the police.

Six questions were asked of the respondents to help gauge their opinions regarding the root causes of crime. Two questions dealt with the possibility of the Court, through its lenient rulings, as possibly contributing to crime. Another question dealt with whether or not a possible liberal bias of the media was a cause. Another two questions examined economic-related matters as influences on crime: respondents were asked whether or not they believe poverty to be a cause of crime, and whether or not they believe spending more on prisons would help lower the crime rate. The sixth question asked whether discrimination against the poor and members of minority groups led to crime.

Table 4.1 presents the differences in opinion between the mass public and lawyers concerning these questions on the causes of crime. Table 4.2 presents these opinions among the public for respondents according to their level of education and knowledge. Table 4.3 presents these opinions among the public for respondents by differing racial categories (all tables are at the end of this chapter).

The Court System as Cause

As the results of the survey reveal, one possible explanation for the rise in crime rates since the 1960s, has been that the criminal justice system, rather than serving as the protector of the rights of citizens to live in a crime-free society, has substantially found loopholes in the law to allow suspected criminals to go free. Many point to the correlation between the rise in crime rates from the 1960s to the 1980s and the liberal court decisions of this period (Wilson, 1983). In other words, the courts lowered the risk and severity of punishment to such a degree that a rational individual with thoughts of committing a crime would not adequately be deterred based on calculations of costs and benefits.

It is probable that one's race would play a prominent role in formulating one's opinion concerning these issues. Since many in the black community believe that the courts are stacked against minority defendants, it is probable that blacks would not be as likely as whites to be in favor of a court system tougher on defendants.

Looking at Tables 4.1, 4.2, and 4.3 one can see that lawyers were less likely than the public to believe that a "legal system that is too lenient on criminals causes crime" (52% vs. 82%; p=.001). Among the mass public, the differences based upon one's level of education and knowledge were not that large. Individuals with higher levels of education were only slightly less likely to believe that a lenient court system causes crime (82% agree [high and middle] vs. 86% [low], p=.643), while, for reasons that are not apparent, those with middle levels of knowledge were most likely to agree that this is a cause of crime (81% agree [high] vs. 87% [middle] vs. 78% [low], p=.015). Overall, white and Asian respondents were more likely than black and Hispanic respondents to believe that a lenient system causes crime (89% agree [Asian] vs. 85% [white] vs. 83% [Hispanic] vs. 67% [Black]).

It would make sense that lawyers, who have had personal dealings with the Court, would have more direct experience and knowledge than nonlawyers with respect to the alleged bias toward the rights of the accused in the criminal justice system. It is therefore quite telling that members of the legal profession are more than 30 percentage points less likely than the public as a whole to believe that such a bias exists. It is also worth emphasizing that there were not significant differences within the public based upon one's level of education and knowledge. Therefore, to the extent that the legal profession in fact has better information about the consequences of the judicial system, the current mainstream mass media may not be doing their job in bringing accurate information to the public.

Within the criminal justice system, decisions of the United States Supreme Court in particular have come under much criticism. Some argue that decisions such as *Miranda* have undermined the police in their efforts at bringing criminals to justice. In particular, they wonder why individuals should be let free on procedural technicalities, when evidence points to their guilt.

In response to the second question dealing with the effect of courts on crime, lawyers were much less likely than the public to believe that "liberal Supreme Court decisions that have hurt the efforts of law enforcement" help cause crime (30% vs. 65%; p=.001). Here, again, the differences in opinion based upon knowledge and education were not that large. Respondents with higher levels of education (62% agree [high] vs. 69% [middle] vs. 66% [low], p=.171), and knowledge (60% agree [high] vs. 69% [middle] vs. 65% [low], p=.084) were only slightly less likely to believe that liberal Supreme Court decisions have helped spur crime. Analyzing the results by race, black respondents were least likely to believe liberal Supreme Court decisions cause crime (74% agree [Hispanic] vs. 68% [white] vs. 50% [Asian] vs. 44% [black]).

There are a few possible explanations for the differences between the mass public and lawyers. First, it is possible that lawyers do not believe that the Court has been deciding cases in a decisively liberal direction. Second, even if the Court has been deciding cases in this manner, lawyers may not believe that there is a causal connection between the decisions and crime. It should be noted that lawyers are more likely to follow United States Supreme Court decisions, and are therefore more likely, than others, to know the philosophical direction of recent Court decisions. Again, it is the job of the legal elite to pass along the true facts to members of the mass public.

In sum, members of the mass public, regardless of their level of education and knowledge, are much more likely than those in the legal profession to perceive that the legal system in general, and Supreme Court decisions in particular, are too lenient and are important causes of crime today.

The Media

Another popular target as a cause of the rising crime rate has been the mass media. Many believe that the media have a liberal bent and, as applied to issues of criminal justice, are permissive toward violence and deviant behavior and protective of rights. Critics point to the fact that journalists, as well as most of the Hollywood elite, have opinions that are much more to the Left, on average, than the rest of society. Many have argued that this bias is apparent in the reporting of the news. Further, since modern society has become inundated by mass communication, the media can have a great influence in shaping society's values and norms.

Lawyers were less likely than members of the mass public to believe that "the media's emphasis on the rights of the accused and not on the rights of the victim" leads to crime (37% vs. 70%, p=.000). Among the public, there were only slight differences based upon levels of education and knowledge, with individuals with higher levels of education and knowledge slightly and insignificantly less likely than others to believe the media's protectiveness of criminals' rights to be a cause of crime (education: 69% agree [high] vs. 70% [middle] vs. 73% [low], p=.654; knowledge: 68% agree [high] vs. 73% [middle] vs. 69% [low], p=.394). Also, Blacks were again less likely to believe this to be a cause of crime (90% believe that the media are a cause of crime [Asian] vs. 82% [Hispanic] vs. 71% [white] vs. 58% [black]).

There are at least two plausible explanations for the public being almost twice as likely as lawyers to believe the media's focus on the rights of the accused causes crime. One possibility is that the public's opinions concerning this issue might be related to individuals' attitudes measured by other questions in the survey—especially prior ones. Since more among the public than lawyers are convinced that the courts are too lenient on criminal defendants, they might be inclined to perceive that any story on the news which emphasizes the rights of the accused is unnecessary and superfluous. Second, members of the legal profession, unlike the public, are likely to have acquired detailed knowledge of crime from studying the legal system in law school, as well as firsthand knowledge from the practice of criminal law. Therefore, lawyers would have much more information and more complex schema regarding the causes of crime, so they might not give as much credence to the notion that the media causes crime.

Economic Explanations

As opposed to accusations that the courts and media have caused the rise of crime, others place the blame on underlying economic conditions. Economic reasons are distinguished from the others in that they do not argue that crime can be solved by imposing harsher sentences and by changing societal opinion to be more sympathetic toward the rights of victims. Rather, the United States is considered a society that denies economic opportunity and well being for many people, and this leads to crime.

Lawyers were 9 percentage points more likely than the public to agree that "the lack of economic opportunities for the poor and for members of minority groups leads to crime" (66% vs. 57%, p=.003). Within the public, differences based upon education were larger than the differences varying by knowledge. Respondents with high levels of education were 11 percentage points more likely than those with low levels to believe that lack of opportunity can lead to crime (59% agree [high] vs. 58% [middle] vs. 48% [low], p=.088), while only 3 percentage points separated respondents with different levels of knowledge (59% agree [high] vs. 57% [middle] vs. 56% [low], p=.719). Blacks were more likely than whites to believe lack of opportunity to be a cause of crime (71% agree [Hispanic] vs. 67% [black] vs. 56% [white] vs. 50% [Asian]).

In sum, the differences between lawyers and the public were greater when the alleged cause was the media and the criminal justice system than when the issue was the American economic system. In addition, education seemed to matter more for the question dealing with economic issues. One possible explanation is that the reasoning of this question is less tied to the technical legal knowledge that one might possess, than to one's ideology regarding economic issues. It is worth noting that a majority of individuals in all subgroups (except those in the lowest category of education) agree that lack of opportunity is a cause of crime, a traditionally liberal position. Also, members of minority groups were more likely than others to believe this to be a source of crime. Again, many in these communities believe that the system is still biased against members of minority communities.

Another possible explanation for crime, some argue, is the economic structure of the United States. Inherent in capitalism in the United States is inequality of income. Inequality, in addition to poverty and subsistence, can turn many to a life of crime, since they see others in society with more than they possess. In other words, relative poverty, a situation wherein one feels deprived since others are seen with more, can also lead an individual to crime (Banfield, 1970).

The mass public and legal elite were evenly split on the issue of whether or not "the lack of income equality" causes crime: 52% of lawyers vs. 53% of the mass public responded that poverty causes crime. Among the mass public, there was not much difference in opinion based upon one's party or ideology. There was only a 4 percentage point difference based on the public's different levels of knowledge (54% agree [high and middle] vs. 50% [low], p=.626), and 2 percentage points separating individuals with different levels of education (54% agree [high] vs. 52% [middle and low], p=.823). In addition, there was little difference in opinion based upon race (64% believe that poverty causes crime [Hispanic] vs. 53% [white] vs. 52% [black] vs. 50% [Asian]).

Unlike the other results described earlier, there was little difference based upon legal education, general education, knowledge, or race. This is the first question bearing on attitudes toward crime on which lawyers and the mass public do not disagree. There are two possible explanations for this. First, this opinion is not dependent upon a legal education per se. Second, knowledge and education would have little basis for playing a distinctive role in the formulation of an individual's opinion regarding this issue. While the better educated might understand the problems of poverty in society, and the travails faced by the poor, they might not think this justifies the commission of illegal activity. In contrast, individuals with less education and income, while not condoning such behavior outright, might be more understanding of such activity since they might have experienced similar predicaments. Also, though it is shown from earlier questions that blacks believe the system to be unjust, they still do not believe that poverty is an excuse for crime.

In sum, a majority of both the mass public and lawyers believed that both economic issues and lack of opportunity and poverty are causes of crime. Both of these causes of crime would fall under traditionally liberal explanations for crime. There was, however, much greater support for the traditionally conservative explanations of crime among members of the mass public (i.e., lenient court system, liberal Supreme Court decisions, mass media's emphasis on the rights of the accused), regardless of level of education and knowledge. This was not the case for members of the legal profession, who were more likely to affirm the liberal explanation for crime.

Government Spending

Another commonly expressed explanation for the rise in crime has been the claim that the government has been spending money in the wrong places in its war on crime (Wilson, 1985). Many conservatives argue that if the government would spend more money on building prisons, as opposed to spending money on social programs that have not worked, crime would drop. The presumption here is that deterrence is very important to eliminate crime, and imprisonment is an important part of the solution.

Interestingly, neither the mass public nor legal elite agreed overall that "money being spent on social spending instead of on building prisons" causes crime (31% of lawyers vs. 24% of the public, p=.021). Within the public, individuals with higher levels of education, by 13 percentage points, were less likely to agree that social spending vs. building prisons is a cause of crime (26% agree [high] vs. 35% [low] vs. 39% [low], p=.005), while the differences were only half as great for differing levels of knowledge (27% agree [high] vs. 31% [middle] vs. 33% [low], p=266). Though Blacks were slightly less likely to believe that this is a cause of crime, all races did not believe this to be cause of crime (32% agree [Hispanic] vs. 31% [white] vs. 30% [Asian] vs. 23% [black]).

There are a few ways to interpret these results. First, it is possible that the public does not believe that building more prisons can alleviate crime; rather, focusing on social programs is needed. Another explanation is that the public believes it is important to build prisons, but spending on social programs is also of importance. In addition, it is possible that the public blames neither prisons nor social programs for rising crime rates, rather, they believe that the lack of enough police officers to apprehend criminals combined with a court system too lenient on defendants who are apprehended are the main causes of crime.

In all, lawyers, on average, took a more liberal view than the public on the causes of crime. In general, the public took a conservative position when asked about the legal system, the Supreme Court, and the mass media. However, when dealing with poverty, social programs vs. prisons, and economic opportunities for the poor and members of minority groups, the public was more liberal. Therefore, it seems that the public associates the terms "legal system," "mass media," and "Supreme Court" with liberalism. The public attributes blame to these institutions for what the public perceives as an environment with a rising crime rate.

FAIRNESS OF THE COURT SYSTEM

This section examines responses to questions regarding the fairness of the criminal justice system. Specifically, two questions were asked concerning race and the courts, and another concerning the courts more generally. The hypothesis here is that respondents who believe that the criminal justice system is unfair to minorities would be less likely to give the police great leeway in their procedures, since they would believe that society must be extremely vigilant in who it arrests, because justice will not take place in the courtroom. Conversely, one who believes in the fairness of the court system would give more leeway to the police. Table 4.4 presents the responses for the mass public and lawyers, Table 4.5 breaks down the public's results by different levels of education and knowledge, and Table 4.6 reports the public's results for different racial groups.

Race

As discussed in Chapter 3, one of the most controversial issues in the war on crime has been the imposition of the death penalty for individuals accused of murder. Specifically, the way in which the death penalty is administered is allegedly racially biased, since, proportionally, blacks are sentenced and administered the death penalty more than whites. One counterargument is that the fact that blacks are sentenced to the death penalty in greater numbers than their numbers within the population is not reflective of discrimination; rather, it is caused by blacks being more likely than whites to commit crimes which are punishable by the death penalty.

As with the causes of crime, lawyers were also more liberal than the mass public on the issue of the death penalty. When asked "with regard to the death penalty, would you say blacks have generally been treated the same as whites, less well than whites, or better than whites," the majority of lawyers (63%) believe that blacks get treated less well than whites in the administration of the death penalty. However, only 40% of the mass public believed that blacks get treated less well than whites, a 23 percentage point difference from lawyers (p. =000). Within the mass public, differences based upon knowledge and, to an even greater degree, education were quite large. Respondents with low levels of education were 20 percentage points more likely than those with high levels of education to believe that all are treated equal when it comes to the death penalty (68% all treated same [low] vs. 57% [middle] vs. 48% [high], p=.000), while those with high levels of education were 23 percentage points more likely to believe that blacks are treated less well (46% less well [high] vs. 37% [middle] vs. 23% [low], p=.000). The same pattern existed for knowledge, though the numbers are not as striking (47% all treated the same [high] vs. 55% [middle] vs. 58% [low]; 48% less well [high] vs. 37% [middle] vs. 35% [low], p=.030). Interestingly, Black respondents had opinions similar to lawyers (61% less well [black] vs. 54% [Hispanic] vs. 37% [white] vs. 10% [Asian]).

This issue in particular has received a great deal of attention in the news media. A probable reason for the great differences based on one's legal training, as well as general education, is probably the mass media's coverage of this issue. Individuals with greater levels of education would have a greater propensity to follow "newsworthy" issues within the mass media, and would, therefore, have a greater chance of becoming exposed to the cases of alleged bias in carrying out the death penalty. Another possibility is that the more educated and members of the legal profession have learned the "politically correct" response, which is that the death penalty is unfair to the poor and to members of minority groups. It is also possible that the death penalty is genuinely unfair to the poor and members of minority groups and the educated and lawyers are able to see this to a greater degree than others.

This issue is one that has acquired, over time, a great deal of salience, as well as a "correct" answer that might cause some, especially the more educated, to provide the "correct" answer. Hence the issue becomes, what does the public think about racial justice when the question is presented in more general terms, uncontaminated by a possible need to provide the "acceptable" response.

When asked if they "believe blacks are accused and convicted of criminal acts more than whites, simply because they are black," a majority of both groups, lawyers and the mass public, believed this not to be true (61% system fair [lawyers] vs. 62% [mass public], p=.579). Among the public, only 7 percentage points separated respondents based upon levels of education (61% say system fair [high] vs. 58% [middle] vs. 65% [low], p=.467), while there was an 8 percentage point difference based upon levels of knowledge (62% say system fair [high] vs. 63% [middle] vs. 55% [low], p=.145). However, a majority of black respondents from within the mass public believed that the system was unfair toward black defendants (64% say system unfair [Hispanic] vs. 61% [black] vs. 40% [Asian] vs. 36% [white]).

The results to this question are quite interesting and, to a certain degree, contradictory to the responses to the question concerning the death penalty. It would seem quite illogical for an individual to believe that the court system is basically fair toward blacks, except when it comes to the death penalty. The apparent contradiction was most noticeable for members of the legal profession. One possible explanation is that the lawyers and more educated respondents felt that they had to argue that the current death penalty system was biased, since they would otherwise look unknowledgeable or racist, while in answering the question concerning the overall fairness of the system toward black defendants, they were free to state their true opinions. Others might argue that even the most educated are unknowledgeable concerning biases in the court system in general, and have obtained only enough information regarding discrimination in applying the death penalty due the great amount of coverage it has received in the mass media.

Local Criminal Courts

As mentioned earlier, many blame the courts for the high crime rates nationwide. In addition, if people feel that the courts are letting criminals off based on technicalities in the law, as opposed to actual innocence, there would be an inclination to give greater leeway to the police, especially concerning having useful, but illegally obtained, evidence thrown out of court.

Some 61% of lawyers as opposed to 37% of the public believe that "in relation to crime, the courts in their area" were about right, while 30% of lawyers versus 58% of the public believe that the courts in their area were not harsh enough in dealing with criminals (p=.000). Interestingly, fewer than 10% in either survey thought that the courts were too harsh. Differences in opinion based upon levels of education and knowledge were not as large. There were 9 to 12 percentage point differences based upon level of education among those answering that the courts are about right or not harsh enough (39% about right [high] vs. 37% [middle] vs. 30% [low]; 57% not harsh enough [high] vs. 58% [middle] vs. 69% [low], p=.108). There were smaller differences based upon levels of knowledge. Individuals with low levels of knowledge were slightly less likely to believe that the courts were about right and as likely to believe that the courts were not harsh enough (40% about right [high] vs. 38% [middle] vs. 33% [low]; 58% not harsh enough [high and low] vs. 60% [middle], p=.003). Still, less than 10% of these subgroups believed the courts to be too harsh. However, once more, black respondents had opinions slightly different than other respondents. Blacks were more likely than others to believe that the courts in their area were too harsh on criminal defendants (15% too harsh [black] vs. 4% [Hispanic] vs. 3% [white]).

Again, members of the legal profession are more likely to have personal knowledge of the legal system, while members of the public at large receive information about the courts to a greater extent through the mass media. Usually this occurs when the media cover sensational cases, and especially when there is a perception that the court system has failed. This causes the public to have a low opinion of the court system, and to believe that the civil liberties of criminal defendants are overly protected. The most notable of the sensational cases was the O.J. Simpson trial, which was still ongoing during the same time period as these surveys. Clearly, it would be helpful for those who know the intricacies of the criminal justice system to pass along this information to others.

TRUST IN INSTITUTIONS

Another possible influence on opinions concerning civil liberties is the level of trust individuals have in the relevant institutions. Specifically, one explanation for lawyers having opinions that are more civil libertarian than the mass public, as well as more consistent with recent Supreme Court decisions, might be affected partially by lawyers having less respect for the police and more trust in the Supreme Court. One who has less confidence in the police would be more likely to give the police less leeway in the tactics they use to apprehend potential criminal defendants. Table 4.7 presents the relevant findings here for the mass public and lawyers; Table 4.8 reports the results for different levels of education and knowledge.

Police

The job and duties of the police officer have long been a controversial subject. Many people within minority communities have long been suspicious of police officers. Others see the police as saviors, making the difference between a safe community and a community riddled by crime. Hence, one can surmise that there should be a strong relationship between the trust and respect people have for police officers and the discretion they would give to the police in fighting crime.

Lawyers were, in fact, 21 percentage points less likely than the mass public to have a great deal of respect for the police (44% vs. 65%), and 20 percentage points more likely to have only some respect (47% vs. 27%, p=.000). About 10% or fewer among lawyers and the public had hardly any respect for the police. Within the mass public, an interesting trend emerged. Respondents with higher levels of education were less likely to have a great deal of respect for the police (65% great deal [high] vs. 61% [middle] vs. 72% [low], and were more likely to have only some respect for the police [27% only some [high] vs. 31% [middle] vs. 20% [low], p=.262). In contrast, respondents with higher levels of knowledge had more respect for the police than the less educated (66% great deal [high] vs. 68% [middle] vs. 60% [low]; 29% only some [high] vs. 26% [middle] vs. 28% [low], p=.031). Only individuals in the low knowledge category had more than 10% of respondents with hardly any confidence in the police (13%).

The fact that lawyers are less respectful of police is consistent with the notion that those with more education are less likely to defer to authority. In addition, that many lawyers have personal dealings with the police might have led them to a more cynical opinion. It should also be noted that since blacks made up a disproportionate number of the respondents in the low categories for both education and knowledge, and were less likely than others to respect the police, the pattern was slightly skewed. In other words, if only whites were included the more educated and knowledgeable would be less respectful of the police to a greater degree. In all, this may help explain why lawyers are more civil libertarian and less willing than the mass public to give leeway to the police during the course of a criminal investigation.

The Supreme Court

Another possible cause for civil libertarian attitudes is the confidence that one has in the United States Supreme Court. Having a great deal of respect for this Court, would seem to lead people to be deferential to the Court and to give more leeway to the police, since there would be less worry that innocent people would be improperly convicted.

Interestingly, an overwhelming majority of lawyers (75%) are most confident in the Supreme Court, while only a plurality of the mass public (41%)

chose that branch. Also, 28% of the mass public vs. only 8% of lawyers could not choose any branch of government in which to be confident (p=.000). Among the public, the more knowledgeable and more educated were more likely to be most confident in the Supreme Court (education: 53% [high] vs. 29% [middle] vs. 22% [low]; knowledge: 50% [high] vs. 41% [middle] vs. 29% [low]), and less likely to be most confident in the presidency (education: 8% [high] vs. 15% [middle] vs. 24% [low]; knowledge: 9% [high] vs. 12% [middle] vs. 18% [low]), and no branch at all (education: 20% [high] vs. 36% [middle and low] p=.000; knowledge: 21% [high] vs. 29% [middle] vs. 33% [low], p=.000).

It is quite interesting to find that lawyers, as well as the more educated of the public, are much more confident in the Supreme Court and less likely not to be confident in any branch of government than others. This could lead one to be more civil libertarian. However, one caveat to bear in mind is that the Court itself has been less supportive of civil liberties, and its supporters might therefore be more inclined to follow its lead.

Court Discretion

Another likely contributor to the formation of one's opinion concerning agreement with the Court's decision, regardless of one's own opinion, is the role one envisions for the Court. The question that has been the subject of great debate among scholars has been whether or not the Court should take public opinion into account in its decision-making process. Some have argued that since the Court is composed of some great thinkers, they need only base their decisions on their own view of what the law should be. Others have argued that in deciding law for the entire nation, the Court should take the opinions of the nation into account.

When asked whether the Court should follow the wishes of society or its own, lawyers were 28 percentage points more likely to state that the Court should follow its own judgment (78% vs. 51%), and the mass public was three time as likely to believe that the Court should follow society's wishes (39% vs. 12%, p=.000). Only 10% of the mass public and 3% of lawyers volunteered that it depends on the situation. Individuals with higher levels of education, and to an even greater extent knowledge, were more likely to believe that the Court should follow its wishes (education: 58% [high] vs. 42% [middle] vs. 44% [low], p=.000; knowledge: 60% [high] vs. 53% [middle] vs. 37% [low], p=.000).

The responses to this question are consistent with the results to the previous question which asked respondents to choose the branch of government in which they were most confident. If the less educated and knowledgeable are less trusting in government in general, and the Supreme Court in particular, it follows that they would also give the court less leeway in decision making. Possible explanations, again, include that the more educated have a more sophisticated understanding of the criminal justice system in general, and the courts in particular, while the less educated merely obtain their information from the mass media, especially television, that at times focus on the sensational cases, which tend to give the courts a bad name. In sum, lawyers have more confidence, than others, in the Supreme Court, are more willing to allow the Court to follow its own interpretation of the law, and have less confidence in the police. This may help explain why lawyers are generally less likely to grant police more leeway while investigating a crime, yet more inclined to follow the ruling of a court, even when the court rules against what would be considered civil libertarian norms. This will be examined further in Chapters 5 and 6.

PERSONAL FEELINGS TOWARD CRIME

Another likely set of influences on opinions concerning civil liberties in the area of criminal procedure are personal experiences and fear of crime. One might surmise that individuals who have had more personal exposure to crime, or are otherwise more fearful of crime, would be less civil libertarian. Table 4.9 presents the results for the lawyers and the mass public, Table 4.10 reports the responses for differing categories of education and knowledge within the mass public, and Table 4.11 reports the responses for the question concerning fear of walking alone at night for differing categories of race, age, and gender.

Personal Experience

The most dramatic and disturbing event an individual might encounter in life is being a crime victim. Among the many personal effects this might have are on beliefs concerning the "rules of the game" in fighting crime. If an individual or one of his family members has been victimized, he might become more willing to grant great leeway to the police in fighting crime.

Ironically, considering the civil libertarian positions held by many lawyers, lawyers are more likely to have had crimes committed against them personally. While 48% of the public reported having had no crime committed against them or their families, only 11% of lawyers were as fortunate; 34% of lawyers reported having their car vandalized while only 11% among the public. Lawyers were also twice as likely to be mugged (11% vs. 5%), and were 50% more likely to have had a robbery committed in their home (32% vs. 20%, p=.000). Among the mass public, a related pattern emerged. Individuals with less education and knowledge were much more likely not to have had crimes committed against them or their families (education: 37% [high], 57% [middle], 68% [low]; knowledge: 38% [high], 48% [middle], 59% [low]), and they were less likely to have been victims of robbery in the home (education: 25% [high] vs. 15% [middle] vs. 14% [low]; knowledge: 26% [high] vs. 22% [middle] vs. 11% [low]), or of car vandalism (education: 14% [high] vs. 10% [middle] vs. 5% [low], p=.000; knowledge: 18% [high] 7% [middle] vs. 10% [low], p=.000). Also, the more educated were more likely to have been the victims of a mugging or physical assault.

While the results are possibly surprising, they are explicable, since one can assume that lawyers, as well as the more educated and more knowledgeable, are likely to be better off financially and to have nicer homes and cars, and carry more money, as well as have and wear more expensive jewelry, than the less successful members of society, so that they are more likely targets of crime. In addition, it is possible that lawyers, who are more likely than the mass public to live in urban areas, might live and work in high-crime areas. These variations in opinion, however, are quite interesting in light of the fact that the more educated and knowledgeable remain more civil libertarian than others.

Fear of Crime

One of the consequences of societal fear of violent crime is the limitations it puts on the freedom to move about as one wishes. Many wonder why they should be locked in their homes at night, unable to move about freely, while criminal are free to roam the streets. It is reasonable to suspect that respondents who were more fearful to walk alone at night would be less protective of the civil liberties of criminal defendants.

When asked whether or not there "is any area near where you live—that is, within a mile—where you would be afraid to walk alone at night," 42% of the public vs. 45% of lawyers responded that they were fearful (p=.329). Within the public, the less educated and knowledgeable were more fearful to walk alone at night (education: 41% [high] vs. 38% [middle] vs. 55% [low], p=.009; knowledge: 37% [high] vs. 41% [middle] vs. 47% [low], p=.085). Within the mass public, blacks (51% fear walking [black] vs. 41% [white] 40% [Asian] vs. 36% [Hispanic], women (50% fear walking [women] vs. 33% [men], and the elderly (55% fear walking [65 and older] vs. 41% [44-64] vs. 39% [18-24] vs. 38% [25-33] vs. 37% [34-43], were most fearful walking at night (see Table 4.11).

This helps explain why lawyers and the more educated are more civil libertarian despite the fact that they have had more crimes committed against them and their families. Ironically, they are less afraid to walk alone at night. This might be due, in part, to the fact that lawyers and the more educated, most probably, live in safer and more upscale communities, despite the fact that they are more likely to be the victims of crime. A possible cause for the higher crime rate among lawyers, is that lawyers do not perceive crime to be as large of a problem as do the public, and therefore are less cautious and find themselves in riskier situations. An explanation for the discrepancy between the public's perception of the crime problem and its actual rate of victimization is that the nature of the crimes of which lawyers are more likely to be victims are those against one's property (car, robbery, muggings), while the public or their family members are more likely to be the victims of murder (5% vs. 3%), and rape

(4% vs. 2%), and are almost as likely to be the victims of physical assault (7% [public] vs. 9% [lawyers]). One murder or rape can cause great fear and panic within a community, while a car being stolen or a robbery of one's home will not cause so great an uproar.

An even greater fear of crime can occur when an individual is fearful of intruders while home at night. Some have argued that we are living in a society void of morality when the elderly, as well as individuals in poorer communities, cannot feel safe in their own homes.

When asked whether or not they felt safe at home at night, 91% of the public and legal elite (p=.975) answered in the affirmative. Among the public, the more educated and knowledgeable were slightly more likely than others to feel safe at home at night (education: 91% [high] vs. 94% [middle] vs. 86% [low], p=.093; knowledge: 93% [high and middle] vs. 88% [low], p=.049).

In sum, lawyers, as well as the more educated and more knowledgeable, are more likely to have had crimes committed against them or their families. Yet they are not more fearful of crime than the public at large. The fact that lawyers are not more fearful of crime than others, might explain why they are not less civil libertarian.

SOURCES OF INFORMATION

Average Americans almost certainly obtain most of their information regarding the situation of crime in America from the mass media. They do not normally have access to, or an interest in, complicated statistical data regarding crime. As a result, the method in which the mass media present the current crime situation is quite pertinent. Responses to questions bearing on this, asked only of the mass public, are reported in Table 4.12.

Favorite Medium

It is well known that television in particular covers the state of crime in a quite sensational fashion. On many evenings, the local nightly news begins with reports of various crimes, especially rape and murder (see Frankel, 1997). Since many people obtain all their "hard news" during this time, the perception of even higher crime rates might exist. In fact, even if crime was indeed on the decline, it would not be noticeable to the average television viewer since the nightly news would still begin in the same fashion. In addition, television reports rarely examine the causes and nature of crime in a sophisticated manner. In contrast, individuals who obtain their information from newspapers would be more likely to have acquired a deeper understanding of the state as well as causes of crime, since these outlets examine these issue with much greater depth and complexity.

Members of the public were asked: "Where do you usually get *most* of your information on crime in the United States? From the newspapers, radio, television, magazines, talking to people, or where?" Table 4.12 reports that respondents with higher levels of knowledge were more likely to obtain their information regarding crime from the newspapers (education: 25% [high] vs. 18% [middle] vs. 14% [low]; knowledge: 30% [high] vs. 18% [middle] vs. 17% [low]), as opposed to the television, which was more likely to be the source of information for the less educated and knowledgeable (education: 53% [high] vs. 64% [middle] vs. 71% [low], p=.024; knowledge: 48% [high] vs. 64% [middle and low], p=.000). More educated and knowledgeable respondents were also slightly more likely to obtain their information from the radio (education: 10% [high and middle] vs. 9% [low]; knowledge: 14% [high] vs. 8% [middle and low]), and from magazines (education: 3% [high] vs. 1% [middle and low]; knowledge: 3% [high] vs. 2% [middle] vs. 1% [low]).

These results can be quite helpful in explaining the lesser degree of support for civil liberties among the less educated. Not only are the better educated likely to have a deeper and more sophisticated level and degree of knowledge from their schooling, they also continue to obtain new information from more sophisticated sources.

Another possible related variable is the amount of time one views television each day. Indeed, if television news continues to highlight major crime events, and TV dramas exaggerate loopholes in the current state of law, through which criminal defendants can slip, the amount of TV viewing may be related to a disdain for civil liberties.

When asked "on the average day, how many hours do you personally watch television," the less educated and knowledgeable responded that they watched a greater number of hours than those with more education and knowledge. The less educated and knowledgeable were about four times as likely to say they watched five or more hours per day (education: 4% [high] vs. 12% [middle] vs. 14% [low], p=.000; knowledge: 2% [high] vs. 10% [middle] vs. 13% [low], p=.000), and around twice as likely to view four hours of television per day (education: 6% [high] vs. 11% [middle] vs. 14% [low]; knowledge: 6% [high] vs. 8% [middle] vs. 12% [low]). Also, the more educated and knowledgeable were more likely not to watch any television (education: 9% [high] vs. 7% [middle] vs. 6% [low]; knowledge: 11% [high] vs. 5% [middle] vs. 9% [low]), or 1 hour of television (education: 38% [high] vs. 23% [middle] vs. 25% [low]; knowledge: 37% [high] vs. 31% [middle] vs. 25% [low]). In all, there was substantial correlation between education and knowledge and the amount of hours one watched television; the more educated and knowledgeable the less TV viewing.

Thus, the less educated and knowledgeable are more likely to list TV as their main source of information, and they in fact report that they are likely to watch TV many hours of the day. This group is also less likely than others to support the civil liberties of criminal defendants. Though correlation does not necessarily mean causation, the possibility of such a causal effect will be examined further in Chapters 5 and 6.

IDEOLOGY AND PARTISANSHIP

Interestingly, Table 4.13 indicates that lawyers were slightly more likely than members of the public to identify themselves as Republican identifiers or leaners (Independent, but closer to Republican: 19% [lawyers] vs. 6% [public]; Republican (19% [lawyers] vs. 16% [public]; strong Republican: 8% [lawyers] vs. 18% [public], p=.000). This was the case even though lawyers were more likely to identify themselves as having, or leaning toward, a liberal ideology, more often than the public (strong liberal: 8% [lawyers] vs. 6% [public]; liberal: 10% [lawyers] vs. 11% [public]; moderate, but closer to a liberal: 21% [lawyers] vs. 10% [public], p=.000).

CONCLUSION

In sum, it seems that the liberal beliefs of lawyers stem not from following the ideology of their party, but rather from a combination of other factors. As this bears toward the criminal justice system, lawyers' beliefs that the system is not too lenient on criminals might stem from their personal knowledge of the system, while the public might be swayed by sensational news stories which highlight criminals "getting off easy." In addition, it is possible that some of the opinions lawyers possess might be related to exposure to current elite debate (Zaller, 1992).

For example, lawyers take apparently contradictory opinions on the issues dealing with race. While believing that blacks are treated less well in meting out the death penalty, lawyers also believe that blacks are not generally convicted more than whites. One possible explanation is that lawyers have been exposed to elite discussion (see Zaller, 1992) regarding discriminatory implementation of the death penalty and are therefore more inclined than the public at large to believe that there is discrimination in the administration of the death penalty. However, as direct participants in the legal system, lawyers might be less willing to admit to general inequalities within the system, or these might not be directly visible to them on a regular basis.

Further, as noted, though lawyers have had more crimes committed against them personally, they still wish to uphold the rights of the accused to a greater extent than the rest of the public. Here, this is probably due to their regular awareness of court decisions which have been mindful of the rights and liberties of the suspects and defendants (this awareness is related to their higher level of education as well).

FURTHER ANALYSIS

This chapter has provided the foundations of the analysis by reporting the basic results of the two surveys. The two chapters that follow will investigate further the causal effects on attitudes toward criminal justice procedures of the variables examined in this chapter. Chapters 5 and 6 will also present further results of other subgroup variations and influences such as race, gender, age, income, religion, region, partisan identification, and ideological leaning. These analyses will also compare further the opinions of the elite among the mass public with the opinions of the legal elite. They will examine the possible separate conditional effects of a legal education, as well as that of different experiences and perceptions of crime, and perception of other matters bearing on criminal justice issues that have been identified in this chapter.

Table 4.1
Percent of Mass Public and Legal Elite Opinion Believing
in Six Very Important Factors Causing Crime Today

	Mass Public	Lawyers
1. A legal system that is too lenient on criminals	82% (803)	52% (405)
	chi-square=127.263, df=1, p=.000	
2. Liberal Supreme Court decisions that have hurt the efforts of law enforcement	65% (795)	30% (405)
	chi-square=133.174, df=1, p=.000	
3. The media's emphasis on the rights of the accused and not on the rights of the victim	70% (803)	37% (402)
	chi-square=119.285, df=1, p=.000	
4. The lack of economic opportunities for the poor and for members of minority groups	57% (808)	66% (402)
	chi-square=8.813, df=1, p=.003	
5. Lack of income equality	53% (808)	52% (407)
	chi-square=.110, df=1, p=.740	
6. Money being spent on social programs instead of on building prisons	31% (793)	24% (402)
	chi-square=5.356, df=1, p=.021	

Table 4.2

Percent of Mass Public, by Levels of Education and Knowledge, Believing in Six Very Important Factors Causing Crime Today

	Education			Knowledge		
	High	Middle	Low	High	Middle	Low
1. A legal system that is too lenient on criminals	82%	82%	86%	81%	87%	78%
	(419)	(273)	(111)	(244)	(329)	(230)
	chi-square=.884			chi-square=8.453		
	df=2, p=.643			df=2, p=.015		
2. Liberal Supreme Court decisions that have hurt the efforts of law enforcement	62%	69%	66%	60%	69%	65%
	(417)	(268)	(110)	(242)	(328)	(225)
	chi-square=3.535			chi-square=4.947		
	df=2, p=.171			df=2, p=.084		
3. The media's emphasis on the rights of the accused and not on the rights of the victim	69%	70%	73%	68%	73%	69%
	(421)	(272)	(110)	(243)	(330)	(230)
	chi-square=.851			chi-square=1.864		
	d=2, p=.654			df=2, p=.394		
4. The lack of economic opportunities for the poor and for members of minority groups	59%	58%	48%	59%	57%	56%
	(424)	(273)	(111)	(244)	(334)	(230)
	chi-square=4.863			chi-square=.659		
	df=2, p=.088			df=2, p=.719		
5. Lack of income equality	54%	52%	52%	54%	54%	50%
	(423)	(273)	(112)	(243)	(333)	(232)
	chi-square=.389			chi-square=.938		
	df=2, p=.823			df=2, p=.626		
6. Money being spent on social programs instead of on building prisons	26%	35%	39%	27%	31%	33%
	(414)	(269)	(110)	(240)	(325)	(228)
	chi-square=10.613			chi-square=2.646		
	df=2, p=.005			df=2, p=.266		

Table 4.3
Percent of Mass Public, Based upon One's Race, Believing in
Six Very Important Factors Causing Crime Today

	White	Black	Asian	Hispanic
1. A legal system that is too lenient on criminals	85% (672)	67% (85)	89% (9)	83% (27)
	chi-square=19.526, df=3, p=.000			
2. Liberal Supreme Court decisions that have hurt the efforts of law enforcement	68% (664)	44% (84)	50% (10)	74% (27)
	chi-square=20.202, df=3, p=.000			
3. The media's emphasis on the rights of the accused and not on the rights of the victim	71% (670)	58% (85)	90% (10)	82% (28)
	chi-square=10.422, df=3, p=.015			
4. The lack of economic opportunities for the poor and for members of minority groups	56% (675)	67% (85)	50% (10)	71% (28)
	chi-square=6.382, df=3, p=.094			
5. Lack of income equality	53% (674)	52% (86)	50% (10)	64% (28)
	chi-square=1.463, df=3, p=.691			
6. Money being spent on social programs instead of on building prisons	31% (661)	23% (84)	30% (10)	32% (28)
	chi-square=2.627, df=3, p=.453			

Table 4.4
Mass Public and Legal Elite Opinions Regarding Race and Crime, and Courts and Crime

	Mass Public	Lawyers
1. Blacks have been treated, with regard to the death penalty		
the same as whites	53% (430)	33% (13)
less well than whites	40% (318)	63% (254)
better than whites	7% (55)	4% (18)
Total N	803	404
	chi-square=58.414, df=2, p=.000	
2. Percent believing blacks accused of crimes more than whites?	39% (317)	38% (153)
Total N	806	406
	chi-square=.308, df=1, p=.579	
3. In relation to crime, courts are		
too harsh	4% (34)	9% (34)
about right	37% (298)	61% (245)
not harsh enough	59% (472)	30% (122)
Total N	804	401
	chi-square=86.272, df=2, p=.000	

Table 4.5
Mass Public Opinion, for Different Levels of Knowledge and Education, Regarding Race and Crime, and Courts and Crime

	Education			Knowledge		
	High	Middle	Low	High	Middle	Low
1. Blacks have been treated, with regard to the death penalty the same as whites	48%	57%	68%	47%	55%	58%
	(201)	(154)	(75)	(113)	(184)	(133)
less well than whites	46%	37%	23%	48%	37%	35%
	(193)	(100)	(25)	(115)	(123)	(80)
better than whites	6%	6%	10%	5%	8%	8%
	(27)	(17)	(11)	(12)	(25)	(18)
Total N	421	271	111	240	332	231
	chi-square=21.850			chi-square=10.691		
	df=4, p=.000			df=4, p=.030		
2. Percent believing blacks accused of crimes more than whites	39%	42%	35%	38%	37%	45%
	(193)	(100)	(25)	(90)	(123)	(104)
Total N	421	271	111	240	333	233
	chi-square=1.522			chi-square=3.884		
	df=2, p=.467			df=2, p=.145		
3. In relation to crime, courts are too harsh	4%	6%	2%	3%	2%	9%
	(16)	(16)	(2)	(6)	(8)	(20)
about right	39%	37%	30%	40%	38%	33%
	(164)	(101)	(33)	(95)	(125)	(78)
not harsh enough	57%	58%	69%	58%	60%	58%
	(238)	(158)	(76)	(137)	(200)	(233)
Total N	422	272	111	238	333	233
	chi-square=7.596			chi-square=16.249		
	df=4, p=.108			df=4, p=.003		

Table 4.6
Mass Public Opinion, Based upon One's Race,
Regarding Race and Crime, and Courts and Crime

	White	Black	Asian	Hispanic
1. Blacks have been treated, with regard to the death penalty				
the same as whites	56% (375)	35% (30)	90% (9)	46% (13)
less well than whites	37% (246)	61% (52)	10% (1)	54% (15)
better than whites	7% (48)	5% (4)		
Total N	669	86	10	28
	chi-square=26.820, df=6, p=.000			
2. Percent believing blacks accused of crimes more than whites	36% (240)	61% (52)	40% (4)	64% (18)
Total N	672	86	10	28
	chi-square=27.058, df=6, p=.000			
3. In relation to crime, courts are				
too harsh	3% (19)	15% (13)		4% (1)
about right	38% (256)	29% (25)	40% (4)	39% (11)
not harsh enough	59% (396)	55% (47)	60% (6)	57% (16)
Total N	671	85	10	28
	chi-square=30.432, df=6, p=.000			

Table 4.7
Mass Public and Legal Elite Confidence in the Police
and Various Branches of the Federal Government

	Mass Public	Lawyers
1. How much do you respect police?		
a great deal	65% (521)	44% (178)
only some	27% (219)	47% (190)
hardly any	8% (64)	10% (39)
Total N	804	407
	chi-square=51.860, df=2, p=.000	
2. The branch one is most confident in		
Congress	19% (156)	8% (34)
Supreme Court	41% (327)	75% (304)
presidency	13% (101)	8% (33)
none	28% (224)	8% (34)
Total N	808	405
	chi-square=134.568, df=3, p=.000	
3. The Court should follow		
society's wishes	39% (317)	12% (48)
Court's wishes	51% (408)	78% (314)
depends	10% (82)	3% (13)
the law (write-in)		2% (7)
the constitution (write-in)		5% (21)
Total N	807	403
	chi-square=173.000, df=4, p=.000	

Table 4.8
Mass Public Confidence in the Police and Various Branches of the Federal Government, for Different Levels of Knowledge and Education

	Education			Knowledge		
	High	Middle	Low	High	Middle	Low
1. How much do you respect police?						
a great deal	65%	61%	72%	66%	68%	60%
	(275)	(166)	(80)	(160)	(224)	(137)
only some	27%	31%	20%	29%	26%	28%
	(113)	(84)	(22)	(70)	(86)	(63)
hardly any	8%	8%	8%	6%	6%	13%
	(32)	(23)	(9)	(14)	(21)	(29)
Total N	420	273	111	244	331	229
	chi-square=5.225			chi-square=10.670		
	df=4, p=.262			df=4, p=.031		
2. The branch one is most confident in						
Congress	20%	20%	17%	20%	18%	20%
	(82)	(55)	(19)	(49)	(61)	(46)
Supreme Court	53%	29%	22%	50%	41%	29%
	(223)	(79)	(25)	(122)	(137)	(68)
presidency	8%	15%	24%	9%	12%	18%
	(33)	(41)	(27)	(21)	(39)	(41)
none	20%	36%	36%	21%	29%	33%
	(84)	(99)	(41)	(51)	(96)	(77)
Total N	422	274	112	243	333	232
	chi-square=74.931			chi-square=27.810		
	df=6, p=.000			df=6, p=.000		
3. The Court should follow						
society's wishes	33%	49%	41%	31%	39%	49%
	(138)	(136)	(46)	(75)	(128)	(114)
Court's wishes	58%	42%	44%	60%	53%	37%
	(245)	(114)	(49)	(146)	(175)	(87)
depends	10%	9%	15%	9%	9%	9%
	(40)	(25)	(17)	(21)	(29)	(32)
Total N	423	272	112	242	332	233
	chi-square=24.083			chi-square=26.841		
	df=4, p=.000			df=4, p=.000		

Table 4.9
Mass Public and Legal Elite's Fear of Crime and Worst Crime Suffered

	Mass Public	Lawyers
1. Worst crime suffered by respondent or member of family		
car	11% (92)	34% (138)
mugging	5% (37)	11% (36)
robbery in home	20% (162)	32% (129)
physical assault	7% (55)	9% (35)
murder	5% (44)	3% (11)
rape	4% (30)	2% (8)
none	48% (391)	11% (46)
Total N	811	403
chi-square=208.765, df=6, p=.000		
2. Percent fearful walking alone		
at night	42% (338)	45% (182)
Total N	811	407
chi-square=.953, df=1, p=.329		
3. Percent feeling safe at home at night	91% (741)	91% (373)
Total N	811	408
chi-square=.001, df=1, p=.975		

Table 4.10
Mass Public's Fear of Crime and Worst Crime Suffered,
for Different Levels of Knowledge and Education

	Education			Knowledge		
	High	Middle	Low	High	Middle	Low
1. Worst crime suffered by respondent or member of family						
car	14%	10%	5%	18%	7%	10%
	(58)	(28)	(6)	(44)	(24)	(24)
mugging	6%	3%	3%	3%	5%	5%
	(26)	(8)	(3)	(8)	(18)	(11)
robbery in home	25%	15%	14%	26%	22%	11%
	(105)	(41)	(16)	(63)	(74)	(25)
physical assault	8%	7%	5%	7%	8%	5%
	(32)	(18)	(5)	(16)	(27)	(12)
murder	6%	5%	2%	6%	5%	6%
	(27)	(15)	(2)	(15)	(16)	(13)
rape	4%	3%	4%	3%	4%	4%
	(17)	(9)	(4)	(6)	(14)	(10)
none	37%	57%	68%	38%	48%	59%
	(159)	(156)	(76)	(92)	(161)	(138)
Total N	424	275	112	244	334	233
	chi-square=49.078			chi-square=46.138		
	df=12, p=.000			df=12, p=.000		
2. Percent fearful walking alone	41%	38%	55%	37%	41%	47%
at night	(173)	(104)	(61)	(91)	(137)	(110)
Total N	424	275	112	244	334	233
	chi-square=9.352			chi-square=4.922		
	df=2, p=.009			df=2, p=.085		
3. Percent feeling safe at	91%	94%	86%	93%	93%	88%
home at night	(387)	(257)	(97)	(227)	(310)	(204)
Total N	424	275	112	244	257	233
	chi-square=4.742			chi-square=6.042		
	df=2, p=.093			df=2, p=.049		

Table 4.11
Mass Public's Fear of Crime by Race, Age, and Gender

	White	Black	Asian	Hispanic
1. Percent fearful walking alone at night	40% (276)	51% (44)	40% (4)	36% (10)
Total N	677	86	10	18
chi-square=3.834, df=3, p=.280				

	Male		Female	
2. Percent fearful walking alone at night	36% (139)		50% (199)	
Total N	415		396	
chi-square=23.413, df=1, p=.000				

	18-24	25-33	34-43	44-64	65–
3. Percent fearful walking alone at night	39% (38)	38% (58)	37% (68)	41% (100)	55% (74)
Total N	97	153	184	243	134
chi-square=12.975, df=4, p=.011					

Table 4.12

Mass Public's Sources of Information, for Different Levels of Education and Knowledge

	Education			Knowledge		
	High	Middle	Low	High	Middle	Low
1. Where do you get most of your information?						
papers	25%	18%	14%	30%	18%	17%
	(107)	(50)	(16)	(74)	(59)	(40)
TV	53%	64%	71%	48%	64%	64%
	(223)	(176)	(79)	(118)	(212)	(148)
radio	10%	10%	9%	14%	8%	8%
	(40)	(28)	(10)	(34)	(25)	(19)
magazines	3%	1%	1%	3%	2%	1%
	(12)	(3)	(1)	(6)	(7)	(3)
talking to people	6%	4%	3%	3%	5%	7%
	(26)	(12)	(3)	(6)	(18)	(17)
other	4%	2%	3%	2%	4%	3%
	(15)	(6)	(3)	(5)	(13)	(6)
Total N	423	275	112	243	334	233
	chi-square=20.599			chi-square=35.052		
	df=10, p=.024			df=10, p=.000		
2. How many TV hours per day?						
0	9%	7%	6%	11%	5%	9%
	(37)	(20)	(7)	(26)	(17)	(21)
1 hour	38%	23%	25%	37%	31%	25%
	(159)	(64)	(28)	(91)	(102)	(58)
2 hours	29%	30%	23%	30%	28%	27%
	(121)	(81)	(26)	(73)	(92)	(63)
3 hours	14%	17%	17%	13%	19%	14%
	(61)	(47)	(19)	(31)	(63)	(33)
4 hours	6%	11%	14%	6%	8%	12%
	(26)	(30)	(16)	(16)	(28)	(28)
5 hours	4%	12%	14%	2%	10%	13%
	(20)	(33)	(16)	(7)	(32)	(30)
Total N	424	275	112	244	334	233
	chi-square=39.432			chi-square=35.263		
	df=10, p=.000			df=10, p=.000		

Table 4.13

Mass Public and Legal Elite's Party Identification and Ideology

	Mass Public	Lawyers
1. Party Identification		
Strong Democrat	10% (78)	12% (50)
Democrat	21% (164)	16% (65)
Independent leaning Democrat	7% (55)	16% (65)
Independent	22% (175)	9% (38)
Independent leaning Republican	6% (50)	19% (78)
Republican	17% (134)	19% (78)
Strong Republican	18% (140)	8% (31)
Total N	796	405
	chi-square=112.949, df=6, p=.000	
2. Political Ideology		
Strong liberal	7% (51)	8% (32)
Liberal	12% (90)	10% (41)
Moderate leaning liberal	10% (75)	21% (85)
Moderate	24% (188)	17% (69)
Moderate leaning Conservative	10% (82)	21% (85)
Conservative	24% (189)	17% (70)
Strong Conservative	14% (105)	5% (22)
Total N	780	404
	chi-square=75.596, df=6, p=.000	

Chapter 5

Causal Influences on the Mass Public's Attitudes Toward Issues of Criminal Justice

Using multivariate analysis and scales based on multiple measures, this chapter will investigate more fully than the previous two chapters the important causal influences at work on attitudes toward criminal justice procedures.

MEASURING OVERALL MASS AND LEGAL OPINIONS

Based on the analysis in Chapter 3, three simple scales were developed to measure opinions toward criminal procedures: one for the responses to all the questions that were included in the analysis, one for the eight search and seizure items, and another based on the remaining four criminal rights questions. For the analysis here, an additional scale is also used to measure support of United States Supreme Court decisions, which is different conceptually from support for civil liberties broadly defined, since the Court has put some limits on such liberties as noted in Chapters 2 and 3. For the new measure, one point is added for each instance in which the respondents' opinions matched the opinion of the Court. Thus, four criminal procedure scales are utilized in the analysis that follows. For each, higher scores indicate either civil libertarian viewpoints or support of the Court.

Though one would expect members of the legal profession to be more civil libertarian than members of the mass public, it is possible that as the Court has decided more and more cases on the side of law enforcement, members of the legal profession may have also moved to the Right. This accords, as noted in Chapter 3, with the notion that members of the elite are more protective of civil liberties due to their exposure to "mainstream norms" (Zaller, 1992). As the court has moved to the right, it has altered mainstream norms along with it.

Table 5.1 presents results for the attitude scales from responses to the questions related to Supreme Court decisions on criminal procedures (all tables are at the end of this chapter). For reasons explained in Chapter 3, the questions dealing with police trickery and mental health were excluded from the summary measures. Also, as noted earlier (see Ch. 3), although the opinions of lawyers did not yield exactly identical factors as the responses of the mass public, the search and seizure scale and the rights of the accused scale consist of the same items in both surveys. This provides a way for comparing the overall results of the two surveys in terms of the public's versus lawyers' overall opinions.

For the summary criminal procedure scale, based on the full twelve questions, lawyers scored, on average, 1.34 points higher than members of the mass public (6.56 [lawyers] vs. 5.32 [public], p=.000). Lawyers also scored higher than the public on both the separate search and seizure scale, as well as the rights of the accused scale. On the searche scale, lawyers averaged 3.53, compared with 2.75 for the public (p=.000). On the accused scale, they scored 3.02, compared with 2.36 for members of the public (p=.000). Lawyers were more likely to take the civil libertarian position than were members of the mass public, and were also slightly more likely to be in agreement with recent Supreme Court decisions. Lawyers scored 7.74 on the agreement scale compared with 7.60 for members of the mass public. This is peculiar, since, as will be seen later, individuals within various subgroups are more likely to be in disagreement with Court decisions in direct relation with scoring higher on the civil libertarian scale. In other words, the more civil libertarian the individual, the more likely she or he will be in disagreement with Court decisions. This is, of course, quite logical, since the Court has been moving to the Right on a number of different of issues. A possible explanation for the lawyers' agreement with the Court, despite being more civil libertarian, is that the lawyers were extremely civil libertarian when the court sided with the civil libertarian alternative, while they were only marginally against the civil libertarian alternative when the Court ruled against the civil libertarian alternative.

SOURCES OF VARIATION IN SUPPORT

In addition to education and knowledge, the other factors that might be expected to have an effect on one's support for criminal procedures included gender, marital status, race, region, community type, source of information about crime, in addition to the other potential independent variables described in chapter 4. As mentioned in Chapter 4, traditional explanations for variance in support toward civil liberties do not explain enough of the variation, so that an examination of other explanations, including various demographic variables, is necessary. Ideological factors can be expected to influence opinions toward criminal procedures as well. These included, that is, identifiable dimensions of liberal-conservative ideology. The question wordings and the coding of the measures of these variables are reported in Appendix 1.

Education and Knowledge

Table 5.2 presents the means for knowledge and education on the four scales. For the overall scale based on twelve questions, the more politically knowledgeable are only slightly (but not significantly) more civil libertarian than respondents with lower levels of knowledge. Those with high levels of knowledge scored a 5.52 vs. 5.28 for those with middle levels of knowledge vs. 5.18 for those with low levels of knowledge (p=.431). But there are no appreciable differences on the separate search and seizure and rights of the accused scales (search and seizure: 2.77 [high and low] vs. 2.72 [middle], p=.935; rights of the accused: 2.43 [high] vs. 2.32 [middle] vs. 2.36 [low], p=.617). This anomaly has to do with the fact that the results are for all twelve questions, not just the eight or four in the other two scales. The earlier analysis, based on Table 3.2, which indicated that the more knowledgeable are less civil libertarian when the court rules against the civil libertarian alternative, is part of the reason for lack of differences among the groups. The more knowledgeable were also more likely to agree with recent Court decisions (7.74 [high] vs. 7.66 [middle] vs. 7.38 [low], p=.063).

The effect of education is clearer and more consistent, with holding at least a high school diploma showing the greatest relation with support for civil liberties. Those with the highest level of education had a mean on the criminal procedure scale of 5.48 vs. 5.37 for respondents in the middle level category vs. 4.55 for respondents in the low level category (p=.014). The same pattern exists for the relationship between education and the search and seizure and rights of the accused scale: for search and seizure those with high levels of education had a mean of 2.82 vs. 2.83 in the middle level category vs. 2.30 in the low level category (p=.050); for the rights of the accused we find the same pattern (2.46 [high] vs. 2.33 [middle] vs. 2.09 [low], p=.019). In general, education is associated with somewhat more civil libertarian positions when it comes to criminal procedure. In the case of agreement with Court decisions, the least educated are more likely than others to have opinions in line with the Supreme Court (7.65 [high] vs. 7.44 [middle] vs. 7.82 [low], p=.121).

In sum, bivariately, education has a greater positive effect than knowledge concerning opinions toward civil liberties. On the other hand, knowledge was of greater consequence than education in causing one to have greater agreement with Supreme Court decisions. This is consistent with past research, in the sense that education, based upon past literature, has been associated with higher levels of support for civil liberties. More knowledgeable respondents, per se, would have greater levels of information concerning recent Court decisions, and might therefore be more inclined to support them (see Zaller, 1992).

The interesting finding, however, is that knowledge and education do not have as great an effect as might be expected. Therefore, it is necessary to examine other variables—other demographics and attitudinal factors—which might affect opinions concerning the civil liberties delineated by criminal justice procedures.

Region

Reporting on the relationships with region, Table 5.3 reveals that those in the Pacific region score highest on the criminal procedure scale, while those in the South score lowest. Respondents living in the Pacific area had a mean of 6.31 vs. 5.74 for New England residents vs. 5.44 for Mountain residents, 5.30 for mid-Atlantic residents, 5.20 for the West North Central residents, and 5.00 for Southern residents (p=.017). In addition, while Pacific residents scored highest for issues dealing with search and seizure (3.43 [Pacific] vs. 3.05 [New England] vs. 2.80 [mid-Atlantic] vs. 2.74 [Mountain] vs. 2.67 [West North Central] vs. 2.48 [South], p=.010), residents in New England scored highest for issues dealing with the rights of the accused (2.83 [New England] vs. 2.56 [Mountain] vs. 2.53 [Pacific] vs. 2.37 [West North Central] vs. 2.33 [mid-Atlantic] vs. 2.25 [South] p=.049). Residents of the South scored lowest on both these scales.

In addition, in accord with the Court's recent move to the Right, southerners were the group most in agreement with recent Court decisions, with Pacific residents the least likely to support the Court (7.81 [South] vs. 7.75 [West North Central] vs. 7.68 [Mountain] vs. 7.51 [New England] vs. 7.19 [Pacific], p=.043).

The results are consistent with a recent study conducted by the National Opinion Research Center on public attitudes in the 1990s (Myerson, 1996, p. 5), which found that people in the West not only identify themselves as liberal more than residents of other parts of the country, but also have more liberal attitudes on a wide range of specific social issues (see also Page and Shapiro, 1992, Ch. 7). The data also accord well with documented strong support among southerners for maintaining law and order.

Marital Status

Table 5.3 shows that respondents who were never married or are currently divorced scored highest on all three scales, followed by those who are separated. For the general criminal procedure scale, there was a full 1.5 point difference between respondents who were married and those who were divorced (6.41 [divorced] vs. 6.26 [never married] vs. 5.27 [separated] vs. 4.92 [married] vs. 4.48 [widowed] p=.000). Similar patterns occur for both the search and seizure and rights of the accused scales, though the differences are greater for the search and seizure scale (search and seizure: 3.62 [divorced] vs. 3.45 [never married] vs. 2.86 [separated] vs. 2.45 [married] vs. 2.08 [widowed] p=.000; rights of the accused: 2.65 [never married] vs. 2.64 [divorced] vs. 2.38 [separated] vs. 2.23 [married and widowed] p=.000). In accord with the Court moving to the Right, married and widowed respondents were also more likely than others to agree with recent Supreme Court decisions (7.87 [widowed] vs. 7.80 [married] vs. 7.18 [never married] vs. 7.14 [divorced] vs. 7.09 [separated], p=.000).

There are a number of possible reasons for the striking differences between the married (including widowed) and divorced or separated respondents. First, divorced individuals are more likely to fear an intrusive government. It is possible that they would not want various personal matters revealed during a personal investigation related to their divorce and privacy more generally. This explanation might also help explain why divorced individuals would be more protective regarding search and seizure issues. Also, even if the divorce investigation has already ended, their exposure to the system may have left a lasting impression. Another possibility is that those who have experienced divorce or separation are more likely to have had additional stress in their lives due to unsuccessful marriages, and they might be extremely wary of any government action that might cause further stress. It is also possible that individuals who have divorced or who have never married might be less likely to adhere to authority or restrictive norms.

Respondents who were separated were consistently more civil libertarian than those who were married, yet less civil libertarian than respondents who were divorced. They were, apparently, in the middle of a metamorphosis in their lives, and their opinions fell in-between.

Gender

In Table 5.3, men scored higher than women on all three scales: on the criminal procedure scale men averaged 5.70 compared to 4.91 for women (p=.000); the same pattern is found for both the search and seizure and rights of the accused scale (search: 2.98 [male] vs. 2.51 [female], p=.002; accused: 2.47 [male] vs. 2.25 [female], p=.011). Also, females are only slightly more likely to agree with recent Court decisions (7.62 [female] vs. 7.58 [male], p=.740).

This finding that men are somewhat more civil libertarian than women corresponds with past survey research (Stouffer, 1955) that also found men to be more tolerant than women. This may be attributable to the past finding that women are more concerned than men with personal and family safety, thus seeing the rights tradeoff differently than men (cf. Shapiro and Mahajan, 1986). The survey data also reveal that women are more afraid to walk alone at night (see section below on Fear of Crime), and therefore might be more inclined to give the police more leeway in combating crime.

Community Type

The data reported in Table 5.3 also show that residents of rural areas scored lower on all three scales than did suburban or urban residents. They had a mean of 4.86 on the overall criminal procedure scale vs. 5.44 for city dwellers and 5.58 for suburbanites, (p=.015). This pattern, of suburban residents more supportive than others of civil libertarian norms, was also apparent regarding search and seizure (2.96 [suburb] vs. 2.79 [city] vs. 2.44 [rural], p=.017). For the rights of the accused, city and suburban dwellers were most civil libertarian (2.45 [city] vs. 2.42 [suburb] vs. 2.19 [rural], p=.043). In contrast, rural residents were most likely to be supportive of recent conservative leaning Supreme Court decisions (7.81 [rural] vs. 7.57 [city] 7.45 [suburb], p=.066).

It is, then, the case that residents of rural communities are less supportive of the civil liberties of criminal defendants, even though they are much less personally fearful of walking alone at night. It is possible that education (less) and other personal characteristics (white, protestant), which are correlated with lower levels of support for civil liberties, help explain this. It is also possible that people in rural communities do not have the same fear of government or law enforcement officials that people in larger metropolitan areas have. In small communities people may be much more likely to know some of their police and government officials, and as a result do not have the fear of an intrusive police force.

That city dwellers are most supportive of the rights of the accused might be attributable to their exposure to high-profile cases in which the police have been accused of mischief during a number of postarrest situations.

Race

The racial differences reported in Table 5.3 are clearly among the most striking. Blacks scored higher on all three scales than members of all other races. On the criminal procedure scale, blacks had a mean of 6.58 compared to 5.54 for Hispanics, 5.17 for whites, 4.50 for Asians (p=.000). Especially notable was the search and seizure scale, on which blacks scored a 3.66 vs. 2.93 for Hispanics vs. 2.63 for whites vs. 2.50 for Asians (p=.000). The same pattern, though not as striking, emerged for the rights of the accused scale (2.68 [black] vs. 2.41 [Hispanic] vs. 2.34 [white] vs. 1.60 [Asian], p=.021). Whites and Asians were also more likely than others to agree with recent Supreme Court decisions (7.69 [white] vs. 7.50 [Asian] vs. 7.38 [Hispanic] vs. 6.96 [black], p=.003).

Clearly the probable reasons for the greater support of civil liberties among blacks is the feeling among many blacks of unfairness of the criminal justice system as a whole (see Dawson, 1994, on "shared fates") in relation to the black community. Many blacks might feel that if the police were given great leeway in the area of search and seizure, blacks might be singled out merely due to racial prejudices. It has been alleged that police officers single out blacks, especially young black males, as suspects during criminal investigations, merely because they are black. These and other factors have led blacks to be wary of figures of societal authority in general, and the police in particular. Along these lines, blacks have much less respect for police officers compared to other subgroups. As a result, blacks give police officers much less leeway during a criminal investigation than do whites, and therefore they tend to be more civil libertarian. Blacks have yet to reach economic equality with whites within society (Grofman, Handley, and Niemi, 1992; Hacker, 1992), therefore, they continue to live, on average, in low-income areas which have high crime rates. In addition, blacks are the victims and the perpetrators of crimes to a greater degree than whites (Wilson, 1983; Wilson and Herrstein, 1985), and, therefore, on average, have more day-to-day experience—direct and indirect—with police: the idea of giving up protections from the police, during the course of a criminal investigation, is clearly less probable than for individuals for whom the issues involved are more academic.

Due to the small number of cases (Ns of 10) one can only speculate that the finding that Asians scored much lower than other groups on all three scales, especially on the rights of the accused scale, might be attributed to Asians' tending to be recent immigrants from countries where suspected criminals have little or no rights. Asian-Americans may be less acculturated into mainstream American norms and values regarding criminal justice and rights.

Religion

In the case of religion, individuals who reported themselves as atheists were the group that scored highest on the criminal procedure scale: 6.59 vs. 5.30 for Catholics vs. 5.26 for others vs. 5.16 for Protestants vs. 4.95 for Jews (p= .008). A similar pattern emerged for search and seizure issues (3.57 [atheist] vs. 2.85 [other] vs. 2.72 [Catholic] vs. 2.65 [Protestant] vs. 2.25 [Jewish], p= .013). A different pattern appears for the rights of the accused, where, interestingly, Jews were more civil libertarian, ranking only second behind atheists (2.75 [atheist] vs. 2.50 [Jewish] vs. 2.33 [Protestant] vs. 2.32 [Catholic] vs. 2.24 [other], p=.106). Also of interest, atheists and others were least likely to agree with recent Court decisions (7.68 [Jewish] vs. 7.67 [Protestant] vs. 7.62 [Catholic] vs. 7.28 [atheist] vs. 7.26 [other], p=.388).

It is clear that across the board, atheists are more civil libertarian than individuals associated with an organized religion. Atheists are individuals who are critical in their thought in ways that have led them to have rejected organized religion—in a nation so dominated by religion. Atheists might feel like outsiders in this religious nation, and, therefore, might be more suspicious of governmental intrusion into the private lives of its citizens. With this theory in mind, it is quite peculiar that Jews would be the least civil libertarian group on all but the rights of the accused scale, and that is probably correlated with the fact that Jews are more likely to live in cities where, as we have seen, residents are more civil libertarian regarding the rights of the accused. One can surmise that Jews have begun to feel acculturated into the mainstream, and therefore no longer feel as outsiders. It is also possible that the small N (19) distorted the true picture of Jewish opinion.

Sources of Information

Individuals who say television is their main source of information about crime scored lower on all three scales than those who mainly acquire their information from reading, radio, and talking to people. Those who said television was their main source of information had a mean of 5.11 on the criminal procedure scale compared to 5.48 for those who listen to the radio vs. 5.67 for newspapers vs. 6.00 for talking to people vs. 6.64 for magazines vs. 4.86 for those who acquired their information from "other" sources (p = .063). This same pattern held for both the search and seizure and rights of the accused scales (search: 3.79 [magazines] vs. 2.98 [papers] vs. 2.94 [talking] vs. 2.90 [radio] vs. 2.74 [other] vs. 2.60 [TV], p = .115; accused: 2.73 [magazines] vs. 2.58 [talking] vs. 2.51 [papers] vs. 2.41 [radio] vs. 2.30 [TV] vs. 1.87 [other], p = .076). Respondents who listed TV as their main source of information were also most inclined to agree with the holdings of recent Court decisions (7.67 [TV] vs. 7.59 [other] vs. 7.57 [papers] vs. 7.45 [radio] v.7.24 [talking] vs. 7.21 [magazines], p = .620).

Thus people who obtain their information from magazines are more civil libertarian than individuals who obtain their information from the newspapers, and all are more civil libertarian than respondents who obtained their information from TV. Clearly, one of the reasons for the greater support of civil liberties among those who said their primary source of information was reading a newspaper or magazine is that these individuals have much higher levels of education than those who cited television as their primary source. However, another possible explanation may be the sensationalism attached to much of the television coverage of crime. The saliency of crime on TV news may also lead many whose main source of information is television to perceive crime to be a greater threat than it actually is, which in turn makes this group more willing to give greater discretion to the authorities.

Talk Radio

Of late, talk radio has emerged as an alternative source of information among a small but vocal segment of the population. Respondents who listen to talk radio were somewhat less likely to support civil liberties than those who do not listen to talk radio. On the criminal justice scale, listeners scored a 5.42 vs. 5.16 for those who did not listen (p = .222). The same pattern held for both the search and rights of the accused scales (search: 2.79 [don't listen] vs. 2.68 [listen], p = .487; accused: 2.41 [don't listen] vs. 2.29 [listen], p = .165). Both groups were about equal in their support of recent Court decisions (7.59 [don't listen] vs. 7.65 [listen], p = .941).

People who listen to talk radio, it would seem, are self-selected, in particular, of more politically conservative dispositions, and therefore less civil libertarian, since prior to the survey most talk show hosts were conservative. It should be emphasized, clearly, that the differences in attitudes here are not as great as might have been expected. One reason for this may be that conservatives, especially in the Western part of the country, have been quite critical and skeptical of an overreaching government, and are as civil libertarian as many politically liberal citizens.

Fear of Crime

Not surprisingly, as shown in Table 5.3, individuals who responded that they were afraid to walk alone at night scored lower on all three scales than those who were not afraid. Those who were not averaged 5.58 on the criminal procedure scale, compared to 4.95 for those who were (p=.003). The same pattern held for both the search and seizure and rights of the accused scales (search: 2.90 vs. 2.54, p=.014; accused: 2.46 vs. 2.22, p=.006). There was no real difference between the two groups of respondents in their support of recent Supreme Court decisions (7.62 [afraid] vs. 7.59 [not afraid], p=.785). The differences are noteworthy but not enormous, indicating that self-interest is a noticeable but hardly a predominant concern here. Other influences are evidently at work producing variation from individual to individual.

A differing pattern of results was found based upon whether or not one feels safe at home at night. Respondents who were afraid at home at night were more civil libertarian than those not fearful (5.45 [not fearful] vs. 5.31 [fearful], p=.689). The same pattern holds true in the area of search and seizure (3.25 [not fearful] vs. 2.70 [fearful], p=.038), but not regarding the rights of the accused (2.38 [fearful] vs. 2.22 [not fearful], p=.298). Also, of interest, those fearful in their homes at night were much more likely to agree with recent Court decisions (7.66 [fearful] vs. 7.02 [not fearful], p=.003).

Personal Experience with Crime

A quite intriguing finding in Table 5.3 is that there was no relationship between one's personal experience with crime and one's opinion regarding civil liberties. In fact, those who themselves or whose families had experienced robbery, assault, murder, rape and muggings were more civil libertarian than those who had no crimes committed against them (5.89 [rape] vs. 5.59 [mugged] vs. 5.53 [physical assault] vs. 5.31 [robbery in home] vs. 5.26 [murder] vs. 5.25 [no crime] vs. 5.21 [car], p=.912). Further, respondents who had not been victimized were least civil libertarian on the search and seizure scale (3.21 [rape] vs. 2.98 [physical assault] vs. 2.97 [mugged] vs. 2.75 [robbery in home] vs. 2.72 [murder] vs. 2.69 [car] vs. 2.67 [no crime], p=.797). There was little difference on the rights of the accused and agreement with Court scales (accused: 2.43 [physical assault] vs. 2.38 [robbery] vs. 2.37 (rape and no crime) vs. 2.35 [murder] vs. 2.33 [mugged] vs. 2.28 [car], p=.996; agreement: 7.71 [mugged] vs. 7.64 [car] vs. 7.63 [no crime] vs. 7.58 [robbery in home] vs. 7.53 [murder] vs. 7.46 [rape] vs. 7.45 [physical assault], p=.987).

The notion that personal experience with crime does not have an effect on one's opinion concerning how we as a society should deal with crime is well documented (see GSS data). People's ideas about crime are apparently more likely to be affected by other factors.

Respect for Police

Along with racial differences the apparent effect of respect for the police is also most striking. Respondents with greater respect for the police were more likely to give leeway to police during their investigations of criminal investigations. On the criminal procedure scale, those who had great respect for police had a mean of 4.94 compared with 5.96 for those with only some respect and 6.40 for those with hardly any (p=.000). This same pattern held for the search and seizure scale (3.62 [hardly any] vs. 3.22 [only some] vs. 2.46 [great deal], p=.000), and to a lesser degree the rights of the accused scale (2.59 [hardly any] vs. 2.52 [only some] vs. 2.27 [great deal], p=.015). Respondents with a great deal of trust in the police were the group most inclined to support the Court's decisions (7.79 [great deal] vs. 7.30 [only some] vs. 7.24 [hardly any], p=.000).

Thus, the more one trusts the police, the less civil libertarian one is. It also makes some sense that trust in police would have a greater effect on issues of search and seizure than rights of accused, since police officers are more directly involved and have greater personal autonomy in the decision-making process.

Age

Table 5.3 also reports that respondents under age 43 scored quite a bit higher on the overall criminal procedure scale than respondents over 43. Respondents aged 18-24 scored a 6.15 vs. 5.45 for those 25-33 vs. 5.78 for those 34-43 vs. 4.99 for those 44-64 vs. 4.49 for those over 64 (p=.001). The same pattern held for search and seizure and, to a lesser degree, the rights of the accused (search: 3.25 [18-24] vs. 3.16 [34-43] vs. 2.87 [25-33] vs. 2.46 [44-64] vs. 2.17 [over 64], p=.000; accused: 2.65 [18-24] vs. 2.51 [34-43] vs. 2.34 [25-33] vs. 2.29 [44-64] vs. 2.11 [over 64], p=.008). Older respondents were also more likely to agree with recent Supreme Court decisions (7.80 [44-64] vs. 7.73 [over 64] vs. 7.60 [25-33] vs. 7.37 (18-24 and 33-43), p=.070).

Clearly younger adults are more civil libertarian, but the reasons for this are subject to debate. Several possible explanations are at work. First, generational effects may cause a major part of the variation. Older Americans may see the crime problem as greater than young people, since they grew up during a time when crime was not perceived to be the problem that it is today. Therefore, older cohorts may feel a greater need to fight crime, in an attempt to bring back the past.

Another generational influence may also be at work. Individuals who reached adulthood in the post-1960s era were socialized in an environment that accepted the existence of constitutional safeguards for criminal defendants. A 1976 survey revealed that "91% of all American thirteen-year-olds knew they had a right to remain silent" (Walker, 1989, p. 124). The obvious reason, of course, is that the Miranda warning has been widely visible in movies and television. Most of the landmark civil liberties decisions occurred in the 1960s, whereas Americans born before the 1960s became politically aware during a much different time period.

It is also possible that older people, related to aging, may be more fearful of crime, and therefore less civil libertarian: thus a life-cycle effect. The fact that this fear of crime did not exist so generally to such a degree when these older individuals were young, as it does today, has very likely added to this groups apprehension about crime.

In addition, "period effects," most probably, have an affect on opinions concerning crime-fighting techniques across all age groups. On the one hand, the United States Supreme Court in its decisions of the 1960s, which established landmark procedural and substantive guarantees for criminal defendants, should have led to higher levels of support for procedural safeguards for criminal defendants among all cohorts, and especially within cohorts socialized within that era. The information concerning these opinions was disseminated to the mass public to a greater extent during that period, due to the publicity many of the rulings received in the mass media, movies, and other outlets. However, reports of higher crime rates, and the gruesome nature of some of the highlighted crimes, may cause a drop in support for procedural protections among respondents of all age groups.

Income

Table 5.3 shows that income is only slightly but not significantly related to attitudes toward civil liberties. Those earning less than $10,000 scored 5.11 on the criminal procedure scale, vs. 5.34 for $10,000-$20,000, vs. 5.57 for $20,000-$30,000, vs. 5.19 for $30,000-$40,000 vs. 5.04 for $40,000-$50,000, vs. 5.92 for $50,000-$60,000, vs. 5.24 for those earning more than $60,000 ($p=.555$). The same pattern, or lack of, held for the search and seizure and rights of the accused scales (search: 3.00 [$50,000-$60,000] vs. 2.94 [$20,000-$30,000] vs. 2.83 [$10,000-$20,000] vs. 2.73 [less than $10,000] vs. 2.64 [$30,000-$40,000] vs. 2.60 [more than $60,000] vs. 2.44 [$40,000-$50,000], $p=.517$; accused: 2.55 [$50,000-$60,000] vs. 2.40 [$20,000-$30,000] vs. 2.38 [$40,000-$50,000] vs. 2.36 [more than $60,000] vs. 2.34 [less than $10,000] vs. 2.33 [$10,000-$20,000] vs. 2.30 [$30,000-$40,000], $p=.933$). In addition, respondents with higher levels of income were only slightly more likely to support recent Court decisions (7.89 [$40,000-$50,000] vs. 7.75 [$50,000-$60,000] vs. 7.67 [more than 60 and $30,000-$40,000] vs. 7.50 [$20,000-$30,000] vs. 7.48 [less than $10,000] vs. 7.45 [$10,000-$20,000], p=.488).

The reason why people with higher incomes might tend to be more civil libertarian is most likely due to their higher levels of education and knowledge. The effect may be diminished by the fact that those with more income have more possessions and therefore have more to lose from criminal activity. In addition the possibility that individuals with greater income would be more understanding of the possible societal aspects to the root causes of crime, and therefore be more civil libertarian, is counterbalanced by their being more likely to be Republicans and conservatives and therefore less prone to support civil liberties.

Involvement in Crime

In the mass survey, about half of the respondents were asked whether they, or a member of their family, were ever indicted or convicted of a crime. The data reveal that respondents who answered in the affirmative were more likely to hold civil libertarian opinions, by 5.88 vs 5.09 (p=.054; n=295). The relationship was stronger on issues dealing with search and seizure than for the rights of the accused (search: 3.26 [yes] vs. 2.54 [no], p=.013; accused: 2.52 [yes] vs. 2.35 [no], p=.366). Those who had not had this experience of running into the law were also more likely to agree with recent Court decisions (7.78 [no] vs. 7.29 [yes], p=.039).

It is not surprising that respondents, or a family member, who have been accused or convicted of a crime are more civil libertarian than others. They may readily have believed that members of their family were wrongly accused, since it may be hard to fathom that someone you know so well is capable of criminal behavior. Since this group was more civil libertarian on search issues in particular, it may be that many in this group might believe that the police should be prevented from intruding on their families in ways that are shady and that should be illegal.

Confidence in Government/Court

Also, in a sense not surprisingly, respondents who had more confidence in government were less likely to hold civil libertarian opinions than others. Those who had hardly any confidence in government averaged a 5.48 on the criminal procedure scale vs. 5.28 who had only some confidence vs. 4.78 for those who had a great deal of confidence (p=.170). The differences were apparent, however, on the search and seizure scale, not for the rights of the accused (search: 2.92 [hardly any] vs. 2.66 [only some] vs. 2.54 [great deal], p=.168; accused: 2.33 [hardly any] vs. 2.40 [only some] vs. 2.25 [great deal], p=.573), and the differences were most insignificant in the case of agreement with recent Court decisions (7.66 [only some] vs. 7.60 [hardly any] vs. 7.34 [great deal], p=.346).

The people with more confidence in government, then, are more likely to give the police more leeway during criminal investigations. Respondents with more confidence in government are less likely to believe that wrongdoing is likely during the course of a criminal investigation. A related question asked respondents in which branch of government they had the most confidence. Respondents who said that they did not have confidence in any of the branches of government were more likely to have civil libertarian beliefs than others, followed by those who were most confident in the Supreme Court (5.55 [none] vs. 5.39 [Sup. Ct.] vs. 5.29 [Congress] vs. 4.66 [president], p=.087). This same pattern occurred for search and seizure and less strongly for the rights of the accused (search: 2.89 [none] vs. 2.80 [Sup. Ct.] vs. 2.74 [Congress] vs. 2.34 [president], p=.163; accused: 2.42 [none] vs. 2.41 [Sup. Ct.] vs. 2.32 [Congress] vs. 2.18 [president], p=.346). Respondents who had highest levels of support for Congress, unexpectedly, due to their higher levels of support for civil liberties, were slightly more likely to agree with recent Court decisions, though no significant differences existed (7.71 [Congress] vs. 7.66 [president] vs. 7.59 [Sup. Ct.] vs. 7.49 [none], p=.655).

It is understandable that respondents who do not have confidence in any branch of government would be more civil libertarian than others. They have less trust in government and its institutions, and are therefore less willing to give over rights to governmental representatives. Similarly it makes sense that respondents who have more confidence in the Court, than the other branches, would be more inclined to believe that if the Court decided a case in the civil libertarian direction, it was doing the right thing.

Role of Supreme Court

Examining further the role of the Supreme Court, the data reveal that respondents who believed that the court should follow society's wishes (5.64) were more civil libertarian than those who said that the Court should follow its own preferences (5.18). Interestingly, respondents who stated that it depends upon the situation were less civil libertarian than those in the other two groups (4.68, p=.017). The same pattern occurred for search and seizure and rights of the accused (search: 3.01 [society] vs. 2.63 [Court] vs. 2.27 [depends], p=.005; accused: 2.49 [society] vs. 2.29 [Court] vs. 2.22 [depends], p=.057). Respondents who answered "depends" were more likely, based upon their less civil libertarian views, to agree with past Court decisions (7.95 [depends] vs. 7.62 [Court] vs. 7.49 [society], p=.113).

There are two possible explanations for why respondents who would give less power to the courts are more civil libertarian. Respondents who believe that the Court should follow society's wishes are less likely to give over authority to political institutions. Also, they are less likely to have as much confidence in the Court and would therefore be less likely to have trust in the Court's decisions, which would cause them to be more civil libertarian.

PARTISANSHIP AND IDEOLOGY

Contrasting sharply with the possible effects of knowledge, education, and other demographic characteristics, what seem to matter most are certain attitudes and ideological concerns more targeted than political partisanship and liberal-conservative ideological labels. Table 5.4 reports the results of the relevant cross-tabulations.

Party

First, Table 5.4 shows that respondents who identified themselves as Democrats were more supportive of civil liberties than were Republicans and Independents, with this pattern holding for all three scales. On the criminal procedure scale, Democrats had a mean of 5.57, compared with 5.30 for Independents and 5.06 for Republicans (p=.134). The range was even greater when the seven-point party scale was used (6.01 [strong Democrat] vs. 5.37 [Democrat] vs. 5.29 [Independent but closer to Democrat] vs. 5.44 [Independent] vs. 4.90 [Independent but closer to Republican] vs. 5.10 [Republican] vs. 5.02 [strong Republican], p=.111). The same pattern held for the search and seizure and rights of the accused scales (search: 2.90 [Democrat] vs. 2.80 [Independent] vs. 2.54 [Republican], p=.114; accused: 2.50 [Democrat] vs. 2.36 [Independent] vs. 2.23 [Republican], p=.054). Republicans were also more likely to agree with the Supreme Court decisions (7.82 [Republican] vs. 7.50 [Independent] vs. 7.47 [Democrat], p=.034).

It was expected that predictably more conservative respondents who identify with the Republican party would be less civil libertarian. It is also reasonable to expect Republicans to be more likely to agree with the relatively recent Court decisions, since most of the Court members were appointed by Republicans. What is quite interesting, and perhaps unexpected to a degree, is that the effect of partisanship (self-identified) is not as large as might be expected. One possible explanation is the rise of libertarianism among some Republican party identifiers.

Ideology

The differences for self-identified ideology were slightly larger: liberals had a mean of 5.65 on the criminal procedure scale, compared with 5.47 for moderates and 4.99 for conservatives (p=.039). Again, the differences were slightly greater on the seven-point scale (5.04 [strong conservative] vs. 6.49 [strong liberal]). The same patterns held for the other scales (search: 3.07 [liberal] vs. 2.77 [moderate] vs. 2.54 [conservative], p=.041; accused: 2.52 [liberal] vs.

2.45 [moderate] vs. 2.21 [conservative], p=.018). Conservatives were also most likely, but not significantly, to agree with past Court decisions (7.78 [conservative] vs. 7.57 [moderate] vs. 7.40 [liberal], p=.081).

While the direction of the results were as expected, the strength of the correlation was not extremely large. It was necessary to see whether or not specific dimensions of ideology, in addition to the Democrat-Republican and conservative-liberal constructs, were useful considerations as well in explaining attitudes toward criminal procedures.

Racial Justice, Economic Equality, and Fairness of Criminal Justice System

To examine other ideological considerations, additional ideological scales were created from survey items on the causes of crime, attitudes concerning race, and questions about crime and the courts (see Appendix 1). Factor analysis was used to develop three measures. Responses to the two racial issues ("With regard to the death penalty, would you say blacks have generally been treated the same as whites, less well than whites, or better than whites," and "In general, do you believe that blacks are accused and convicted of criminal acts more than whites, simply because they are black") loaded on one factor; the two economic issues ("Please tell me whether or not you believe it is a very important factor causing crime today: the lack of income equality; the lack of economic opportunities for the poor and for members of minority groups) on a second factor; and the four crime items ("Please tell me whether or not you believe it is a very important factor causing crime today: The media's emphasis on the rights of the accused and not on the rights of the victim; a legal system that is too lenient on criminals; liberal Supreme Court decisions that have hurt the efforts of law enforcement," and "In general, do you think the courts in your area deal too harshly, about right, or not harshly enough") loaded on a third factor. Based on these results, three scales were created: racial liberalism, economic liberalism, and criminal justice liberalism. Table 5.4 clearly shows that these ideological scales matter more when it comes to criminal procedure than do party ID and self-described ideology. This is especially so for the racial liberalism and criminal liberalism scales. Those who scored a zero on the criminal liberalism scale had a mean of 4.58 on the overall criminal procedure scale, whereas those who scored a four on criminal liberalism had a mean of 9.40 (p= .000). A similar relationship occurred for the search and seizure and rights of the accused scales (search: 2.22 [0] vs. 5.80 [4], p=.000; accused: 2.14 [0] vs. 3.50 [4], p=.001). Last, the higher a respondent scored on the scale, the less he or she agreed with recent Court decisions (7.92 [0] vs. 6.00 [4], p=.000).

A possible explanation for why the criminal liberalism measure makes more of a difference than more general self-identification measures is that there are crossover individuals within the traditional categories of ideology. As was seen when analyzing the responses of respondents who listened to talk radio, many self-identified conservatives were quite civil libertarian. In addition, many liberals might have labeled themselves as liberal for other reasons. A similar, though not as striking, pattern held for the racial liberalism scale. Those who scored a zero on racial liberalism had a mean of 4.90 on the Criminal procedure scale compared to those who scored a two, who had a mean of 6.21 (p=.000). A similar pattern occurred for the other scales as well (search: 2.45 [0] vs. 3.25 [2], p=.000; accused: 2.05 [0] vs. 2.74 [2], p=.000). There was only a weak and insignificant relationship with the Court (7.80 [0] vs. 7.46 [2], p=.471).

A probable explanation for the more civil libertarian opinions of those who are more likely to believe that racial discrimination does exist, is their belief that it is important to be watchful of both the courts and the police, since they also perceive that violations of rights or even trumped-up charges against members of minority groups still occur. Therefore, according to these individuals, the less power given to the police and the courts the better.

A similar, though less decisive, pattern occurred for the economic liberalism scale. Respondents who scored 0 on the scale averaged 4.82 on the criminal procedure scale vs. 5.37 for those who scored 1 vs. 5.62 for those who scored 2 (p=.007). Similar patterns emerged for the search and seizure and rights of the accused scales (search: 2.46 [0] vs. 2.80 [1] vs. 2.90 [2], p=.045; accused: 2.11 [0] vs. 2.38 [1] vs. 2.53 [2], p=.000). Given these results it was unexpected that there would be no significant difference concerning agreement with the Court (7.65 [0] vs. 7.63 [1] vs. 7.56 [2], p=.809).

This set of results is important and quite explicable. Opinions concerning issues of criminal justice should have a greater effect than one's opinions concerning issues of racial justice, on one's opinion concerning civil liberties in the area of criminal procedure, given the direct correlation. In turn, the effect of one's opinions concerning issues of economic justice might still have an effect upon one's opinions concerning civil liberties in the area of criminal procedure, but not nearly as great an effect as that of issues of race and criminal justice. More narrowly targeted beliefs are at work here from broad abstract ideologies.

In sum, the bivariate analysis reveals that race, gender, marital status, opinions regarding the root causes of crime, as well as other demographic variables are quite important determinants of one's opinions regarding civil liberties in the area of criminal procedure. In contrast, traditional explanations such as one's knowledge and education were not as important as one might expect. To determine the independent effects of different independent variables, multivariate analysis follows.

MULTIVARIATE ANALYSIS

Criminal Justice, Searches and Seizure Scale, and Accused Scale

The results of the multivariate analysis reported in Table 5.5 show which variables independently affect opinions toward criminal procedures once other variables are controlled. Also, based upon the various regression models presented in this chapter, a path diagram was created (see Table 5.18 and analysis of the path model later in this chapter). For the regression equation presented in Table 5.5, all of the identified and measured independent variables have been included in the regression models. These results confirm what is largely apparent in the description of the bivariate findings. Education and knowledge per se matter remarkably little in explaining differences in support for protections against intrusive surveillance and searches and protections for the rights of the accused.

What is apparently also happening is that any effects of education and knowledge are likely mediated by exposure to information of a relatively detailed sort (in contrast to television), from reading newspapers and magazines that lead people—apparently—to be aware of government intrusions, and violations of privacy and procedural rights. Since use of print media is related to education, knowledge, and income $R^2 = .23$), the indirect effects of these latter variables are noteworthy, but these effects are still less than those of other variables.

The set of variables that makes the substantively most important differences regarding criminal procedure are the attitudinal variables: racial liberalism (b = .413*), criminal justice liberalism (b = .394**), fear of crime (b = -.525*), and respect for police (b = .672**). They have consistently high betas, with respect for police having the highest (beta = .15 for the overall scale in Table 5.5). When these attitudinal variables are excluded the demographic variables alone explain less variance in the dependent variables. The R^2 was .072 lower for the overall scale, .068 lower for the search and seizure scale, and .024 lower for the rights of the accused scale. In other words, racial and ideological attitudes, fear of crime, and respect for police are quite important variables in predicting one's opinion regarding issues of civil liberties, however, demographic variables are still quite important.

The nonattitudinal characteristics of respondents that still have clear effects on opinion toward criminal procedure when other variables are controlled are: race, with blacks more protective (b = .810*); sex, with men more protective (b = .683**); region, with the largest difference between the West (Pacific and Mountain) and the South (base = South, variable = Pacific b = .961*, variable = Mountain .618); type of community, with suburbs most protective (base = suburb, variable = rural b = -.555, variable = city b = -.484); marital status, with divorced or separated people most protective (base = married, variable = divorced/separated b = .952*). The effects of these characteristics occur independently of attitudes bearing on issues of race, crime, the police, or personal safety. The effects of sex and community type variables may be related to unmeasured perceptions of high crime that might lead people to support greater government intrusiveness. In all, that partisanship and liberal-conservative ideology do not independently affect opinion toward criminal procedures further confirms how distinctive these issues are (ideology b = -.017, party b = -.048).

Education and Knowledge

Tables 5.6-5.11 present the regression analyses for the different levels of knowledge and education. The results reveal that the effect of most independent variables diminishes as one's level of education rises. A possible explanation is that the less educated need to rely on different shortcuts (race, gender), are more easily swayed by environmental factors (area, region, fear of crime), and have their opinions more easily influenced by new pieces of information (source of information, talk radio), than the more educated, since their opinions are not as firmly established (see Sniderman, Brody, and Tetlock, 1991).

Some interesting trends emerge within the different education categories (see Table 5.6). First, of the different ideological scales, the criminal justice liberalism scale has the greatest effect, though it diminishes as one's education rises (b=1.256* [low] vs. .395* [middle] vs. .408* [high]). Also, residents of the Pacific and Mountain regions were consistently more civil libertarian than others, though, again, the effect diminishes as education rises (base=South, variable=Pacific b=1.973 [low] vs. 1.087 [middle] vs. .252 [high]). Respondents who feared walking alone at night (b=-2.107* [low] vs. -1.436** [middle] vs. .203 [high]), and those who listened to talk radio (b=-690 [low] vs. -.150 [middle] vs. -.129 [high]), were less civil libertarian, and again, the effect diminished with education.

In contrast, residents who lived in the suburbs were less civil libertarian than residents of other communities among the less educated, but were more civil libertarian within other categories of education (base=suburb, variable= city b=.920 [low] vs. -.694 [middle] vs. -.549 [high]; variable=rural b=.830 [low] vs. -.342 [middle] vs. -.642 [high]). The same pattern appeared regarding TV viewing, with individuals who are less educated more likely to be civil libertarian, if their main source of information was the television, while the opposite was true for respondents in the other education categories (base=TV, variable=reading b=-.049 [low] vs. .725 [middle] vs. .595 [high]). Across the board, divorced and separated respondents were more civil libertarian, with the greatest effect among the most educated respondents (base=married, variable= divorced/separated b=.824 [low] vs. .680 [middle] vs. 1.216 [high]). Blacks were more civil libertarian, about evenly across all levels of education (base= white, variable=black b=.820 [low] vs. 1.190 [middle] vs. .929 [high]), while men were more civil libertarian as well (b=.555 [low] vs. 1.042** [middle] vs. 226 [high]), though the effect was not as large for those in the highest level of education. Also of interest was that the factor of whether or not one respects the police had a greater effect on respondents with more education, with those who respect the police more being less civil libertarian (b=.166 [low] vs. .517 [middle] vs. .643** [high]).

In general, with some variations in the numbers, the same basic pattern held for the differing levels of knowledge, though the patterns were not as clear and linear as they were for the differing levels of education (see Tables 5.9-5.11).

Agreement with Court Scale

As articulated earlier, it would be expected that the same factors that would cause one to be more civil libertarian would also cause one to be less supportive of recent Supreme Court decisions. This is because the Court has been moving consistently to the Right over the past couple of decades.

The regression equation results presented in Table 5.12 are consistent with this notion. First, the higher one scores on the criminal justice liberalism scale, the less one agrees with the Court (b=-.198**). In addition, respondents in the South, who are least civil libertarian, are most likely to agree with Court decisions, while respondents from the Pacific region are least likely to be in agreement (base=South, variable=Pacific b=-.743**). Those who cite TV as their main source of information are most likely to agree with recent Court decisions (base=TV, variable=reading b=-.287). Also, whites (base=white, variable=black b=-.338), females (base=female, variable=male b=-.022), married people (base=married, variable=divorced/separated b=-.512*), less educated (b=-.047), as well as those who have less respect for the police (b=-.291**), are most likely to be in agreement with recent Court decisions. All these groups were also less supportive of civil liberties.

There do not seem to be any major differences when the regression equations were run for the different levels of education and knowledge (see Tables 5.13 and 5.14). One interesting point is that the effect of fear of crime declines as one's education and knowledge grows (b=.498 [low education] vs. .105 [middle] vs. .030 [low]; b=.534 [low knowledge] vs. .0026 [middle] vs. -.010 [high]). This is probably because the more educated and knowledgeable have the ability to see crime in broader societal terms, thus mitigating the effect personal experience with crime might have on their general opinions concerning the issue.

RELATED EFFECTS

To estimate possible indirect effects and causes of spuriousness, additional regressions were performed (see Tables 5.15-5.17). This led to the creation of the causal flow graph presented in Table 5.18.

Party ID, political ideology, income, source of information concerning crime, fear of crime, and respect for the police, as well as the three ideology scales were all specified as dependent variables on race, gender, area, region, listening to talk radio, marital status, knowledge, education, age, and TV viewing. Party ID, political ideology, income, source of information, fear of crime, and respect for police were included as independent variables when each was not specified as a dependent variable, as shown in the path model.

The logic behind the flow graph is that the causally prior variables are used as independent variables, while the variables that might be affected by the independent variables are specified as dependent variables. Race, gender, area, region, and religion are variables that are quite stable and at times cannot be changed. They are therefore specified as independent variables. As one moves rightward on the flow graph, one sees that the variables are more amenable to change and are likely to be affected by the variables to the left on the flow graph. For example, it is quite logical for one's gender, race, area, or religion to influence one's party ID, political ideology, or fear of crime, but not vice versa.

Ideology Scales

When the criminal justice liberalism scale was used as the dependent variable (see Table 5.15), gender (males less liberal), race (blacks more liberal), religion (atheists more liberal), marital status (divorced people more liberal), education (the more educated more liberal), party, and ideology (conservatives and Republicans less liberal) were all statistically significant.

The same pattern held when the dependent variable was the racial justice scale, with the addition of region (all areas more liberal than the South) as being a significant explanation for changes in the dependent variable.

The pattern was slightly different when the dependent variable was the economic liberalism scale. Most important indicators of change in the dependent variable were region (South most conservative), listening to talk radio (listeners more conservative), age (older people more conservative), party (Republicans more conservative), and respect for the police (the less respect, the more liberal).

Other Significant Variables

To further assess possible indirect effects, other variables which were significant in the original regression equation were also analyzed as dependent variables.

The three most important factors in predicting the level of respect for police officers (see Table 5.16), were region (New Englanders less respectful), knowledge (the more knowledgeable the less respectful), and age (the young less respectful). Fear of crime was affected by one's gender (women more fearful), area (rural dwellers least fearful), and income (poorer people more fearful). Source of information was predicted by one's gender (women get more information from TV than men), listening to talk radio (listeners obtain less info from TV than others), amount of TV hours viewed, and income (poorer people obtain more information from TV than the more well off). Level of income (see Table 5.17) is predicted by gender (men with higher levels), race (whites with higher incomes), religion (Protestants with lower incomes), area (Southerners earning the least and Pacific coast dwellers the most), marital status (married individuals earning more than others), knowledge, education (the more knowledge and education, the higher the income), age (the older earn more), and party (Republicans earn more).

In all, the results from this analysis, as presented in the flow graph in Table 5.18, are in line with the previous regression equations. Though the effects of education, party identification, and political ideology are more apparent, lending support to the hypothesis that their effect is negated by the inclusion of the ideology scales in the previous regressions, the demographic variables found significant in the previous regression models still play a quite prominent role.

RACIAL DIFFERENCES

To assess causal differences based upon race, regressions were run separately for black and white respondents (see Tables 5.19-5.21). Generally, the results indicate similar effects on one's opinion regarding issues of criminal justice, regardless of race. There are a few noteworthy differences.

Blacks and whites who scored higher on the racial liberalism scale and criminal justice liberalism scale were both more likely to score higher on the three scales measuring one's support for civil liberties (criminal justice liberalism scale: whites=.330, blacks=1.286**; racial liberalism scale: whites=.339, blacks=1.015). However, differences occurred when the independent variable was the economic liberalism scale. The higher white respondents scored on the economic liberalism scale, the higher they scored on the civil liberties scales (b=.111, p=.448). In contrast, the higher blacks scored on economic liberalism, the less support they had for civil liberties (b=-.815, p=.031). A possible explanation, as revealed in the bivariate analysis, is that blacks scored much higher than whites on the racial liberalism and criminal justice liberalism scales, but did not score higher than whites on the economic liberalism scales. In other words, blacks were more likely to believe that racial injustice, in the courts as well as in society, were more likely than poverty to be a cause of crime.

Other differences between the races were based upon region (southern blacks were more civil libertarian than blacks in other regions [base=South, Pacific=-2.197, Mountain=-3.899, West North Central=1.446, mid-Atlantic= -1.174, New England=-.623], while the opposite was true for white respondents [base=South, Pacific=1.107, Mountain=.756, West North Central=.562, mid-Atlantic=.294, New England=.155]); area (suburban whites were more civil libertarian than city whites [base=suburb, city=-.609, rural=-.560], while the opposite is true for blacks [base=suburb, city=.631, rural=-.249]); religion (white Protestant were less civil libertarian than whites of other religions [base=Protestant, Catholic=.201, atheist=.521, Jewish=-.495, other=-.058], while black Protestants were more civil libertarian than others [base=Protestant, Catholic=-1.041, Atheist=-1.072, other=-.889]); gender (white men were more civil libertarian [.664], while among blacks women were more civil libertarian [-.304]); and talk radio (black listeners were more civil libertarian than non-listeners [.406], while among whites listeners were less civil libertarian [-.315]).

CONCLUSION: WHAT DO EDUCATION AND KNOWLEDGE HAVE TO DO WITH IT?

Education and more recently political knowledge have been the workhorses of theories about attitude formation and opinion change (see Zaller, 1992; and Page and Shapiro, 1992, for reviews and appraisals). In this chapter, we see, however, that they do not matter much when it comes to the specifics of criminal justice procedures. I have offered reasons why this is so in emphasizing the greater effects of other variables. In general, the reason that education and political knowledge seem to foster support for civil liberties and civil rights is that these variables represent the exposure to and subsequent acquisition of values that are part of an elite or existing societal consensus that certain rights and liberties ought to be protected. Moreover, there are also connections between and among different rights, such that protections of rights are sweepingly defined. In contrast, this is not now the case for criminal justice procedures in which the protection of rights or the allowance of government intrusion is conditional, and thus there is no sweeping norm or value for protection or for allowing systematic and increasing invasion of privacy.

This lack of elite consensus means that simple exposure to this dissensus—as measured by education and knowledge—will not have a predictable effect on opinion. While we still have to examine whether the effect of this exposure is contingent on one's ideology and values (by testing their interactions; see Zaller, 1992), such that we would expect exposure to further polarize those already predisposed to accept or reject arguments for or against protecting people from government intrusion, one should not be surprised that other influences on opinion take hold. In reacting to threats to privacy and procedural fairness, it makes much sense that blacks and those who have less respect for police authority are more likely than others to be protective. In addition, those who are liberal when it comes to racial attitudes and other attitudes toward crime (in contrast to economic concerns) are quite explicitly more defensive on criminal procedures and intrusions as well. In contrast, people who are sensitive to the threat posed by crime are more willing to trade-off rights and freedom from intrusion for measures that would ostensibly promote public safety. These trade-offs involve considerations that are unrelated to knowledge or education per se, nor are they guided by principals of conduct to which the educated and knowledgeable are more likely than others to be exposed.

Chapter 6 uses similar bivariate and multivatriate analysis to examine further the legal elite.

Table 5.1
Means for Overall Mass Survey

Both Surveys	All Lawyers	Mass Public
Criminal procedure scale (0-12)	6.56 (369)	5.32 (720)
	F=46.272, df=1, p=.000	
Search and seizure scale (0-8)	3.53 (375)	2.75 (751)
	F=36.353, df=1, p=.000	
Accused scale (0-4)	3.02 (396)	2.36 (771)
	F=39.162, df=1, p=.000	
Agreement w/Ct scale (0-12)	7.74 (369)	7.60 (720)

Note: Including lawyer survey, mass survey by knowledge and education for overall criminal procedure scale, search and seizure scale, rights of the accused scale, and agreement with Court scale.

Table 5.2
Mass Survey for Different Levels of Knowledge and Education

	Education			Knowledge		
	High	Middle	Low	High	Middle	Low
Overall criminal procedure scale	5.48	5.37	4.55	5.52	5.28	5.18
	(374)	(250)	(96)	(212)	(299)	(209)
	F=4.326, df=2, p=.014			F=.844, df=2, p=.431		
Search and seizure scale (0-8)	2.82	2.83	2.30	2.77	2.72	2.77
	(388)	(259)	(104)	(219)	(310)	(222)
	F=3.014, df=2, p=.050			F=.068, df=2, p=.935		
Accused scale (0-4)	2.46	2.33	2.09	2.43	2.32	2.36
	(402)	(264)	(105)	(230)	(319)	(222)
	F=3.975, df=2, p=.019			F=.484, df=2, p=.617		
Agreement w/Ct scale (0-12)	7.65	7.44	7.82	7.74	7.66	7.38
	(374)	(250)	(96)	(212)	(299)	(209)
	F=2.120, df=2, p=.121			F=2.773, df=2, p=.063		

Table 5.3
Means for All Scales and Variables

Region	New England	Mid-Atlantic	West North Central	South	Mountain	Pacific
Criminal procedure scale	5.74 (35)	5.30 (242)	5.20 (59)	5.00 (269)	5.44 (34)	6.31 (75)
			F=2.777, df=5, p=.017			
Search scale	3.05 (39)	2.80 (255)	2.67 (60)	2.48 (277)	2.74 (35)	3.43 (79)
			F=3.063, df=5, p=.010			
Accused scale	2.83 (41)	2.33 (266)	2.37 (62)	2.25 (280)	2.56 (34)	2.53 (81)
			F=2.237, df=5, p=.049			
Agreement w/Ct scale	7.51 (35)	7.46 (242)	7.75 (59)	7.81 (269)	7.68 (34)	7.19 (75)
			F=2.306, df=5, p=.043			

Marital Status	Married	Widowed	Divorced	Separated	Never Married
Criminal procedure scale	4.92 (416)	4.48 (69)	6.41 (80)	5.27 (11)	6.26 (144)
		F=11.446, df=4, p=.000			
Search scale	2.45 (432)	2.08 (72)	3.62 (81)	2.86 (14)	3.45 (152)
		F=13.496, df=4, p=.000			
Accused scale	2.23 (440)	2.23 (75)	2.64 (87)	2.38 (13)	2.65 (156)
		F=5.077, df=4, p=.000			
Agreement w/Ct scale	7.80 (416)	7.87 (69)	7.14 (80)	7.09 (11)	7.18 (144)
		F=6.280, df=4, p=.000			

Gender	Male	Female
Criminal procedure scale	5.70 (369)	4.91 (351)
	F=14.637, df=1, p=.000	
Search scale	2.98 (383)	2.51 (368)
	F=10.083, df=1, p=.002	
Accused scale	2.47 (394)	2.25 (377)
	F=9.559, df=1, p=.011	
Agreement w/Ct scale	7.58 (369)	7.62 (351)
	F=.110, df=1, p=.740	

Community Type	City	Suburb	Rural
Criminal procedure scale	5.44 (274)	5.58 (239)	4.86 (207)
	F=4.204, df=2, p=.015		
Search scale	2.79 (287)	2.96 (249)	2.44 (215)
	F=4.071, df=2, p=.017		
Accused scale	2.45 (292)	2.42 (255)	2.19 (224)
	F=3.161, df=2, p=.043		
Agreement w/Ct scale	7.57 (274)	7.45 (239)	7.81 (207)
	F=2.729, df=2, p=.066		

Race	White	Black	Asian	Hispanic
Criminal procedure scale	5.17 (600)	6.58 (78)	4.50 (10)	5.54 (24)
	F=6.313, df=3, p=.000			
Search scale	2.63 (623)	3.66 (83)	2.50 (10)	2.93 (27)
	F=6.684, df=3, p=.000			
Accused scale	2.34 (645)	2.68 (81)	1.60 (10)	2.41 (27)
	F=3.254, df=3, p=.021			
Agreement w/Ct scale	7.69 (600)	6.96 (78)	7.50 (10)	7.38 (24)
	F=4.720, df=3, p=.003			

continued . . .

Table 5.3 (continued)

Religion	Protestant	Catholic	Jewish	Atheist	Other
Criminal procedure scale	5.16 (421)	5.30 (191)	4.95 (19)	6.59 (58)	5.26 (27)
		$F=3.476$, $df=4$, $p=.008$			
Search scale	2.65 (439)	2.72 (199)	2.25 (20)	3.57 (61)	2.85 (27)
		$F=3.173$, $df=4$, $p=.013$			
Accused scale	2.33 (452)	2.32 (201)	2.50 (20)	2.75 (64)	2.24 (29)
		$F=1.917$, $df=4$, $p=.106$			
Agreement w/Ct scale	7.67 (421)	7.62 (191)	7.68 (19)	7.28 (58)	7.26 (27)
		$F=1.036$, $df=4$, $p=.388$			

Source of Crime Information	Papers	Radio	TV	Mags	Talking	Other
Criminal procedure scale	5.67 (157)	5.48 (67)	5.11 (430)	6.64 (14)	6.00 (29)	4.86 (22)
			$F=2.108$, $df=5$, $p=.063$			
Search scale	2.98 (162)	2.90 (69)	2.60 (446)	3.79 (14)	2.94 (36)	2.74 (23)
			$F=1.776$, $df=5$, $p=.115$			
Accused scale	2.51 (167)	2.41 (71)	2.30 (458)	2.73 (15)	2.58 (36)	1.87 (23)
			$F=2.002$, $df=5$, $p=.076$			
Agreement w/Ct scale	7.57 (157)	7.45 (67)	7.67 (430)	7.21 (14)	7.24 (29)	7.59 (22)
			$F=.705$, $df=5$, $p=.620$			

Do You Listen to Talk Radio?	Yes	No
Criminal procedure scale	5.16 (281)	5.42 (439)
	$F=1.497$, $df=1$, $p=.222$	
Search scale	2.68 (291)	2.79 (460)
	$F=.483$, $df=1$, $p=.487$	
Accused scale	2.29 (297)	2.41 (474)
	$F=1.928$, $df=1$, $p=.165$	
Agreement w/Ct scale	7.59 (281)	7.60 (439)
	$F=.005$, $df=1$, $p=.941$	

Scared to Walk Alone at Night	Yes	No
Criminal procedure scale	4.95 (300)	5.58 (420)
	F=8.915, df=1, p=.003	
Search scale	2.54 (314)	2.90 (437)
	F=6.051, df=1, p=.014	
Accused scale	2.22 (318)	2.46 (453)
	F=7.514, df=1, p=.006	
Agreement w/Ct scale	7.62 (300)	7.59 (420)
	F=.074, df=1, p=.785	

Do You Feel Safe Home at Night?	Yes	No
Criminal procedure scale	5.31 (656)	5.45 (64)
	F=.160, df=1, p=.689	
Search scale	2.70 (686)	3.25 (65)
	F=4.337, df=1, p=.038	
Accused scale	2.38 (702)	2.22 (69)
	F=1.084, df=1, p=.298	
Agreement w/Ct scale	7.66 (656)	7.02 (64)
	F=8.775, df=1, p=.003	

Worst Crime Suffered	Car	Mugged	Robbery in Home	Physical Assault
Criminal procedure scale	5.21 (85)	5.59 (34)	5.31 (142)	5.53 (47)
Search scale	2.69 (87)	2.97 (34)	2.75 (150)	2.98 (49)
Accused scale	2.28 (89)	2.33 (36)	2.38 (154)	2.43 (51)
Agreement w/Ct scale	7.64 (85)	7.71 (34)	7.58 (142)	7.45 (47)

continued . . .

Table 5.3 (continued)

Worst Crime Suffered (continued)	Murder	Rape	None
Criminal procedure Scale	5.26 (38)	5.89 (28)	5.25 (346)
	F=.347, df=6, p=.912		
Search scale	2.72 (39)	3.21 (29)	2.67 (363)
	F=.516, df=6, p=.797		
Accused scale	2.35 (40)	2.37 (30)	2.37 (371)
	F=.106, df=6, p=.996		
Agreement w/Ct scale	7.53 (38)	7.46 (28)	7.63 (346)
	F=.162, df=6, p=.987		

Respect for Police	Great Deal	Only Some	Hardly Any
Criminal procedure scale	4.94 (466)	5.96 (195)	6.40 (53)
	F=13.745, df=2, p=.000		
Search scale	2.46 (488)	3.22 (202)	3.62 (55)
	F=16.087, df=2, p=.000		
Accused scale	2.27 (497)	2.52 (209)	2.59 (59)
	F=4.251, df=2, p=.015		
Agreement w/Ct scale	7.79 (466)	7.24 (195)	7.30 (53)
	F=8.710, df=2, p=.000		

Age	18-24	25-33	34-43	44-64	Over 64
Criminal procedure scale	6.15 (87)	5.45 (139)	5.78 (165)	4.99 (216)	4.49 (113)
		F=6.588, df=4, p=.000			
Search scale	3.25 (92)	2.87 (141)	3.16 (174)	2.46 (225)	2.17 (119)
		F=7.155, df=4, p=.000			
Accused scale	2.65 (93)	2.34 (147)	2.51 (175)	2.29 (229)	2.11 (127)
		F=3.483, df=4, p=.008			
Agreement w/Ct scale	7.37 (87)	7.60 (139)	7.37 (165)	7.80 (216)	7.73 (113)
		F=2.181, df=4, p=.070			

Income	Less Than $10,000	$10-20,000	$20-30,000	$30-40,000
Criminal procedure scale	5.11 (71)	5.34 (144)	5.57 (137)	5.19 (118)
Search scale	2.73 (74)	2.83 (154)	2.94 (142)	2.64 (123)
Accused scale	2.34 (79)	2.33 (154)	2.40 (145)	2.30 (122)
Agreement w/Ct scale	7.48 (71)	7.45 (144)	7.50 (137)	7.67 (118)

Income (continued)	$40-50,000	$50-60,000	More Than $60,000
Criminal procedure scale	5.04 (84)	5.92 (48)	5.24 (102)
		$F=.819$, df=6, p=.555	
Search scale	2.44 (85)	3.00 (49)	2.60 (106)
		$F=.869$, df=6, p=.517	
Accused scale	2.38 (94)	2.55 (51)	2.36 (105)
		$F=.308$, df=6, p=.933	
Agreement w/Ct scale	7.89 (84)	7.75 (48)	7.67 (102)
		$F=.909$, df=6, p=.488	

Did You or Member of Family Commit a Crime?	Yes	No
Criminal procedure Scale	5.88 (58)	5.09 (237)
	$F=3.750$, df=1, p=.054	
Search scale	3.26 (58)	2.54 (238)
	$F=6.182$, df=1, p=.013	
Accused scale	2.52 (58)	2.35 (243)
	$F=.819$, df=1, p=.366	
Agreement w/Ct scale	7.29 (58)	7.78 (237)
	$F=4.314$, df=1, p=.039	

continued . . .

Table 5.3 (continued)

Confidence in Government	Great Deal	Only Some	Hardly Any
Criminal procedure scale	4.78 (67)	5.28 (362)	5.48 (289)
		F=1.776, df=2, p=.170	
Search scale	2.54 (69)	2.66 (379)	2.92 (298)
		F=1.788, df=2, p=.168	
Accused scale	2.25 (68)	2.40 (393)	2.33 (306)
		F=.556, df=2, p=.573	
Agreement w/Ct scale	7.34 (67)	7.66 (362)	7.60 (289)
		F=1.064, df=2, p=.346	

People Most Confident In	Congress	Supreme Court	President	None
Criminal procedure scale	5.29 (143)	5.39 (296)	4.66 (90)	5.55 (190)
		F=2.198, df=3, p=.087		
Search scale	2.74 (148)	2.80 (303)	2.34 (95)	2.89 (203)
		F=1.710, df=3, p=.163		
Accused scale	2.32 (148)	2.41 (315)	2.18 (96)	2.42 (211)
		F=1.105, df=3, p=.346		
Agreement w/Ct scale	7.71 (143)	7.59 (296)	7.66 (90)	7.49 (190)
		F=.540, df=3, p=.655		

Role of Court	Society Wishes	Court Wishes	Depends
Criminal procedure scale	5.64 (286)	5.18 (365)	4.68 (66)
		F=4.072, df=2, p=.017	
Search scale	3.01 (295)	2.63 (378)	2.27 (75)
		F=5.382, df=2, p=.005	
Accused scale	2.49 (306)	2.29 (387)	2.22 (74)
		F=2.870, df=2, p=.057	
Agreement w/Ct scale	7.49 (286)	7.62 (365)	7.95 (66)
		F=2.183, df=2, p=.113	

Table 5.4
Means on Selected Scales and Variables

Party	Democrat	Independent	Republican
Criminal procedure scale	5.57 (222)	5.30 (242)	5.06 (248)
		F=2.014, df=2, p=.134	
Search scale	2.90 (230)	2.80 (255)	2.54 (256)
		F=2.176, df=2, p=.114	
Accused scale	2.50 (234)	2.36 (267)	2.23 (260)
		F=2.928, df=2, p=.054	
Agreement w/Ct scale	7.47 (222)	7.50 (242)	7.82 (248)
		F=3.392, df=2, p=.034	

Ideology	Liberal	Moderate	Conservative
Criminal procedure scale	5.65 (124)	5.47 (300)	4.99 (269)
		F=3.251, df=2, p=.039	
Search scale	3.07 (131)	2.77 (315)	2.54 (276)
		F=3.218, df=2, p=.041	
Accused scale	2.52 (133)	2.45 (328)	2.21 (281)
		F=4.048, df=2, p=.018	
Agreement w/Ct scale	7.40 (124)	7.57 (300)	7.78 (269
		F=2.525, df=2, p=.081	

Party (7-point)	Strong Democrat	Democrat	Independent, but Closer to Democrat	Independent
Criminal procedure scale	6.01 (70)	5.37 (152)	5.29 (48)	5.44 (150)
Search scale	3.18 (73)	2.77 (157)	2.84 (49)	2.82 (159)
Accused scale	2.61 (74)	2.45 (160)	2.13 (54)	2.48 (164)
Agreement w/Ct scale	7.30 (70)	7.55 (152)	7.46 (48)	7.44 (150)

continued . . .

Table 5.4 (continued)

Party (7-point continued)	Independent, but Closer to Republican	Republican	Strong Republican
Criminal procedure scale	4.90 (41)	5.10 (121)	5.02 (127)
	F=1.313, df=6, p=.249		
Search scale	2.73 (44)	2.49 (125)	2.58 (131)
	F=1.105, df=6, p=.358		
Accused scale	2.22 (46)	2.24 (126)	2.23 (134)
	F=1.829, df=6, p=.091		
Agreement w/Ct scale	7.83 (41)	7.93 (121)	7.72 (127)
	F=1.731, df=6, p=.111		

Ideology (7-point)	Strong Liberal	Liberal	Moderate, but Closer to Liberal	Moderate
Criminal procedure scale	6.49 (47)	5.13 (77)	5.92 (62)	5.56 (166)
Search scale	3.71 (48)	2.70 (83)	3.03 (66)	2.84 (173)
Accused scale	2.90 (49)	2.30 (84)	2.61 (70)	2.46 (183)
Agreement w/Ct scale	6.74 (47)	7.81 (77)	7.56 (62)	7.48 (166)

Ideology (7-point continued)	Moderate, but Closer to Conservative	Conservative	Strong Conservative
Criminal procedure scale	4.89 (73)	4.97 (173)	5.04 (95)
	F=3.167, df=6, p=.005		
Search scale	2.36 (77)	2.52 (178)	2.59 (97)
	F=3.181, df=6, p=.004		
Accused scale	2.26 (76)	2.21 (180)	2.21 (100)
	F=3.211, df=6, p=.004		
Agreement w/Ct scale	7.79 (73)	7.75 (173)	7.82 (95)
	F=3.218, df=6, p=.004		

Criminal Justice Liberalism Scale	Low (0)	.5	1.0	1.5	Middle (2)
Criminal procedure scale	4.58 (225)	5.24 (100)	5.06 (132)	5.49 (84)	5.98 (56)
Search scale	2.22 (236)	2.70 (103)	2.53 (134)	2.80 (87)	3.34 (59)
Accused scale	2.14 (234)	2.30 (109)	2.37 (141)	2.44 (90)	2.55 (62)
Agreement w/Ct scale	7.92 (225)	7.70 (100)	7.67 (132)	7.61 (84)	7.30 (56)

Criminal Justice Liberalism Scale (continued)	2.5	3.0	3.5	High (4)
Criminal procedure scale	5.95 (43)	7.38 (21)	6.85 (26)	9.40 (10)
		$F=8.601$, df$=8$, p$=.000$		
Search scale	3.15 (46)	4.43 (21)	3.79 (28)	5.80 (10)
		$F=9.549$, df$=8$, p$=.000$		
Accused scale	2.51 (49)	2.88 (24)	2.74 (27)	3.50 (10)
		$F=3.392$, df$=8$, p$=.001$		
Agreement w/Ct scale	7.26 (43)	6.43 (21)	6.92 (26)	6.00 (10)
		$F=4.745$, df$=8$, p$=.000$		

Racial Liberalism Scale	Low (0)	.5	Middle (1)	1.5	High (2)
Criminal procedure scale	4.90 (40)	4.84 (293)	5.23 (106)	5.41 (93)	6.21 (180)
		$F=7.270$, df$=4$, p$=.000$			
Search scale	2.45 (44)	2.43 (301)	2.84 (111)	2.84 (99)	3.25 (188)
		$F=5.225$, df$=4$, p$=.000$			
Accused scale	2.05 (42)	2.19 (312)	2.27 (114)	2.35 (96)	2.74 (196)
		$F=7.260$, df$=4$, p$=.000$			
Agreement w/Ct scale	7.80 (40)	7.70 (293)	7.47 (106)	7.58 (93)	7.46 (180)
		$F=.887$, df$=4$, p$=.471$			

continued . . .

Table 5.4 (continued)

Economic Liberalism Scale	Low (0)	Middle (1)	High (2)
Criminal procedure scale	4.82 (204)	5.37 (236)	5.62 (276)
		$F=5.024$, df=2, p=.007	
Search scale	2.46 (212)	2.80 (246)	2.90 (287)
		$F=3.125$, df=2, p=.045	
Accused scale	2.11 (215)	2.38 (253)	2.53 (299)
		$F=7.682$, df=2, p=.000	
Agreement w/Ct scale	7.65 (204)	7.63 (236)	7.56 (276)
		$F=.213$, df=2, p=.809	

Note: Including criminal procedure scale, search and seizure scale, rights of the accused scale, by
party, ideology, racial liberalism scale, economic liberalism scale, criminal justice liberalism
scale, and role of the Court.

Table 5.5
**Multivariate Regression Models, for Mass Sample with Criminal Procedure,
Search and Seizure, and Rights of the Accused Scales
as Dependent Variables**

	Criminal Procedure		Search		Rights of Accused	
	b	Beta	b	Beta	b	Beta
Economic liberalism scale	.031	.001	-.047	-.020	.098	.066
Racial liberalism scale	.413*	.101	.226	.076	.161*	.076
Criminal justice liberalism	.394**	.153	.306**	.163	.110*	.096
Region (base=South)						
New England	.274	.022	.352	.041	.430	.084
Mid-Atlantic	.190	.033	.296	.071	.055	.022
West North Central	.293	.031	.326	.046	.100	.023
Mountain	.618	.050	.416	.046	.372	.066
Pacific	.961*	.104	.801**	.120	.141	.035
Scared walking at night	-.525*	-.096	-.292	-.073	-.249*	-.102
Talk radio	-.185	-.034	-.034	-.009	-.087	-.035
Area (base=suburb)						
Rural	-.555	-.093*	-.354	-.082	-.217	-.082
City	-.484	-.087	-.354	-.087	-.139	-.056

	Criminal Procedure		Rights of Search		Accused	
	b	Beta	b	Beta	b	Beta
Source of info (base=TV)						
Radio	.626	.066	.543*	.078	.192	.045
Talking with people	.502	.037	.272	.030	.170	.030
Reading	.611**	.099	.493**	.109	.179	.065
Marital status (base=married)						
Divorced/Separated	.952**	.118	.746**	.128	.246	.070
Widowed	.124	.013	-.170	-.025	.188	.046
Never married	.292	.042	.154	.031	.091	.030
Religion (base=Protestant)						
Jewish	-.610	.037	-.536	-.044	-.011	-.001
Catholic	.102	.017	.024	.005	-.102	-.038
Atheist	.295	.030	.036	.005	.227	.052
Other	-.175	-.012	.075	.007	-.297	-.047
Race (base=white)						
Black	.810*	.091	.567*	.089	.228	.057
Asian	-1.460	-.062	-.506	-.029	-.982*	-.091
Hispanic	.374	.024	.281	.026	.033	.005
Male	.683**	.127	.414*	.105	.204*	.085
Political knowledge	.009	.005	-.050	-.038	-.015	-.018
Income	-.058	-.041	-.079	-.077	-.007	-.011
Education	-.033	-.018	.034	.025	-.013	-.015
Age	-.146	-.067	-.089	-.056	-.055	-.057
Ideology	-.017	-.011	-.016	-.014	-.010	-.014
Party	-.048	-.036	-.020	-.021	-.019	-.033
TV hours per day	-.141	-.054	-.054	-.038	-.141	-.072
Respect for police	.672**	.154	.509**	.160	.088	.046
R^2	.216		.207		.123	
Adjusted R^2	.169		.161		.074	
F	4.593**		4.516**		2.515**	
N	602		623		641	

$*p<.05; **p<.01$

Note: The b's are unstandardized regression coefficients, the Betas are standardized coefficients.

Table 5.6
Multivariate Regression Models for Differing Levels of Education, with Criminal Procedure Scale as Dependent Variable

	Low		Middle		High	
	b	Beta	b	Beta	b	Beta
Economic liberalism scale	-.286	-.083	-.0049	-.001	.036	.012
Racial liberalism scale	.253	.053	.564	.135	.333	.086
Criminal justice liberalism	1.256*	.366	.395*	.140	.408*	.178
Region (base=South)						
New England	.075	.004	.978	.084	-.584	-.051
Mid-Atlantic	-.194	-.031	.255	.042	.083	.016
West North Central	1.275	.084	.845	.067	.025	.003
Mountain	1.523	.100	.566	.031	.200	.020
Pacific	1.973	.129	1.087	.118	.282	.034
Scared walking at night	-2.107*	-.349	-1.436**	-.243	.203	.040
Talk radio	-.690	-.114	-.150	-.026	-.129	-.025
Area (base=suburb)						
Rural	.830	.121	-.342	-.059	-.624	-.107
City	.920	.153	-.694	-.118	-.549	-.105
Source of info (base=TV)						
Radio	-2.568	-.214	1.319	.128	.559	.066
Talking with people	-2.737	-.105	1.820*	.137	.204	.017
Reading	-.049	-.006	.725	.105	.595	.110
Marital status (base=married)						
Divorced/Separated	.824	.110	.680	.079	1.216*	.115
Widowed	.494	.068	-.707	-.070	.723	.074
Never married	1.452	.109	-.163	-.021	.218	.037
Religion (base=Protestant)						
Jewish	-7.181	-.276	-.119	-.006	.025	.002
Catholic	1.018	.153	-.734	-.115	.590	.104
Atheist	5.488*	.360	.510	.049	.219	.025
Other	-3.579	-.137	-1.409	-.049	.297	.028
Race (base=white)						
Black	.820	.107	1.190	.139	.929	.094
Asian	-4.221	-.162	-5.925*	-.145	-.171	-.009
Hispanic	1.528	.082	1.789	.114	-.572	-.040
Male	.555	.092	1.042**	.184	.226	.045
Income	.434	.224	.008	.004	-.141	-.105
Age	.202	.077	-.130	-.059	-.141	-.067
Ideology	.304	.165	-.008	-.050	.012	.009
Party	-.056	-.039	-.088	-.062	-.052	-.042
TV hours per day	-.400	-.197	.045	.023	-.214	-.104
Respect for police	.166	.030	.517	.118	.643**	.234

	Low		Middle		High	
	b	Beta	b	Beta	b	Beta
R²		.464		.369		.242
Adjusted R²		.055		.254		.157
F		1.135		3.229**		2.842**
N		74		209		317

*p<.05; **p<.01
Note: The b's are unstandardized regression coefficients, the Betas are standardized coefficients.

Table 5.7
Multivariate Regression Models for Differing Levels of Education,
with Search and Seizure Scale as Dependent Variable

	Low		Middle		High	
	b	Beta	b	Beta	b	Beta
Economic liberalism scale	.117	.051	-.095*	-.039	-.123	-.051
Racial liberalism scale	.041	.015	.406*	.139	.187	.063
Criminal justice liberalism	.738*	.333	.245	.127	.367**	.206
Region (base=South)						
New England	.281	.023	.604	.076	.034	.004
Mid-Atlantic	.760	.184	.08	.019	.300	.073
West North Central	.864	.084	.389	.044	.219	.036
Mountain	2.204	.198	-.357	-.030	.270	.034
Pacific	1.198	.134	.919*	.145	.243	.037
Scared walking at night	-1.234*	-.312	-.951**	-.232	.218	.055
Talk Radio	-.165	-.042	-.080	-.020	.003	.008
Area (base=suburb)						
Rural	-.027	-.006	-.122	-.030	-.290	-.064
City	.364	.093	-.443	-.109	-.369	-.091
Source of info (base=TV)						
Radio	-.251	-.034	1.043*	.144	.377	.057
Talking with people	-2.629	-.150	1.239	.133	.217	.026
Reading	.065	.012	.525	.108	.542*	.128
Marital status (base=married)						
Divorced/Separated	.453	.095	.542	.092	1.337*	.218
Widowed	-.029	-.006	-.544	-.077	.369	.049
Never married	.188	.021	.134	.026	.119	.026

continued . . .

Table 5.7 (continued)

	Low		Middle		High	
	b	Beta	b	Beta	b	Beta
Religion (base=protestant)						
Jewish	-4.924*	-.281	.008	.001	-.152	-.015
Catholic	.189	.043	-.741*	-.168	.510	.115
Atheist	2.081	.203	-.073	-.010	.218	.032
Other	-3.281	-.187	-.799	-.039	.566	.067
Race (base=white)						
Black	1.138	.228	.540	.094	.796	.101
Asian	-1.966	-.112	-3.065	-.106	.573	.039
Hispanic	-.356	-.035	1.471*	.133	-.385	-.035
Male	.938	.238	.655*	.166	-.013	-.003
Income	.257	.199	-.036	-.029	-.130*	-.126
Age	.132	.075	-.051	-.034	-.138	-.084
Ideology	.226	.192	-.092	-.082	.023	.022
Party	-.083	-.088	-.040	-.041	-.016	-.017
TV hours per day	-.211	-.158	.023	.017	-.076	-.047
Respect for police	.464	.134	.454*	.148	.404*	.126
R^2	.464		.355		.153	
Adjusted R^2	.055		.241		.065	
F	1.135		3.129**		1.743*	
N	74		214		340	

*p<.05; **p<.01
Note: The b's are unstandardized regression coefficients, the Betas are standardized coefficients.

Table 5.8
**Multivariate Regression Models for Differing Levels of Education,
with Rights of the Accused Scale as Dependent Variable**

	Low		Middle		High	
	b	Beta	b	Beta	b	Beta
Economic liberalism scale	-.061	.040	.02	.013	.191	.136
Racial liberalism scale	.141	.068	.139	.076	.184	.105
Criminal justice liberalism	.243	.162	.111	.090	.103*	.099
Region (base=South)						
New England	.292	.034	.557	.111	.280	.059
Mid-Atlantic	-.240	-.088	.150	.056	.012	.005
West North Central	.289	.041	.441	.082	-.124	-.034
Mountain	.726	.103	.768	.094	.042	.009
Pacific	.793	.129	.345	.086	-.148	-.040
Scared walking at night	-.658	-.249	-.566**	-.219	-.0015	-.001
Talk radio	.063	.024	.038	.015	-.152	-.066
Area (base=suburb)						
Rural	.388	.129	-.131	-.052	-.285	-.107
City	.152	.058	-.234	-.090	-.150	-.064
Source of info (base=TV)						
Radio	-1.042	-.206	.538	.123	.066	.017
Talking with people	-.866	-.101	.870*	.148	-.048	-.009
Reading	-.053	-.015	.279	.091	.129	.052
Marital status (base=married)						
Divorced/Separated	.113	.035	.196	.053	.267	.077
Widowed	.241	.076	-.023	-.005	.287	.064
Never married	1.071	.175	-.139	-.042	.057	.022
Religion (base=protestant)						
Jewish	-2.692	-.224	-.275	.030	.344	.058
Catholic	.329	.109	-.246	-.088	-.036	-.014
Atheist	1.640	.223	.260	.057	.195	.051
Other	-.052	-.005	-.713	-.055	-.298	-.063
Race (base=white)						
Black	.179	.053	.414	.109	.253	.056
Asian	-.863	-.072	-2.763*	-.152	-.660	-.076
Hispanic	-.792	-.113	.118	.017	.258	.042
Male	.401	.152	.413*	.167	.0012	.001
Income	.046	.053	.0018	.002	-.034	-.056
Age	.023	.020	-.077	-.081	-.03	-.031
Ideology	.025	.031	-.0091	-.013	-.0016	-.003
Party	-.052	-.080	-.051	-.083	-.014	-.024
TV hours per day	-.172	-.196	.034	.040	-.057	-.061
Respect for police	.213	.090	.025	.013	.127	.069

continued . . .

Table 5.8 (continued)

	Low		Middle		High	
	b	Beta	b	Beta	b	Beta
R^2		.273		.249		.153
Adjusted R^2		-.192		.119		.065
F		.587		1.913**		1.743*
N	82		217		340	

*p<.05; **p<.01
Note: The b's are unstandardized regression coefficients, the Betas are standardized coefficients.

Table 5.9
Multivariate Regression Models for Differing Levels of Knowledge, with Criminal Procedure Scale as Dependent Variable

	Low		Middle		High	
	b	Beta	b	Beta	b	Beta
Economic liberalism scale	-.101	-.028	-.111	-.034	.098	.031
Racial liberalism scale	.367	.085	.468	.115	.559	.143
Criminal justice liberalism	.484*	.179	.265	.100	.307	.126
Region (base=South)						
New England	-.166	-.015	1.810	.104	-1.447	-.146
Mid-Atlantic	-.014	-.002	.605	.110	-.430	-.078
West North Central	-1.544	-.102	.967	.113	-.479	-.056
Mountain	.541	.029	1.084	.097	-.047	-.004
Pacific	-.248	-.021	1.584**	.185	1.058	.126
Scared walking at night	-1.623**	-.277	-.298	-.056	-.434	-.079
Talk Radio	.036	.006	-.181	-.034	-.421	-.080
Area (base=suburb)						
Rural	-.456	-.072	-.391	-.067	-.937	-.165
City	.220	.037	-.470	-.075	-1.038*	-.186
Source of info (base=TV)						
Radio	1.832	.154	-.070	-.000	.888	.114
Talking to people	-.043	-.004	1.723*	.143	-2.306	-.091
Reading	.428	.059	.930*	.143	.546	.101
Marital status (base=married)						
Divorced/Separated	1.488*	.181	.662	.083	1.125	.142
Widowed	-.329	-.038	.142	.015	.340	.034
Never married	-.237	-.033	.410	.060	.027	.004

	Low		Middle		High	
	b	Beta	b	Beta	b	Beta
Religion (base=Protestant)						
Jewish	-.197	-.009	-.012	-.001	-1.322	-.090
Catholic	-.198	-.030	.084	.014	.604	.102
Atheist	-.467	-.039	1.004	.109	.061	.006
Other	-1.130	-.053	1.494	.099	-.972	-.088
Race (base=white)						
Black	.895	.125	.873	.095	1.877	.127
Asian	.388	.018	-3.027	-.124	-.885	-.035
Hispanic	.572	.048	1.158	.081	n.a.	
Male	.747	.128	.796*	.152	.404	.076
Income	.0057	-.003	-.075	-.051	-.103	-.072
Age	-.361	-.170	.044	.021	-.284	-.092
Ideology	.029	.018	.022	.015	.014	.010
Party	-.088	-.059	.038	.029	-.191	-.150
TV hours per day	-.067	-.035	-.106	-.055	-.262	-.114
Respect for police	.828*	.199	.681*	.156	.246	.052
R^2	.369		.240		.295	
Adjusted R^2	.205		.133		.152	
F	2.252**		2.254**		2.062**	
N	155		261		184	

*p<.05; **p<.01   n.a.=not available

Note: The b's are unstandardized regression coefficients, the Betas are standardized coefficients.

Table 5.10
Multivariate Regression Models for Differing Levels of Knowledge,
with Search and Seizure Scale as Dependent Variable

	Low		Middle		High	
	b	Beta	b	Beta	b	Beta
Economic liberalism scale	-.111	-.034	-.086	-.036	.089	.062
Racial liberalism scale	.468	.115	.314	.104	.170	.095
Criminal justice liberalism	.265	.100	.261*	.136	.032	.027
Region (base=south)						
New England	1.810	.104	1.580*	.131	.879	.127
Mid-Atlantic	.605	.110	.679*	.168	.084	.035
West North Central	.967	.113	.780	.122	.309	.079
Mountain	1.084	.097	.861	.106	.475	.093
Pacific	1.584**	.185	1.217**	.196	.268	.072
Scared walking at night	-.298	-.056	-.256	-.066	-.164	-.070
Talk radio	-.181	-.034	-.053	-.013	-.020	-.009
Area (base=suburb)						
Rural	-.391	-.067	-.367	-.086	-.161	-.062
City	-.407	-.075	-.435	-.109	-.150	-.063
Source of info (base=TV)						
Radio	-.070	-.000	.494	.067	-.180	-.039
Talking with people	1.723*	.143	1.087*	.130	.191	.039
Reading	.930*	.143	.833**	.172	.261	.091
Marital status (base=married)						
Divorced/Separated	.662	.083	.496	.085	.259	.075
Widowed	.142	.015	.077	.011	.103	.026
Never married	.410	.060	.0032	.001	.155	.053
Religion (base=Protestant)						
Jewish	-.012	-.001	-.522	-.042	.364	.053
Catholic	.084	.014	-.129	-.030	.091	.035
Atheist	1.004	.109	.191	.028	.527	.130
Other	1.494	.099	1.239	.109	.399	.058
Race (base=white)						
Black	.873	.095	.488	.074	.170	.041
Asian	-3.027	-.124	-1.726	-.094	-1.152	-.103
Hispanic	1.158	.081	.575	.054	.179	.027
Male	.796*	.152	.454	.118	.210	.091
Income	-.075	-.051	-.005	-.047	.0099	.015
Age	.044	.021	.0077	.005	.014	.015
Ideology	.022	.015	-.061	-.056	.013	.021
Party	.038	.029	.062	.065	.00059	.001
TV hours per day	-.106	-.055	-.013	-.009	.0018	.002
Respect for police	.681*	.156	.542**	.168	.104	.054

	Low		Middle		High	
	b	Beta	b	Beta	b	Beta
R^2		.240		.242		.126
Adjusted R^2		.133		.139		.012
F		2.254**		2.363**		1.110
N		261		269		279

*p < .05; **p < .01
Note: The b's are unstandardized regression coefficients, the Betas are standardized coefficients.

Table 5.11
Multivariate Regression Models for Differing Levels of Knowledge, with Rights of the Accused Scale as Dependent Variables

	Low		Middle		High	
	b	Beta	b	Beta	b	Beta
Economic liberalism scale	.033	.021	.089	.062	.099	.070
Racial liberalism scale	.145	.077	.170	.095	.076	.043
Criminal justice liberalism	.106	.090	.032	.027	.151	.137
Region (base=South)						
New England	.483	.105	.879	.035	-.266	-.060
Mid-Atlantic	-.013	-.005	.084	.035	.0036	.001
West North Central	-.512	-.075	.309	.079	-.208	-.053
Mountain	.291	.035	.475	.093	.097	.019
Pacific	-.146	-.028	.268	.072	.217	.058
Scared walking at night	-.536*	-.208	-.164	-.070	-.401*	-.162
Talk radio	-.029	-.011	-.020	-.009	-.278	-.117
Area (base=suburb)						
Rural	-.292	-.105	-.161	-.062	-.303	-.119
City	-.107	-.041	-.150	-.063	-.162	-.064
Source of info (base=TV)						
Radio	.784	.146	-.180	-.039	.381	.111
Talking with people	.426	.083	.191	.039	-.481	-.050
Reading	.202	.064	.261	.091	.230	.094
Marital status (base=married)						
Divorced/Separated	.479	.132	.259	.075	.197	.056
Widowed	.108	.028	.103	.026	.332	.072
Never married	.072	.023	.155	.053	-.147	-.046

continued . . .

Table 5.11 (continued)

	Low		Middle		High	
	b	Beta	b	Beta	b	Beta
Religion (base=Protestant)						
Jewish	-.379	-.040	.364	.053	-353	-.055
Catholic	-.223	-.076	.091	.035	-.195	-.073
Atheist	-.055	-.011	.527	.130	-.023	-.006
Other	-.502	-.052	.399	.058	-.666	-.140
Race (base=white)						
Black	.275	.087	.170	.041	.677	.098
Asian	-.142	-.015	-1.152	-.103	-1.504	-.128
Hispanic	.161	.033	.179	.027	-1.204	-.072
Male	.248	.096	.210	.091	.094	.038
Income	-.046	-.059	.099	.015	-.015	-.023
Age	-.137	-.147	.014	.015	-.102	-.092
Ideology	.037	.054	.013	.021	-.085	-.130
Party	-.052	-.079	.0005	.001	-.0084	-.014
TV hours per day	-.0068	-.083	.0018	.002	-.157	-.152
Respect for police	.130	.070	.104	.054	.0081	.001
R²		.225		.126		.201
Adjusted R²		.036		.012		.046
F		1.192		1.110		1.295
N		163		279		197

*p<.05; **p<.01

Note: The b's are unstandardized regression coefficients, the Betas are standardized coefficients.

Table 5.12
Multivariate Regression Models (full mass sample),
with Agreement with Court as Dependent Variable

	b	Beta
Economic liberalism scale	.107	.054
Racial liberalism scale	-.017	-.007
Criminal justice liberalism	-.198**	-.127
Region (base=South)		
New England	-.293	-.040
Mid-Atlantic	-.347*	-.101
West North Central	-.204	-.035
Mountain	-.313	-.042
Pacific	-.743**	-.143
Scared walking at night	.113	.034
Talk radio	-.088	-.026
Area (base=suburb)		
Rural	.135	.038
City	.218	.065
Source of info (base=TV)		
Radio	-.504*	-.088
Talking with people	-.337	-.041
Reading	-.287	-.077
Marital status (base=married)		
Divorced/Separated	-.512*	-.106
Widowed	.010	.002
Never married	-.119	-.029
Religion (base=Protestant)		
Jewish	.075	.008
Catholic	.128	.035
Atheist	.169	.028
Other	-.282	-.032
Race (base=white)		
Black	-.338	-.063
Asian	-.021	-.001
Hispanic	-.299	-.033
Male	-.022	-.007
Political knowledge	.113*	.103
Income	.052	.061
Education	-.047	-.041
Age	.0018	.001
Ideology	.028	.013
Party	.074	.037
TV hours per day	-.0068	-.006
Respect for police	-.291**	-.110

continued . . .

Table 5.12 (continued)

	b	Beta
R^2	.115	
Adjusted R^2	.062	
F	2.177	
N	603	

*p<.05; **p<.01
Note: The b's are unstandardized regression coefficients, the Betas are standardized coefficients.

Table 5.13
**Multivariate Regression Models (for different levels of education),
with Agreement with Court as Dependent Variable**

	Education=low		Education=mid		Education=high	
	b	Beta	b	Beta	b	Beta
Economic liberalism scale	-.122	-.069	.173	.089	.197	.094
Racial liberalism scale	-.200	-.083	-.156	-.068	.091	.035
Criminal justice liberalism	-.454	-.260	-.137	-.089	-.274**	-.178
Region (base=South)						
New England	-.796	-.084	-.669	-.104	.352	.045
Mid-Atlantic	-1.300*	-.407	-.204	-.060	-.142	-.040
West North Central	-.602	-.077	-.281	-.040	-.0015	.000
Mountain	-1.736	-.223	-.509	-.050	.083	.012
Pacific	-.465	-.060	-.865*	-.171	-.390	-.069
Scared walking at night	.498	.162	.105	.032	.030	.009
Talk radio	-.732	-.237	.121	.038	-.095	-.027
Area (base=suburb)						
Rural	.622	.178	.066	.020	.079	.020
City	.480	.157	.497	.153	.203	.058
Source of info (base=TV)						
Radio	-.668	-.109	-.567	-.100	-.569	-.100
Talking with people	2.005	.151	-.459	-.063	-.529	-.064
Reading	-.218	-.051	-.014	-.004	-.503*	-.138
Marital status (base=married)						
Divorced/Separated	-.850	-.223	-.281	-.060	-.880**	-.167
Widowed	-.200	-.054	-.315	-.057	-.187	-.029
Never married	.0077	.001	-.296	-.070	.059	.015

	Education=low		Education=mid		Education=high	
	b	Beta	b	Beta	b	Beta
Religion (base=Protestant)						
Jewish	3.459	.261	-1.205	-.106	.191	.021
Catholic	.968	.286	.385	.110	-.294	-.077
Atheist	-.801	-.103	.882*	.155	-.269	-.045
Other	1.456	.110	1.336	.084	-.912*	-.128
Race (base=white)						
Black	-.827	-.212	-.804	-.171	-.247	-.037
Asian	1.434	.108	1.062	.047	-.238	-.019
Hispanic	1.459	.155	-1.224	-.142	.212	.022
Male	-.881	-.288	-.072	-.023	.314	.093
Income	-.114	-.115	-.042	-.043	.098	.109
Age	-.176	-.132	.013	.011	.104	.073
Ideology	.164	.175	-.0067	-.008	.030	.033
Party	.134	.184	.052	.066	-.036	-.044
TV hours per day	-.144	-.139	.140	.132	-.029	-.021
Respect for police	-.438	-.154	-.279	-.115	-.273	-.099
R^2	.492		.165		.159	
Adjusted R^2	.105		.014		.064	
F	1.270		1.096		1.680*	
N	74		209		317	

$*p < .05$; $**p < .01$
Note: The b's are unstandardized regression coefficients, the Betas are standardized coefficients.

Table 5.14
Multivariate Regression Models (for different levels of knowledge), with Agreement with Court as Dependent Variable

	Knowledge=low		Knowledge=mid		Knowledge=high	
	b	Beta	b	Beta	b	Beta
Economic liberalism scale	.229	.118	.091	.043	-.035	-.019
Racial liberalism scale	-.100	-.043	-.045	-.017	-.116	-.051
Criminal justice liberalism	-.193	-.132	-.239*	-.139	-.141	-.099
Region (base=South)						
New England	.135	.022	-1.420	-.125	.906	.157
Mid-Atlantic	-.383	-.114	-.692**	-.193	.364	.113
West North Central	.391	.047	-.285	-.051	.011	.002
Mountain	-1.413	-.141	-.477	-.065	.556	.086
Pacific	.066	.010	-.955*	-.171	-.634	-.129
Scared walking at night	.534	.168	.0026	.001	-.010	-.003
Talk radio	-.068	-.021	-.198	-.056	-.044	-.014
Area (base=suburb)						
Rural	.348	.101	.132	.035	.133	.040
City	.019	.006	.395	.112	.321	.098
Source of info (base=TV)						
Radio	-.474	-.073	-.770	-.118	-.582	-.128
Talking with people	-.150	-.023	-.729	-.093	1.035	.070
Reading	-.200	-.051	-.370	-.088	-.602*	-.191
Marital status (base=married)						
Divorced/Separated	-.352	-.079	-.493	-.095	-.592	-.128
Widowed	.787	.166	-.082	-.014	-.218	-.038
Never married	-.164	-.042	-.081	-.018	.108	.027
Religion (base=Protestant)						
Jewish	-1.437	-.124	.347	.035	.245	.028
Catholic	.997**	.281	.036	.010	-.717*	-.207
Atheist	.901	.139	.204	.034	-.425	-.076
Other	.695	.060	-.917	-.093	-.177	-.027
Race (base=white)						
Black	-.315	-.081	-.493	-.082	-.615	-.071
Asian	-1.233	-.107	.042	.003	.500	.034
Hispanic	-.595	-.092	-.643	-.069	n.a.	
Male	-.125	-.039	-.096	-.028	.279	.089
Income	-.042	-.044	-.022	-.023	.155*	.186
Age	-.084	-.073	-.122	-.090	.265*	.185
Ideology	.074	.087	.066	.068	-.055	-.065
Party	.052	.065	-.083	-.099	.097	.130
TV hours per day	.018	.018	.039	.031	-.190	-.142
Respect for police	-.325	-.144	-.334	-.117	-.224	-.082

	Knowledge=low		Knowledge=mid		Knowledge=high	
	b	Beta	b	Beta	b	Beta
R²		.269		.161		.240
Adjusted R²		.078		.044		.086
F		1.411		1.375		1.556*
N		155		261		184

*p<.05; **p<.01   n.a. =not available
Note: The b's are unstandardized regression coefficients, the Betas are standardized coefficients.

Table 5.15
Multivariate Regression Models with Ideology Scales as Dependent Variables

	Criminal Justice		Racial Justice		Economic Justice	
	b	Beta	b	Beta	b	Beta
Region (base=South)						
New England	.256	.056	.397**	.138	.113	.032
Mid-Atlantic	.118	.053	.131*	.094	.128	.076
West North Central	-.043	-.001	.207*	.086	.202*	.069
Mountain	-.104	-.021	.336*	.106	.186	.050
Pacific	.210	.059	.114	.052	.161	.060
Scared walking at night	-.143	-.067	.035	.004	-.074	-.045
Talk radio	-.025	-.011	-.012	-.009	-.181**	-.110
Area (base=suburb)						
Rural	-.133	-.058	.092	.063	.065	.037
City	.054	.025	.023	.017	.093	.056
Source of info (base=TV)						
Radio	.060	.017	.087	.039	-.066	-.024
Talking with people	-.001	.000	.020	.007	-.145	-.039
Reading	-.0884	.036	-.041	-.027	.006	.004
Marital status (base=married)						
Divorced/Separated	.285*	.092	.103	.053	.132	.055
Widowed	-.005	-.001	.028	.013	.153	.057
Never Married	.166	.063	.221*	.132	-.001	.000
Religion (base=Protestant)						
Jewish	.048	.007	.099	.024	-.144	-.023
Catholic	-.062	-.026	-.059	-.040	-.013	-.007
Atheist	.546	.143*	.125	.053	.090	.031
Other	.383	.067	.107	.031	.251	.059

continued . . .

Table 5.15 (continued)

	Criminal Justice		Racial Justice		Economic Justice	
	b	Beta	b	Beta	b	Beta
Race (base=white)						
Black	.446**	.129	.354**	.164	.083	.031
Asian	-.414	-.043	-.174	-.030	-.420	-.059
Hispanic	-.114	-.019	.430	.119	.230	.046
Male	.317**	.151	-.043	-.033	-.065	-.040
Income	-.011	-.020	.004	.014	.001	.001
Education	.113	.154	.043	.094	.034	.062
Political knowledge	-.014	-.020	.062	.071	.039	.036
Age	-.006	-.007	-.001	-.003	-.005	-.084
Ideology	-.047	-.081	-.031*	-.084	-.011	-.025
Party	-.084**	-.162	-.033*	-.102	-.044*	-.112
TV hours per day	.021	.028	.007	.015	.005	.010
Respect for police	.022	.013	-.004	-.005	.103*	.081
R^2	.192		.145		.085	
Adjusted R^2	.153		.105		.043	
F	4.967		3.640		2.028	
N	679		699		704	

$*p < .05$; $**p < .01$
Note: The b's are unstandardized regression coefficients, the Betas are standardized coefficients.

Table 5.16
Multivariate Regression Models with Fear of Crime, Source of Information, and Respect for the Police as Dependent Variables

	Fear of Crime		Source of Information		Respect for Police	
	b	Beta	b	Beta	b	Beta
Region (base=South)						
New England	-.118	-.054	-.028	-.013	.284*	.101
Mid-Atlantic	.001	.001	-.013	-.012	.018	.014
West North Central	-.124	-.069	-.019	-.010	.092	.039
Mountain	.199*	.086	.076	.033	.113	.038
Pacific	-.133*	-.080	-.085	-.052	.085	.039
Scared walking at night			.012	.009	.062	.047
Talk radio	-.026	-.025			.007	.006
Area (base=suburb)						
Rural	-.216**	-.199	-.034	-.031	.079	.056
City	.033	.032	-.044	-.044	.092	.069
Source of info (base=TV)						
Radio	.134*	.081			.055	.026
Talking with people	.006	.003			-.142	-.048
Reading	.038	.033			-.030	-.020
Marital status (base=married)						
Divorced/Separated	-.027	-.018	.056	.038	.111	.058
Widowed	.009	.006	-.082	-.050	-.128	-.060
Never Married	-.078	-.062	-.056	-.045	.101	.062
Religion (base=Protestant)						
Jewish	-.048	-.016	-.059	-.020	-.087	-.022
Catholic	-.015	-.013	.021	.019	-.069	-.048
Atheist	-.055	-.031	-.088	-.051	.060	.026
Other	-.050	-.019	.109	.042	-.057	-.017
Race (base=white)						
Black	.014	.008	.025	.016	.027	.013
Asian	.003	.001	.018	.004	.320	.053
Hispanic	-.093	-.034	-.091	-.034	-.181	-.051
Male	-.124**	-.125	-.065	-.066	.071	.056
Income	-.023	-.087	-.027*	-.103	-.063	-.018
Education	.011	.032	-.017	-.050	.009	.021
Political knowledge	-.030	-.045	-.023	-.035	-.063	-.075
Age	.020	.050	-.015	-.038	-.042	-.081
Ideology	.080	.029	-.100	-.038	-.024	-.066
Party	-.007	-.031	.012	.051	-.013	-.042
TV hours per day	-.000	.000			.000	.000
Respect for police	.034	.045	.011	.015		

continued . . .

Table 5.16 (continued)

	Fear of Crime		Source of Information		Respect for Police	
	b	Beta	b	Beta	b	Beta
R^2		.118		.154		.078
Adjusted R^2		.079		.120		.037
F		3.043		4.601		1.908
N		710		710		710

*$p < .05$; **$p < .01$
Note: The b's are unstandardized regression coefficients, the Betas are standardized coefficients.

Table 5.17
Multivariate Regression Models with Party, Income,
and Ideology as Dependent Variables

	Party		Ideology		Income	
	b	Beta	b	Beta	b	Beta
Region (base=South)						
New England	-.157	-.018	-.854**	-.108	.224	.027
Mid-Atlantic	-.137	-.032	-.056	-.015	.052	.013
West North Central	-.078	-.010	-.514*	-.078	.339	.049
Mountain	.408	.043	.016	.002	.236	.027
Pacific	-.064	-.009	-.268	-.044	.411*	.065
Scared walking at night	-.104	-.025	.090	.025	-.222	-.058
Talk radio	.176	.042	.290*	.079	-.095	-.025
Area (base=suburb)						
Rural	-.254	-.057	.057	.014	-.257	-.062
City	-.309	-.074	-.283	-.076	-.100	-.026
Source of info (base=TV)						
Radio	.156	.023	.137	.022	.136	.021
Talking with people	.309	.033	-.120	-.014	-.156	-.018
Reading	-.410*	-.085	.160	.038	.439	.101*
Marital status (base=married)						
Divorced/Separated	.147	.024	-.119	-.022	-.822**	-.146
Widowed	.034	.257	-.096	-.016	-1.116**	-.177
Never Married	.115	.022	-.072	-.017	-1.302**	-.274

	Party		Ideology		Income	
	b	Beta	b	Beta	b	Beta
Religion (base=Protestant)						
Jewish	-1.182**	-.094	-.429	-.038	.530	.045
Catholic	-.615**	-.134	-.099	-.024	.387**	.091
Atheist	-.377	-.052	-.667**	-.104	.245	.036
Other	-.446	-.041	-.228	-.024	.320	.032
Race (base=white)						
Black	-.664**	-.099	-.111	-.019	-.664**	-.099
Asian	-.056	-.003	.767	.048	-.358	-.021
Hispanic	-.071	-.006	-.228	-.023	-.762*	-.073
Male	.196	.048	.253*	.070	.272*	.072
Income	.100*	.093	.052	.054		
Education	-.019	-.013	-.084	-.067	.473	.361**
Political knowledge	.296**	.110	.001	.000	.261**	.104
Age	-.141*	-.086	.089	.061	-.152*	-.100
Ideology	.407**	.361			.045	.043
Party			.330**	.371	.070*	.075
TV hours per day	-.094	-.064	.013	.010	-.037	-.027
Respect for police	.407**	.361	-.151	-.054	-.034	-.012
R²	.274		.255		.412	
Adjusted R²	.242		.222		.386	
F	8.533		7.738		15.894	
N	710		710		710	

*p<.05; **p<.01

Note: The b's are unstandardized regression coefficients, the Betas are standardized coefficients.

Table 5.18
Path Analysis for the Survey of the Mass Public

Results of Path

Race (base=white) (black=.091*)	Overall Criminal Justice Scale
Gender (base=female) (male=.127**)	Overall Criminal Justice Scale
Area (base=suburb) (rural=-.093)	Overall Criminal Justice Scale
Region (base=South) (Pacific=.104*)	Overall Criminal Justice Scale
Religion (base=Protestant) (atheist=-.107**)	Education
Race (base=white) (black=.118*)	Education
Gender (base=female) (male=-.099**)	Income
Religion (base=Protestant) (Catholic=-.134*)	Party ID
Region (base=South) (Northeast=-.108**)	Political Ideology
Region (base=South) (Pacific=.065**)	Income
Education (.361**)	Income
Race (base=white) (black=.164)	Racial Liberalism Scale
Gender (base=female) (male=.151**)	Criminal Liberalism Scale
Economic Scale (.001)	Overall Criminal Justice Scale
Source of Information (base=TV) (reading .099) . . .	Overall Criminal Justice Scale
Respect for Police (.154**)	Overall Criminal Justice Scale
Marital Status (base=married) (divorced=-.118) . . .	Overall Criminal Justice Scale
Fear of Crime (-.096*)	Overall Criminal Justice Scale
Racial Liberalism Scale (.101*)	Overall Criminal Justice Scale
Party ID (-.036)	Overall Criminal Justice Scale
Political Ideology (-.011)	Overall Criminal Justice Scale
Income (-.041)	Overall Criminal Justice Scale
Criminal Liberalism Scale (.153**)	Overall Criminal Justice Scale

*p<.05; **p<.01

Table 5.19
Multivariate Regression Models, for Whites vs. Blacks in Mass Sample with Criminal Procedure Scale as Dependent Variable

	Whites		Blacks	
	b	Beta	b	Beta
Criminal justice liberalism	.330**	.127	1.286**	.545
Racial liberalism scale	.339	.084	1.015	.241
Economic liberalism	.112	.034	-.792*	-.243
Region (base=South)				
New England	.155	.013	-.623	-.050
Mid-Atlantic	.294	.053	-1.174	-.194
West North Central	.562	.062	1.446	.068
Mountain	.756	.065	-3.899	-.163
Pacific	1.107	.124	-2.197	-.200
Scared walking at night	-.328	-.061	-1.103	-.204
Talk radio	-.315	-.058	.406	.073
Area (base=suburb)				
Rural	-.560*	-.098	-.249	-.033
City	-.609*	-.109	.631	.116
Source of info (base=TV)				
Radio	.578	.065	-1.886	-.124
Talking with people	.877	.059	.760	.077
Reading	.544	.090	.484	.071
Marital status (base=married)				
Divorced/Separated	.789*	.097	1.549	.227
Widowed	.363	.042	-2.983*	-.238
Never married	.293	.039	.433	.080
Religion (base=Protestant)				
Jewish	-.495	-.033		
Catholic	.201	.034	-1.041	-.142
Atheist	.521	.051	-1.072	-.118
Other	-.058	-.004	-.889	-.042
Male	.664**	.125	-.304	.056
Political knowledge	.020	.017	.161	.128
Income	-.042	-.030	-.247	-.153
Education	-.084	-.046	.300	.123
Age	-.167	-.074	-.218	-.110
Ideology	-.037	-.025	.439**	.295
Party	-.023	-.018	-.028	-.061
TV hours per day	-.183*	-.091	-.129	-.080
Respect for police	.660**	.001	.354	.096
R^2	.178		.761	
Adjusted R^2	.125		.544	
F	3.374		3.541	
N	513		61	

$*p < .05$; $**p < .01$
Note: The b's are unstandardized regression coefficients, the Betas are standardized coefficients.

Table 5.20
Multivariate Regression Models, for Whites vs. Blacks in Mass Sample
with Search and Seizure Scale as Dependent Variable

	Whites		Blacks	
	b	Beta	b	Beta
Criminal Justice Liberalism	.252**	.134	1.015**	.569
Racial liberalism scale	.200	.069	.514	.163
Economic liberalism scale	.018	.008	-.546	-.219
Region (base=South)				
New England	.107	.271	-.726	-.074
Mid-Atlantic	.349	.087	-.527	-.115
West North Central	.466	.071	1.172	.070
Mountain	.698	.082	-2.283	-.136
Pacific	.887**	.138	-.454	-.053
Scared walking at night	-.160	-.041	-.670	-.163
Talk radio	-.094	-.024	.489	.115
Area (base=suburb)				
Rural	-.376	-.091	-.487	-.082
City	-.450*	-.111	-.170	-.041
Source of info (base=TV)				
Radio	.438	.068	.410	.042
Talking with people	.382	.040	.416	.054
Reading	.408*	.093	.990	.186
Marital status (base=married)				
Divorced/Separated	.755**	.129	.487	.094
Widowed	.045	.007	-2.210	-.225
Never married	.122	.023	.012	.003
Religion (base=Protestant)				
Jewish	-.481	-.044		
Catholic	.169	.039	-1.054	-.192
Atheist	.024	.003	-.911	-.128
Other	.141	.014	-1.819	-.108
Male	.466**	.122	-.059	-.014
Political knowledge	-.002	-.002	-.065	-.072
Income	-.061	-.060	-.240	-.191
Education	-.013	-.010	.303	.163
Age	-.120	-.074	.012	.008
Ideology	-.037	-.034	.258	.229
Party	-.026	-.028	.152	.148
TV hours per day	-.113	-.078	.063	.051
Respect for police	.526**	.165	.121	.042
R^2	.178		.625	
Adjusted R^2	.126		.304	
F	3.460		1.947	
N	528		65	

$*p<.05; **p<.01$
Note: The b's are unstandardized regression coefficients, the Betas are standardized coefficients.

Table 5.21
Multivariate Regression Models, for Whites vs. Blacks in Mass Sample with Rights of the Accused Scale as Dependent Variable

	Whites		Blacks	
	b	Beta	b	Beta
Economic liberalism scale	.134*	.115	.206	.207
Racial liberalism scale	.119	.065	.365	.207
Criminal justice liberalism	.146*	.098	-.038	-.028
Region (base=South)				
New England	.329	.065	.143	.027
Mid-Atlantic	.106	.042	-.597	-.239
West North Central	.215	.052	.205	.023
Mountain	.418	.077	-1.423	-.139
Pacific	.262	.065	-1.564*	-.338
Scared walking at night	-.215*	-.088	-.693	-.309
Talk radio	-.151	-.062	.057	.025
Area (base=suburb)				
Rural	-.221	-.086	-.169	-.052
City	-.175	-.069	.491	.261
Source of info (base=TV)				
Radio	.205	.051	-1.305	-.203
Talking with people	.104	.017	.500	.120
Reading	.180	.066	.183	.064
Marital status (base=married)				
Divorced/Separated	.117	.032	.592	.206
Widowed	.281	.072	-1.056	-.199
Never married	.046	.014	.231	.103
Religion (base=Protestant)				
Jewish	-.007	-.001		
Catholic	-.092	-.034	-.371	-.120
Atheist	.298	.066	-.259	-.067
Other	-.335	-.055	.614	.068
Male	.182	.076	-.193	-.086
Political knowledge	-.042	-.027	.092	.178
Income	-.003	-.005	-.087	-.132
Education	-.025	-.030	.055	.057
Age	-.072	-.071	-.013	-.016
Ideology	-.017	-.025	.166*	.267
Party	-.008	-.014	-.107	-.189
TV hours per day	-.053	-.059	-.042	-.058
Respect for police	.077	.039	.183	.122
R^2	.110		.662	
Adjusted R^2	.057		.373	
F	2.062		1.834	
N	547		63	

*p<.05; **p<.01

Note: The b's are unstandardized regression coefficients, the Betas are standardized coefficients.

Chapter 6

The Influences on the Legal Elite Attitude Toward Issues of Criminal Justice

When one speaks of an elite group within society, one must realize that "to speak of a single elite obviously misrepresents the realities" (McClosky and Brill, 1983, p. 239). McClosky and Brill argue that

> although they (elites) posses certain qualities in common that justify characterizing them as elites, there are, nevertheless, party elites, organizational elites, community elites, national elites, liberal elites, conservative elites, legal elites, and elites devoted to academic affairs, journalism, business, civil rights, and a dozen other major social and economic interests. The point, once stated, seems obvious enough—perhaps too obvious to require statement. But, like many assertions that are virtually self-evident, the observation that we cannot properly speak of "the elite" as though it were a single entity is one we typically tend to overlook.

In this chapter, I will examine further the opinions of the elite for this particular study—members of the legal profession. As McClosky and Brill also note regarding the acquisition of civil libertarian opinions: "lawyers, judges, and members of certain types of social reform groups can be expected to be significantly more libertarian than the members of the mass public who enjoy equivalent degrees of, say, education and income, but who are involved in business, engineering, or land management" (p. 238). Indeed, the explanations articulated by McClosky and Brill illustrate the driving force behind the thesis of the traditional "elite theory of democracy," as well as much of, possibly, the basis for "issue publics." The notion that there is a single elite is not persuasive, according to most who advance the notion of issue publics (Popkin, 1991). Rather, depending upon particular issues, different groups of individuals decide to follow closely the developments of issues and become elite groups for them. As Popkin notes, an issue public is "a subset of the overall public that cares a great deal about a particular issue, and is therefore likely to pay attention to it" (p. 28).

For this study of mass-elite differences concerning civil liberties regarding issues of criminal justice, the elites—a major issue public—are members of the legal profession. Lawyers care more about law in general, and issues of criminal justice in particular, than members of the public who have not devoted a substantial portion of their adult life to the study of the law. This chapter examines differences in opinion between members of the mass public and members of the legal profession; differences among different specialties within the legal profession; and differences among attitudinal demographic subgroups within the legal profession. In addition, the opinions of all the groups and subgroups will be compared with the decisions of the United States Supreme Court. Lawyers who specialize in different legal subfields might be expected to have different opinions.

DIFFERENCES BETWEEN LEGAL PROFESSIONS AND THE MASS PUBLIC

Table 6.1 presents the means for the entire survey of the legal profession on the criminal procedure, search and seizure, rights of the accused, and agreement with the court scales (all tables are at the end of this chapter). The mean was a 6.56 on the criminal procedure scale vs. 3.53 on the search and seizure scale vs. 3.02 on the rights of the accused scale, and 7.74 on the agreement with Court scale. These numbers can be used as a base when analyzing other statistics presented in this chapter.

Legal Specialization

There are a number of reasons why lawyers specializing in different areas of the law would have varying opinions regarding civil liberties. As Popkin (1991) notes, people obtain information from using all sorts of shortcuts. In addition to obtaining information through the traditional routes of reading newspapers, magazines, and the like, people can also obtain information from personal experiences, which include the educational environment, and the day-to-day workplace (Alwin, Cohen, and Newconmb, 1991). Because of this, people's opinions can be affected by their workplace environment. For individuals who work within the criminal justice system the effect might be quite apparent (Walker, 1989).

Relevant to this study, lawyers specializing in different areas of the law naturally have different workplace environments. For example, corporate lawyers and criminal lawyers work in very different venues and, therefore, over time, are likely to develop different opinions regarding issues related to civil liberties.

Another explanation for differing opinions within the legal profession is the self-selection process, whereby lawyers choose their area of specialization. In other words, individuals with a devotion and support of civil liberties may tend to choose specialities that are reflective of these opinions. They may choose fields such as criminal law in contrast to other areas of law. Those for whom the importance of civil liberties is likely to be less, will choose specializations for which defending civil liberties is not as central.

The results presented in Table 6.1 seem to back up these expectations. Specialties which tend to score highest on the civil liberties scales are areas which deal with issues of the civil libertarian sort and are likely to attract individuals for whom these rights are highly valued. Lawyers specializing in criminal defense scored 9.53 on the criminal procedure scale compared with 3.00 for those who specialize in criminal prosecution. Those who identify themselves as generalists within the area of criminal law (not specifying whether or not they worked exclusively for the defense or prosecution), scored an 8.09 on the criminal procedure scale. This was far higher than the score achieved by both the mean lawyer (6.56) or the mean member of the mass public (5.32).

In all, there is a general pattern that lawyers who work in more ostensibly ideologically liberal-minded specialties are more civil libertarian, while the opposite is true for lawyers who have chosen more conservative specializations.

Lawyers who stated that their specialty was poverty law (9.00), criminal defense (9.53), health care (10.00), Indian (10.00), domestic violence (10.00), equal employment (10.00), as well as those who teach law (9.50), traditionally left-leaning professions, all scored well above the mean of 6.56 for all lawyers. On the other hand, lawyers whose specialty was business and commercial law (4.88), bankruptcy (4.67), criminal prosecution (3.00), military law (4.00), are retired (4.21), or out of law (5.23), are all under the means for the entire survey on the criminal justice scale ($p = .000$).

Naturally, respondents with specialties that are generally less civil libertarian are also more supportive of recent United States Supreme Court decisions. This seems to add to the notion that the Court has been moving away from its support of civil libertarian norms.

Region

There were some differences based on the region of the country in which lawyers practice (see Table 6.2). Similar to the mass public, lawyers from the Pacific region were the most civil libertarian (7.28), followed by the mid-Atlantic (6.78), Mountain (6.62), West North Central (6.56), New England (6.25), and South (5.98) ($p = .077$). The same trend, with lawyers from the Pacific being most civil libertarian and those from the South the least, held for the search and seizure (4.11 [Pacific] vs. 3.71 [Mountain] vs. 3.66 [mid-Atlantic] vs. 3.25 [New England] vs. 3.21 [West North Central] vs. 3.14 [South], $p = .042$). For the rights of the accused, however, the most civil libertarian areas were the West North Central and mid-Atlantic states (3.24 vs. 3.14, respectively vs. 3.13 [Pacific], 3.04 [Mountain], 3.00 [New England], and 2.81 [South], p=.238).

Overall, these results for region are similar to those of the mass public. There were large differences between lawyers in the Pacific region and others on the criminal procedure scale and the search scale. Lawyers in the South were consistently less civil libertarian based on all three scales.

Marital Status

There were great differences in support for civil liberties between married and unmarried lawyers. Lawyers who were widowed scored a 6.00 on the criminal procedure scale vs. 6.22 for married lawyers vs. 7.90 for lawyers who were never married vs. 8.08 for those divorced vs. 8.75 for those separated (p= .000). This same pattern, with the same intensity, occurred for the search scale (5.25 [separated] vs. 4.81 [divorced] vs. 4.63 [never married] vs. 3.27 [married] vs. 2.86 [widowed], p=.000); and to a lesser degree on the accused scale (3.60 [separated] vs. 3.32 [divorced] vs. 3.31 [never married] vs. 3.19 [widowed] vs. 2.93 [married], p=.098). Also, there was more support for recent Court decisions among the married respondents (8.71 [widowed] vs. 7.96 [married] vs. 6.70 [never married] vs. 6.58 [divorced] vs. 6.25 [separated] p=.000).

This pattern is the same as it was for the mass public. Again, divorced individuals, who have gone through the strain and pain of the legal system, are less likely to grant the police extensive power to intrude into their private lives. They are perhaps more independent minded and less likely to adhere blindly to authority. The major differences occurred on the search scale, and this is where divorced individuals may fear the greatest intrusiveness, whereas the rights of the accused are less likely to be personally relevant. Among the mass public they were slightly more civil libertarian, while among lawyers they were slightly less civil libertarian. A possible explanation is that separated lawyers know the troubles and complications ahead for them.

Gender

Female lawyers were somewhat, but not significantly, more likely to support civil liberties than male lawyers, averaging 6.93 on the criminal procedure scale vs. 6.45 for males (p=.197). This same pattern held for the search and seizure scale, but not for the rights of the accused scale (search: 3.85 [females] vs. 3.44 [males], p=.113; accused: 3.07 [females] vs. 3.00 [males], p=.634). Males were also slightly more likely to support recent court decisions (7.79 [males] vs. 7.56 [females], p=.325).

This pattern of women being more civil libertarian is strikingly different than it was for the mass public, among whom women were less civil libertarian.

There are at least three plausible explanations. First, career women may be generally more liberal, and therefore more civil libertarian, than women who stay at home. Second, female lawyers, on average, are younger than male lawyers, and when comparisons based upon age are reported later in this chapter, younger lawyers are likely to be more supportive of civil liberties. It is also possible that male lawyers feel more like part of the establishment, while female lawyers might feel more as outsiders, and therefore be less likely than males to grant more rights to the establishment when it comes to intruding into one's private life.

Community Type

Lawyers residing in rural communities were somewhat more civil libertarian than those living in the cities and suburbs. Lawyers from rural areas scored a 7.09 on the criminal procedure scale vs. 6.72 for those in the cities vs. 6.29 for lawyers in the suburbs (p=.183). The same pattern held for the search and seizure and rights of the accused scales (search: 3.93 [rural] vs. 3.60 [city] vs. 3.37 [suburb], p=.232; accused: 3.23 [rural] vs. 3.09 [city] vs. 2.89 [suburb], p=.112). As expected, suburban lawyers were somewhat, though not significantly, more in line with recent court decisions (7.82 [suburb] vs. 7.68 [city] vs. 7.57 [rural], p=.626).

The results here contrast sharply with the results for the mass public in which residents of the suburbs were the most civil libertarian. A possible explanation for rural lawyers holding opinions more civil libertarian than their counterparts in the mass public is their exposure to elite discourse within the area. As mentioned, many in the West, which includes many rural communities, have become quite critical of the federal government, which in turn would cause one to appear civil libertarian. In other words, lawyers may be the vanguard for opinions concerning the police and government in more rural communities.

Race

There were no noticeable differences based upon race among lawyers. It should be noted that there were only a small number of minority lawyers in the survey (23), as there are only a small number in the legal population as a whole. White lawyers scored a 6.54 vs. 6.63 for blacks vs. 6.50 for Hispanics (p= .852). Black lawyers were a bit more civil libertarian than others on the search scale (3.88 [blacks] vs. 3.67 [Hispanics] vs. 3.51 [whites], p=.768), while white lawyers were slightly more civil libertarian on the rights of the accused scale (3.02 [whites] vs. 2.83 [Hispanics] vs. 2.75 [blacks], p=.897). Whites were slightly but not significantly more likely to support recent Court decisions (7.75 [whites] vs. 7.63 [blacks] vs. 7.50 [Hispanics], p=.710).

Though these results should be read with caution due to the small number of minorities in the legal profession, it would seem that minority lawyers are more suspicious of the police during the initial search and seizure period; blacks in the mass population were also most suspicious on search and seizure issues, though within the mass public they were always more civil libertarian than whites.

Age

The main differences in opinions concerning civil liberties based upon the age of lawyers seems to be between those under 65 and those above 65. Those age 25-33 scored a 7.07 on the criminal procedure scale vs. 7.03 for those 34-43 vs. 6.92 for respondents 44-64, compared with 4.96 for respondents over 65 (p=.000). This same pattern held for search and seizure (4.00 [25-33] vs. 3.92 [34-43] vs. 3.73 [44-64] vs. 2.41 [65+], p=.000), and it was only slightly different for the rights of the accused scale (3.21 (44-640 vs. 3.10 [34-43] vs. 3.07 [25-33] vs. 2.49 [65+], p=.000). Older respondents were also more likely to support recent Court decisions (8.30 [65+] vs. 7.73 [44-64] vs. 7.46 [33-43] vs. 7.29 [25-33], p=.009).

This pattern for lawyers generally followed the pattern for the mass public, though there were starker differences for lawyers over 65. A possible explanation is that the older generation might not have been exposed to the decisions of the 1960s and 1970s that expressed great support for civil liberties. There are two possible explanations for the fact that this same group is also more supportive of recent Court decisions. First, it is possible that Court decisions do not have an effect personally on this age group, and therefore it is harder for its members to put themselves in the position of the criminal defendant. Second, it is possible that the Court decisions of the 1980s and 1990s are beginning to resemble the decisions of the time that this age group was acculturated and therefore there is now more support.

Religion

Jews and atheists have opinions quite different from members of other religious groups. In fact, there is a particular ordering in support for civil liberties among the various religions. Atheists (7.93) are more civil libertarian than Jews (7.42), who are more civil libertarian than "others" (7.39), who are more civil libertarian than Catholics (6.79), while Protestants show the least support for civil liberties (5.72). The same pattern held for search and seizure and to a lesser degree the rights of the accused (search: 4.75 [atheist] vs. 4.17 [other] vs. 4.12 [Jewish] vs. 3.65 [Catholic] vs. 2.93 [Protestant], p=.000; accused: 3.26 (Jewish and other) vs. 3.21 [atheist] vs. 3.18 [Catholic] vs. 2.76 [Protestant], p=.007). The Protestants were also most likely to agree with recent court decisions (8.15 [Protestant] vs. 7.72 [Catholic] vs. 7.32 [Jewish] vs. 7.17 [other] vs. 6.79 [atheist], p=.000).

Except for atheists, who were most civil libertarian in both the mass and lawyer surveys, the surveys yield some differing results. Jewish lawyers were more civil libertarian than the small number of Jews within the mass sample (n=20). It is possible that the small number of Jews led to unreliable results. Also, there were quite large differences between Catholics and Protestants within the legal profession, while significant differences did not exist among the mass public.

Fear of Crime

Lawyer respondents who were fearful of walking alone at night were less civil libertarian than those who were not: 6.27 on the criminal procedure scale vs. 6.79 for those who were not fearful (p=.092). The same pattern continued for the search and seizure and rights of the accused scales (search: 3.67 [not fearful] vs. 3.35 [fearful], p=.134; accused: 3.09 [not fearful] vs. 2.91 [fearful], p=.138). Those fearful, however, were no more supportive of recent Court decisions (7.77 [fearful] vs. 7.71 [not fearful], p=.748).

This pattern followed that of the mass public. Individuals who are more fearful are less civil libertarian, but not strikingly so. Both lawyers and non-lawyers alike held opinions that are not on average substantially swayed by personal experiences.

Similarly, lawyers who feel safe at home at night are more civil libertarian than those who do not, averaging a 6.66 on the criminal procedure scale vs. 5.58 (p=.043). They also scored higher on the search and seizure and rights of the accused scales (search: 3.58 [fearful] vs. 3.03 [not fearful], p=.149; accused: 3.06 [fearful] vs. 2.56 [not fearful], p=.017). There was no difference, however, concerning support of recent Court decisions (7.76 [not fearful] vs. 7.73 [fearful], p=.943).

This pattern differed from that of the mass public, among whom more fearful individuals were actually more civil libertarian. Again there is no correlation between personal fear of crime and opinions regarding civil liberties. The fact that there is even less of a correlation between personal fear of crime and opinions regarding how to deal with crime within the legal population, is probably due to the greater complexity and depth that exists in the opinions of lawyers, as opposed to the mass public, regarding issues related to the law.

Personal Experience with Crime

Surprisingly, respondents who did not actually have crimes committed against them or their families were slightly, though not significantly, less civil libertarian than those who had personal experience with crime. Respondents who had a mugging in their family scored 7.18 on the criminal justice scale vs. 6.73 for physical assault vs. 6.67 for car vandalism vs. 6.56 for robbery in the home vs. 6.11 for murder vs. 6.00 for rape as well as for those who had no crime committed against them or their families (p = .727). This same pattern emerged for both the search and seizure and rights of the accused scales (search: 4.12 [mugged] vs. 3.59 [robbery] vs. 3.56 [car] vs. 3.48 [physical assault] vs. 3.25 [rape] vs. 3.11 [murder] vs. 3.12 [none], p = .575; accused: 3.26 [physical assault] vs. 3.11 [mugged] vs. 3.09 [murder] vs. 3.08 [car] vs. 2.93 [robbery] vs. 2.86 [none] vs. 2.75 [rape], p = .669). Those who did not experience crimes personally or in the family were also more in agreement with recent Court decisions (8.05 [none] vs. 8.00 [rape] vs. 7.89 [murder] vs. 7.82 [physical assault] vs. 7.75 [car] vs. 7.64 [robbery] vs. 7.36 [mugged], p = .794).

These results are similar to those found in the survey of the mass public. However, the extent to which individuals without crimes committed against them or their families are less civil libertarian is much more striking in the survey of the lawyers. Again, this highlights the inference that members of society, and especially members of the legal community, do not formulate their opinions about how to fight crime based on emotions raised from personal experiences. It is also possible that individuals who have had crimes committed against them or their families are more civil libertarian, since they believe that the presence of civil liberties will assure that the person who actually committed the crime is in fact the one incarcerated.

Respect for Police

A variable with quite striking effects on one's opinions toward civil liberties is the level of trust one has for the police. Lawyers who had a great deal of confidence in the police scored a 5.80 vs. 6.68 for those who had only some confidence vs. 9.32 for those with hardly any confidence (p = .000). This pattern continued for the search and seizure scale, and to a lesser degree the rights of the accused scale (search: 5.84 [hardly any] vs. 3.60 [only some] vs. 2.93 [great deal], p = .000; accused: 3.51 [hardly any] vs. 3.05 [only some] vs. 2.88 [great deal] ,p = .009). Lawyers who had a great deal of respect in the police were more likely to agree with recent court decisions (8.28 [great deal] vs. 7.65 [only some] vs. 5.81 [hardly any], p = .000).

This pattern is more striking than the related one for the mass public. Lawyers who have more respect for the police accordingly allow them more leeway in apprehending suspected criminals. Another explanation might lead one in the other direction. It is possible that some respondents, who believe that unfair social conditions cause crime, might be less supportive of a large-scale police crackdown on crime. In other words, respect for police officers might be the dependent variable, as opposed to the independent variable.

Confidence in Institutions

Like the mass public sample, lawyers were asked in which branch of government they had the most confidence. Those who answered that they had the most confidence in the president were most civil libertarian (7.34), followed by those who were most confident in the Supreme Court (6.54), and those who did not have confidence in any branch of government (6.33), and the U.S. Congress (6.14) (p=.382). The same pattern held for the search and seizure and rights of the accused scales (search: 4.19 [president] vs. 3.56 [none] vs. 3.49 [Sup. Ct.] vs. 3.12 [Congress], p=.216; accused: 3.18 [president] vs. 3.04 [Sup. Ct.] vs. 2.90 [none] vs. 2.87 [Congress], p=.672). Logically, individuals who have the most confidence in Congress, are least likely to agree with recent Supreme Court decisions (7.93 [Congress] vs. 7.79 [Sup. Ct.] vs. 7.74 [none] vs. 7.16 [president], p=.281).

The probable explanation for lawyers who had the most confidence in the presidency to also be most civil libertarian is ideological. Specifically, this group is also more likely to identify as liberal and Democratic. Along these lines, lawyers who had most confidence in congress were more conservative and Republican. It is probable that conservatives have the most confidence in Congress since at the time of the survey, the Republicans had regained control of the legislative body, while Bill Clinton, a Democrat, was in the White House.

Party

There were large differences among lawyers based upon partisanship (see Table 6.3). Lawyers who were strong Democrats were around three points more civil libertarian than strong Republicans. Strong Democrats scored an 8.89 on the criminal procedure scale vs. 7.14 for weak Democrats, 7.15 for Independents but closer to Democrat, 6.00 for Independents, 5.70 for Independents but closer to Republicans, 5.61 for weak Republicans vs. 5.73 for strong Republicans (p=.000). This same pattern emerges for the search and seizure and rights of the accused scales (search: 5.37 [strong Democrats] vs. 2.50 [weak Republicans], p=.000; accused: 3.55 [strong Democrats] vs. 2.60 [strong Republicans], p=.000). Republicans and Independents also agreed more often with recent Supreme Court decisions than did Democratic party identifiers (6.41 [strong Democrats] vs. 8.00 [Independents] vs. 8.07 [weak Republicans], p=.000).

These results are similar to those found for the mass public, though, again, all the more striking. This accords well with the observation that individuals with greater levels of education are more likely to have and to understand their party ID. It is also interesting that the group that seems different than the rest in Table 6.3, seems to be the strong Democrats, while Independents and Republicans are jointly more supportive of recent Court decisions. In other words, the Court might be moving more to the right, but the question is, whether or not it is now situated to the right of the country or it accords with mainstream opinions.

Political Ideology

Based upon questions in which respondents identified their political ideology along a seven-point scale, strong liberals scored almost five points higher on the criminal procedure scale than conservatives. They averaged 9.77 vs. 8.08 for weak liberals, 7.27 for moderates but closer to liberals, 6.13 for moderates, 5.60 for moderates closer to conservatives, 5.08 for weak conservatives, vs. 5.47 for strong conservatives (p=.000). The same pattern persisted for the search and seizure scale, and to a lesser degree for the rights of the accused scale (search: 6.10 [strong liberal] vs. 3.25 [moderate] vs. 2.48 [weak conserva- tive], p=.000; accused: 3.68 [strong liberal] vs. 2.85 [moderate] vs. 2.48 [strong conservative], p=.000). Conservatives and moderates were more likely than liberals to agree with recent Court decisions (5.77 [strong liberal] vs. 7.81 [moderate] and 8.49 [weak conservatives], p=.000).

Again, this pattern is similar to the one that existed in the mass public, though the results were much more pronounced among the legal elite. Also, one can see that the effect of ideology was almost twice as large among lawyers than the effect of party. This is in line with the notion that for members of the elite, and especially members of the legal elite regarding issues of criminal justice, party identification has less consistent meaning than ideological identification. Again, there seems to be a congruence in opinion between the moderates and conservatives, with the liberals holding different opinions than the rest. This can be seen as more support that the Supreme Court by moving to the Right is merely moderating past Court decisions that were seen by many as too liberal.

Economic Liberalism, Racial Justice, Fairness of Criminal Justice System

Table 6.3 indicates that lawyers who scored higher on the economic liberal- ism scale (see Chapter 5 for detailed description where the measures examined here were defined) were more than two points more civil libertarian than those who were low on economic liberalism. Lawyers who scored a 0 on economic liberalism scored a 5.38 on the criminal procedure scale vs. 5.95 for those who scored a 1 and 7.61 for those who scored 2 (p=.000). This same pattern held for the search and seizure and the rights of the accused scales (search: 4.22 [2] vs. 3.12 [1] vs. 2.78 [0], p=.000; accused: 3.39 [2] vs. 2.87 [1] vs. 2.58 [0], p=.000). Those low on economic liberalism were also more likely to agree with recent Court decisions (8.04 [0] vs. 7.99 [1] vs. 7.40 [2], p=.005).

These results, as with other ideological variables, accord with the results of the mass survey, though the relationships found here are larger. It is somewhat logical for those who are more economically liberal to be more civil libertarian. These individuals who are more economically liberal would believe that a police crackdown on crime would not have much of an effect on the crime rate, since they believe that the underlying economic system is at fault for much of the crime problem.

Lawyers who are more liberal on the racial liberalism scale are fully three and one half points more civil libertarian than those on the conservative side of the scale. Lawyers scoring 0 on the racial liberalism scale scored 4.20 on the criminal procedure scale vs. 5.50 for those scoring .5, 6.73 for those scoring 1, 6.70 for those scoring 1.5, and 7.62 for those scoring 2 (p=.000). The same pattern emerged for the search and seizure and rights of the accused scales (search: 4.22 [2] vs. 3.45 [1.5] vs. 3.69 [1] vs. 2.82 [.5] vs. 2.19 [0], p=.000; accused: 3.43 [2] vs. 3.10 [1.5] vs. 3.07 [1] vs. 2.65 [.5] vs. 1.94 [0], p=.000). However, there was not much difference in one's support for recent court decisions (7.67 [0] vs. 8.09 [.5], 7.69 [1], 7.50 [1.5], 7.46 [2], p=.123).

Again, there is a greater spread in opinions among lawyers than the mass public. Since crime and crime-fighting techniques have been so often linked with race and issues of racial justice, it can be expected that one's opinions regarding issues of race and its relationship to crime would have an effect on opinions regarding civil liberties. It is also understandable that lawyers would be more primed to issues of racial justice since this issue has received much attention in elite and media discourse, and elites are more likely to be aware of such debates.

The largest and most striking differences occurred for categories of criminal justice liberalism. Lawyers scoring 0 on criminal justice liberalism scored a 3.74 on the criminal procedure scale vs. 5.54 for those scoring 1, 5.96 for those scoring 2, 6.65 for those scoring 3, and 10.03 for those scoring 4. A similarly large spread occurred for the search and seizure and rights of the accused scales (search: 6.23 [4] vs. 3.53 [3] vs. 3.08 [2] vs. 3.00 [1] vs. 1.91 [0], p=.000; accused: 3.81 [4] vs. 3.21 [3] vs. 2.83 [2] vs. 2.57 [1] vs. 1.87 [0], p=.000). Lawyers who scored highest on the criminal justice liberalism scale were also least likely to agree with recent court decisions (8.50 [0] vs. 7.82 [1] vs. 7.70 [2] vs. 8.18 [3] vs. 5.77 [4], p=.000).

This is similar to what was found for the mass public, but the results are clearly more pronounced. While it would seem obvious that those who are more liberal regarding issues of civil liberties would be more civil libertarian, it is quite surprising how much more efficient in predicting support for civil liberties this scale works, as opposed to the self-identified liberal/conservative dichotomy. This was especially true in the results for the mass public, for whom traditional labels did not help much in predicting one's opinion.

Role of the Court

Lawyers who believed that the Court should follow its own wishes, as opposed to society's wishes, were more likely to support civil libertarian norms. Those who said the Court should act autonomously scored 6.76 (see Table 6.4) on the criminal procedure scale vs. 5.88 for those who said the Court should follow society's wishes vs. 4.14 for those who said the Court should follow the law vs. 6.41 for those who said it should follow the Constitution (p=.075). The same pattern persisted for the search and seizure and rights of the accused scales (search: 3.76 [Constitution] vs. 3.62 [Court wishes] vs. 3.26 [society wishes] vs. 2.00 [the law], p=.251; accused: 3.13 [Court wishes] vs. 2.72 [society wishes] vs. 2.71 [Constitution] vs. 2.14 [the law], p=.024). However, there is a relatively small difference in the support of the different groups for recent court decisions (8.14 [the law] vs. 7.79 [society wishes] vs. 7.73 [Court wishes] vs. 7.35 [Constitution], p=.783).

These results do not follow the pattern of the mass public, where the more civil libertarian group was those who believed society's wishes should be followed. It is also interesting to note that lawyers who believed that the Court should follow the law were less civil libertarian than the norm, while those who believed that the Court should follow the Constitution were more civil libertarian. One possible explanation is that many conservatives do not believe that the Court has been following the law: rather, it has been creating law as it goes along. On the other hand, many liberals believe that the Constitution does indeed protect one's civil liberties, as interpreted by the Court, and therefore lawyers who believe the Court should follow the constitution are more civil libertarian than others.

MULTIPLE REGRESSION ANALYSIS

The results of the multivariate analysis reveal what is apparent from the previous analysis. In sharp contrast to the results of the analysis of the mass public, self-identified ideology and party do matter, at times to an even greater degree than the other ideological scales. Interestingly, the other effects were all in the same direction as they were in the survey of the mass public. Also, based upon the various regression models presented in this chapter, a path diagram was created (see Table 6.10 and analysis of the path model later in this chapter).

The results of the regression analysis reveal that the measure which has the greatest effect is criminal justice liberalism, followed by the economic liberalism scale, and the racial liberalism scale. The criminal justice liberalism scale was statistically significant on all three scales (criminal procedure [b=.831**], search [b=.488**], accused [b=.335**]). However, the economic liberalism scale had a greater impact on issues of search and seizure (b=.201) than rights of the accused (b=.146), while the racial liberalism scale had a greater impact on issues dealing with the rights of the accused (b=.231*) than search and seizure (b=.037*) (see Table 6.5).

Regionally, residents of New England, the mid-Atlantic region, and the West North Central were most civil libertarian, while lawyers in the mountain and southern states were least civil libertarian (base=South, variable=New England b=.496, variable=mid-Atlantic b=.485, variable=West North Central b=.479, variable=Mountain b=-.022, variable=Pacific b=.273). Lawyers in the rural areas were most civil libertarian, while those in the suburbs were less civil libertarian than lawyers in the cities and rural communities (base=suburb, variable=rural b=.547, variable=city b=.023). Interestingly, rural dwellers were most civil libertarian when it came to issues of search and seizure. Also, lawyers who were afraid to walk alone at night were only slightly less civil libertarian than those who expressed no fear (b=.042).

Demographically, lawyers who are divorced or separated, and to a lesser degree those who were never married, were much more civil libertarian than those who were married or widowed (base=married, variable=divorced/separated b=1.207**, variable=never married b=.693). Also, unexpectedly, Jews were the least civil libertarian among the different religious groups, once other factors were controlled, Protestants were less civil libertarian than Catholics, and atheists were by far the most civil libertarian of all the groups (base=Protestant, variable=Jewish b=-.013, variable=Catholic b=.272, variable=atheist b= 1.009). In addition, men were more civil libertarian than women (b=.297), and older lawyers slightly less civil libertarian than younger ones (b=-.111).

Ideologically, liberals and Republicans are more civil libertarian (ideology b=-.410, party b=.246). Also, those who respect the police are much less civil libertarian than those who have less respect for the police (.790**).

When the general practice lawyer was used as the base, about half the specialties were more civil libertarian. These were lawyers specializing in criminal (b=.362), corporate (b=.341), tax (b=.695), and criminal defense law (b=.410). Those in business law were particularly not supportive of civil liberties (b=1.375**). Also, lawyers retired (b=-.963), out of law (b=-.686), and specializing in family law (b=-.665) were also less supportive of civil liberties.

One can see from the results for the agreement with the Court scale (see Table 6.6) that those groups who were more supportive of civil liberties were less likely to be supportive of recent Court decisions. This, again, brings some support to the notion that the Court has been moving against civil libertarian positions.

CAUSAL ANALYSIS

As with the survey of the mass public, other regressions were performed to measure possible indirect effects (see Tables 6.7-6.9). This led to the creation of the causal flow graph presented in Table 6.10.

Party ID, political ideology, fear of crime, and respect for the police, as well as the three ideology scales were all specified as dependent on race, gender, area, region, marital status, age, and specialty of law practiced. Party ID, political ideology, fear of crime, and respect for police were included as independent variables when each was not specified as a dependent variable, as shown in the path model.

The logic behind the flow graph is that the causally prior variables are used as independent variables, while the variables that might be affected by the independent variables are specified as dependent variables. Race, gender, area, region, and religion are variables that are quite stable and at times cannot be changed. They are therefore specified as independent variables. As one moves rightward on the flow graph, one sees that the variables are more amenable to change and are likely to be affected by the variables to the left on the flow graph. For example, it is quite logical for one's gender, race, area, or religion to influence one's party ID, political ideology or fear of crime, but not vice versa.

First, the three scales were analyzed as dependent variables. When the racial justice liberalism scale was analyzed as a dependent variable, there were significant differences based upon region (Southerners most conservative), race (blacks more liberal), marital status (divorced and separated lawyers more liberal), ideology, and specialty (criminal defense lawyers most liberal). Similar causal factors were found when the other scales were analyzed as dependent variables.

The other regressions performed also produced quite predictable results. Women were more fearful of crime, Republicans and conservatives had more respect for the police, and party and ideology helped predict in which party one was a member.

In all the effects were predictable, and in line with the results of the previously reported bivariate and multivariate analysis.

CONCLUSION

In all, lawyers are more civil libertarian than members of the mass public. This is true within all demographic and ideological variables. In addition, lawyers and the mass public seem to be influenced by similar factors. Specifically the ideological scales as well as one's marital status showed important effects for both groups. Also, as mentioned, traditional party and ideology self-identification were important factors among lawyers, though not as much among the mass public. In sum, the major differences between lawyers and nonlawyers seem to be their opinions regarding the root causes of crime, manifested by the differences in the results on the more targeted ideology scales which were based upon questions regarding the causes of crime.

Now that the results of both surveys, as well as explanations for them, have been presented, the question we turn to is: How can we bring the opinions of the mass public into line with the legal elite? This assumes that lawyers, due to their structured legal education, have opinions that are more knowledgeable and constructive than those of the mass public, who must rely on the mass media for information. We might start by considering further the two groups' opinions regarding the roots of crime. These and other considerations, especially the role of the media in opinion formation, will be considered further in the concluding chapter.

Table 6.1
Means for Criminal Procedure, Search and Seizure,
Rights of the Accused, and Agreement with Court Scales,
for All Lawyers and by Type of Law Practiced

Entire Survey	All Lawyers
Criminal procedure scale	6.56 (369)
Search scale	3.53 (375)
Accused scale	3.02 (396)
Agreement w/Ct scale	7.74 (369)

Type of Law Practiced	Criminal Procedure Scale	Search Scale	Accused Scale	Agreement with Court Scale
Criminal	8.09 n=35	4.60 n=35	3.50 n=36	7.00 n=35
Poverty	9.00 n=4	5.25 n=4	3.67 n=6	6.50 n=4
Corporate	6.36 n=14	3.43 n=14	2.88 n=16	7.64 n=14
Health	10.00 n=1	6.00 n=1	3.00 n=2	6.00 n=1
Family	6.05 n=20	3.15 n=20	2.90 n=20	8.25 n=20
Employment/elder	7.00 n=1	4.00 n=1	3.00 n=1	9.00 n=1
Judge	6.00 n=3	3.00 n=3	3.00 n=3	8.67 n=3
General practice	6.55 n=76	3.50 n=76	3.09 n=80	7.97 n=76
Criminal defense	9.53 n=15	5.73 n=15	3.83 n=18	6.07 n=15
Retired	4.21 n=19	2.26 n=19	2.09 n=23	8.32 n=19
Real estate	5.50 n=16	3.13 n=16	2.37 n=16	7.88 n=16

continued . . .

Table 6.2 (continued)

Type of Law Practiced	Criminal Procedure Scale	Search Scale	Accused Scale	Agreement with Court Scale
Prosecutor	5.33	3.00	2.00	7.33
	n=3	n=3	n=4	n=3
Out of law	5.23	2.47	2.86	8.46
	n=13	n=15	n=14	n=13
Probate	5.85	2.86	2.86	8.00
	n=13	n=14	n=14	n=13
Civil	6.56	3.35	3.14	8.11
	n=36	n=37	n=37	n=36
Personal injury	7.08	3.85	3.33	7.54
	n=13	n=13	n=15	n=13
Bankruptcy	4.67	2.33	2.33	8.00
	n=3	n=3	n=3	n=3
Taxation	6.86	4.07	2.73	6.57
	n=14	n=14	n=15	n=14
Business/commercial	4.88	2.53	2.33	7.94
	n=17	n=17	n=18	n=17
Fiduciary	6.00	3.00	3.00	8.00
	n=1	n=1	n=1	n=1
Personal injury	11.00	7.00	4.00	5.00
	n=3	n=3	n=3	n=3
Government	6.75	3.20	2.75	7.25
	n=4	n=5	n=4	n=4
Labor	6.67	3.50	3.33	8.67
	n=3	n=4	n=3	n=3
Environmental	7.00	5.00	2.00	5.00
	n=1	n=1	n=1	n=1
Consumer	7.00	3.00	4.00	9.00
	n=1	n=1	n=1	n=1
Entertainment	7.50	4.50	3.00	6.50
	n=2	n=2	n=2	n=2
Criminal prosecutor	3.00	1.00	2.00	8.00
	n=2	n=2	n=2	n=2
Intellectual property	7.00	3.00	4.00	9.00
	n=1	n=1	n=1	n=1

Type of Law Practiced	Criminal Procedure Scale	Search Scale	Accused Scale	Agreement with Court Scale
Constitutional	7.00 n=2	5.00 n=2	2.00 n=2	6.00 n=2
Administrative	5.00 n=1	2.00 n=1	3.00 n=1	9.00 n=1
Teach law	9.50 n=4	5.75 n=4	3.75 n=4	6.50 n=4
Legal librarian	6.00 n=1	2.00 n=1	4.00 n=1	10.00 n=1
Tort	5.67 n=3	2.00 n=3	3.67 n=3	9.67 n=3
Patent	5.33 n=3	2.33 n=3	3.00 n=3	9.33 n=3
Dispute resolution	6.00 n=1	2.00 n=1	4.00 n=1	10.00 n=1
Litigation	7.17 n=6	3.50 n=6	3.71 n=7	8.50 n=6
Workmen's compensation	7.33 n=3	3.67 n=3	3.67 n=3	7.33 n=3
Indian	10.00 n=1	6.00 n=1	4.00 n=1	6.00 n=1
Equal employment	10.00 n=1	6.00 n=1	4.00 n=1	6.00 n=1
Domestic violence	10.00 n=1	7.00 n=1	3.00 n=1	6.00 n=1
Legal writer	4.00 n=1	1.00 n=1	3.00 n=1	10.00 n=1
Military	4.00 n=1	2.00 n=1	2.00 n=1	8.00 n=1
Refuse	5.50 n=6	2.83 n=6	2.86 n=7	8.50 n=6
	$F=2.070$ $df=42$ $p=.000$	$F=2.171$ $df=42$ $p=.000$	$F=1.709$ $df=42$ $p=.005$	$F=1.774$ $df=42$ $p=.003$

Table 6.2
Means for Criminal Procedure, Search and Seizure, Rights of the Accused,
and Agreement with Court Scales, by Demographic and
Attitudinal Variables for Respondents to Survey of Lawyers

Region	New England	Mid- Atlantic	West North Central	South	Mountain	Pacific
Criminal procedure scale	6.25 (24)	6.78 (112)	6.56 (18)	5.98 (122)	6.62 (21)	7.28 (72)
			F=2.004, df=5, p=.077			
Search scale	3.25 (24)	3.66 (114)	3.21 (19)	3.14 (124)	3.71 (21)	4.11 (73)
			F=2.327, df=5, p=.042			
Accused scale	3.00 (24)	3.14 (118)	3.24 (21)	2.81 (130)	3.04 (24)	3.13 (79)
			F=1.362, df=5, p=.238			
Agreement w/Ct scale	7.92 (24)	7.79 (112)	7.89 (18)	7.93 (122)	7.67 (21)	7.25 (72)
			F=1.415, df=5, p=.218			

Marital Status	Married	Widowed	Divorced	Separated	Never Married
Criminal procedure scale	6.22 (284)	6.00 (14)	8.08 (36)	8.75 (4)	7.90 (30)
		F=5.911, df=4, p=.000			
Search scale	3.27 (290)	2.86 (14)	4.81 (36)	5.25 (4)	4.63 (30)
		F=8.194, df=4, p=.000			
Accused scale	2.93 (304)	3.19 (16)	3.32 (38)	3.60 (5)	3.31 (32)
		F=1.971, df=4, p=.098			
Agreement w/Ct scale	7.96 (284)	8.71 (14)	6.58 (36)	6.25 (4)	6.70 (30)
		F=9.573, df=4, p=.000			

Gender	Male	Female
Criminal procedure scale	6.45 (286)	6.93 (82)
	F=1.671, df=1, p=.197	
Search scale	3.44 (292)	3.85 (82)
	F=2.526, df=1, p=.113	
Accused scale	3.00 (306)	3.07 (89)
	F=.227, df=1, p=.634	
Agreement w/Ct scale	7.79 (286)	7.56 (82)
	F=.971, df=1, p=.325	

Community Type	City	Suburb	Rural
Criminal procedure scale	6.72 (145)	6.29 (177)	7.09 (46)
	F=1.708, df=2, p=.183		
Search scale	3.60 (147)	3.37 (181)	3.93 (46)
	F=1.468, df=2, p=.232		
Accused scale	3.09 (156)	2.89 (186)	3.23 (53)
	F=2.198, df=2, p=.112		
Agreement w/Ct scale	7.68 (145)	7.82 (177)	7.57 (46)
	F=.470, df=2, p=.626		

Race	White	Black	Asian	Hispanic	Native American
Criminal procedure scale	6.54 (345)	6.63 (8)	8.00 (5)	6.50 (6)	6.00 (4)
		F=.338, df=4, p=.852			
Search scale	3.51 (351)	3.88 (8)	4.60 (5)	3.67 (6)	3.00 (4)
		F=.456, df=4, p=.768			
Accused scale	3.02 (372)	2.75 (8)	3.40 (5)	2.83 (6)	3.00 (4)
		F=.271, df=4, p=.897			
Agreement w/Ct scale	7.75 (345)	7.63 (8)	6.80 (5)	7.50 (6)	8.50 (4)
		F=.535, df=4, p=.710			

continued . . .

Table 6.2 (continued)

Age	25-33	34-43	44-64	65 or More
Criminal procedure scale	7.07 (28)	7.03 (107)	6.92 (157)	4.96 (76)
		F=10.156, df=3, p=.000		
Search scale	4.00 (29)	3.92 (108)	3.73 (159)	2.41 (78)
		F=10.344, df=3, p=.000		
Accused scale	3.07 (30)	3.10 (114)	3.21 (168)	2.49 (83)
		F=7.514, df=3, p=.000		
Agreement w/Ct scale	7.29 (28)	7.46 (107)	7.73 (157)	8.30 (76)
		F=3.914, df=3, p=.009		

Religion	Protestant	Catholic	Jewish	Atheist	Other	Buddhist
Criminal procedure scale	5.72 (155)	6.79 (105)	7.42 (57)	7.93 (28)	7.39 (18)	10.50 (2)
			F=6.224, df=5, p=.000			
Search scale	2.93 (159)	3.65 (105)	4.12 (59)	4.75 (28)	4.17 (18)	6.50 (2)
			F=7.148, df=5, p=.000			
Accused scale	2.76 (170)	3.18 (111)	3.26 (61)	3.21 (29)	3.26 (19)	4.00 (2)
			F=3.280, df=5, p=.007			
Agreement w/Ct scale	8.15 (155)	7.72 (105)	7.32 (57)	6.79 (28)	7.17 (18)	5.50 (2)
			F=4.856, df=5, p=.000			

Scared to Walk Alone at Night	Yes	No
Criminal procedure scale	6.27 (165)	6.79 (202)
	F=2.852, df=1, p=.092	
Search scale	3.35 (167)	3.67 (206)
	F=2.255, df=1, p=.134	
Accused scale	2.91 (175)	3.09 (219)
	F=2.214, df=1, p=.138	
Agreement w/Ct scale	7.77 (165)	7.71 (202)
	F=.103, df=1, p=.748	

Do You Feel Safe Home at Night?	Yes	No
Criminal procedure scale	6.66 (334)	5.58 (33)
	F=4.126, df=1, p=.043	
Search scale	3.58 (340)	3.03 (33)
	F=2.092, df=1, p=.149	
Accused scale	3.06 (360)	2.56 (34)
	F=5.742, df=1, p=.017	
Agreement w/Ct scale	7.73 (334)	7.76 (33)
	F=.005, df=1, p=.943	

Worst Crime Suffered	Car	Mugged	Robbery in Home	Physical Assault
Criminal procedure scale	6.67 (126)	7.18 (33)	6.56 (113)	6.73 (33)
Search scale	3.56 (128)	4.12 (33)	3.59 (116)	3.48 (33)
Accused scale	3.08 (131)	3.11 (35)	2.93 (125)	3.26 (35)
Agreement w/Ct scale	7.75 (126)	7.36 (33)	7.64 (113)	7.82 (33)

Worst Crime Suffered (continued)	Murder	Rape	None
Criminal procedure scale	6.11 (9)	6.00 (8)	6.00 (40)
	F=.604, df=6, p=.727		
Search scale	3.11 (9)	3.25 (8)	3.12 (41)
	F=.794, df=6, p=.575		
Accused scale	3.09 (11)	2.75 (8)	2.86 (44)
	F=.676, df=6, p=.669		
Agreement w/Ct scale	7.89 (9)	8.00 (8)	8.05 (40)
	F=.519, df=6, p=.794		

continued . . .

Table 6.2 (continued)

Respect for Police	Great Deal	Only Some	Hardly Any
Criminal procedure scale	5.80 (161)	6.68 (170)	9.32 (37)
		F=24.777, df=2, p=.000	
Search scale	2.93 (163)	3.60 (173)	5.84 (37)
		F=34.294, df=2, p=.000	
Accused scale	2.88 (170)	3.05 (185)	3.51 (39)
		F=4.755, df=2, p=.009	
Agreement w/Ct scale	8.28 (161)	7.65 (170)	5.81 (37)
		F=32.554, df=2, p=.000	

People Most Confident In	Congress	Supreme Court	President	None
Criminal procedure scale	6.14 (29)	6.54 (278)	7.34 (32)	6.33 (27)
		F=1.024, df=3, p=.382		
Search scale	3.12 (32)	3.49 (281)	4.19 (32)	3.56 (27)
		F=1.492, df=3, p=.216		
Accused scale	2.87 (31)	3.04 (297)	3.18 (33)	2.90 (30)
		F=.515, df=3, p=.672		
Agreement w/Ct scale	7.93 (29)	7.79 (278)	7.16 (32)	7.74 (27)
		F=1.279, df=3, p=.281		

Table 6.3
Means on Criminal Procedure, Search and Seizure, Rights of the Accused, and Agreement with Court Scales, by Party, Ideology, Racial Liberalism, Economic Liberalism, and Criminal Justice Liberalism Scales for Lawyers

Party	Strong Democrat	Weak Democrat	Independent, but Closer to Democrat	Independent
Criminal procedure scale	8.89 (46)	7.14 (57)	7.15 (61)	6.00 (31)
Search scale	5.37 (46)	3.88 (59)	3.90 (61)	3.23 (31)
Accused scale	3.55 (49)	3.26 (62)	3.26 (65)	2.83 (36)
Agreement w/Ct scale	6.41 (46)	7.74 (57)	7.61 (61)	8.00 (31)

Party (continued)	Independent, but Closer to Republican	Weak Republican	Strong Republican
Criminal procedure scale	5.70 (70)	5.61 (69)	5.73 (30)
	$F=9.519$, df=6, p=.000		
Search scale	2.87 (71)	2.80 (71)	3.03 (31)
	$F=10.995$, df=6, p=.000		
Accused scale	2.76 (75)	2.81 (74)	2.60 (30)
	$F=4.662$, df=6, p=.000		
Agreement w/Ct scale	8.16 (70)	8.07 (69)	7.93 (30)
	$F=5.650$, df=6, p=.000		

Ideology	Strong Liberal	Weak Liberal	Moderate, but Closer to Liberal	Moderate
Criminal procedure scale	9.77 (30)	8.08 (39)	7.27 (74)	6.13 (63)
Search scale	6.10 (30)	4.62 (39)	3.87 (75)	3.25 (64)
Accused scale	3.68 (31)	3.49 (41)	3.41 (83)	2.85 (66)
Agreement w/Ct scale	5.77 (30)	7.21 (39)	7.84 (74)	7.81 (63)

continued . . .

Table 6.2 (continued)

Ideology (continued)	Moderate, but Closer to Conservative	Weak Conservative	Strong Conservative
Criminal procedure scale	5.60 (75)	5.08 (65)	5.47 (19)
		$F=16.690$, df=6, p=.000	
Search scale	2.83 (78)	2.48 (65)	2.90 (20)
		$F=18.518$, df=6, p=.000	
Accused scale	2.75 (80)	2.62 (69)	2.48 (21)
		$F=8.111$, df=6, p=.000	
Agreement w/Ct scale	8.08 (75)	8.49 (65)	7.79 (19)
		$F=10.116$, df=6, p=.000	

Economic Liberalism Scale	Low (0)	Middle (1)	High (2)
Criminal procedure scale	5.38 (97)	5.95 (94)	7.61 (174)
		$F=23.822$, df=2, p=.000	
Search scale	2.78 (101)	3.12 (94)	4.22 (176)
		$F=19.739$, df=2, p=.000	
Accused scale	2.58 (105)	2.87 (97)	3.39 (186)
		$F=18.844$, df=2, p=.000	
Agreement w/Ct scale	8.04 (97)	7.99 (94)	7.40 (174)
		$F=5.390$, df=2, p=.005	

Racial Liberalism Scale	Low (0)	.5	Middle (1)	1.5	High (2)
Criminal procedure scale	4.20 (15)	5.50 (108)	6.73 (100)	6.70 (10)	7.62 (130)
			$F=11.249$, df=4, p=.000		
Search scale	2.19 (16)	2.82 (111)	3.69 (101)	3.45 (11)	4.22 (130)
			$F=9.117$, df=4, p=.000		
Accused scale	1.94 (16)	2.65 (115)	3.07 (109)	3.10 (10)	3.43 (138)
			$F=11.603$, df=4, p=.000		
Agreement w/Ct scale	7.67 (15)	8.09 (108)	7.69 (100)	7.50 (10)	7.46 (130)
			$F=1.826$, df=4, p=.123		

Criminal Justice Liberalism Scale	Low (0)	.5	1.0	1.5	Middle (2)
Criminal procedure scale	3.74 (42)	4.68 (37)	5.54 (28)	5.64 (28)	5.96 (23)
Search scale	1.91 (43)	2.35 (37)	3.00 (29)	2.68 (28)	3.08 (24)
Accused scale	1.87 (47)	2.38 (40)	2.57 (28)	3.00 (29)	2.83 (23)
Agreement w/Ct scale	8.50 (42)	8.30 (37)	7.82 (28)	8.43 (28)	7.70 (23)

Criminal Justice Liberalism Scale (continued)	2.5	3.0	3.5	High (4)
Criminal procedure scale	6.85 (52)	6.65 (17) $F=23.596$, df=8, p=.000	7.88 (99)	10.03 (30)
Search scale	3.55 (53)	3.53 (17) $F=19.697$, df=8, p=.000	4.33 (100)	6.23 (30)
Accused scale	3.27 (55)	3.21 (19) $F=16.518$, df=8, p=.000	3.52 (109)	3.81 (31)
Agreement w/Ct scale	7.92 (52)	8.18 (17) $F=7.837$, df=8, p=.000	7.43 (99)	5.77 (30)

Table 6.4
Means for Criminal Procedure, Search and Seizure, Rights of the Accused, and Agreement with Role of the Court Scales

Role of the Court	Society Wishes	Court Wishes	Neither	The Law	Consti- tution
Criminal procedure scale	5.88 (42)	6.76 (291)	6.25 (8)	4.14 (7)	6.41 (17)
		$F=2.142$, df=4, p=.075			
Search scale	3.26 (43)	3.62 (296)	3.25 (8)	2.00 (7)	3.76 (17)
		$F=1.350$, df=4, p=.251			
Accused scale	2.72 (47)	3.13 (305)	2.80 (10)	2.14 (7)	2.71 (21)
		$F=2.852$, df=4, p=.024			
Agreement w/Ct scale	7.79 (42)	7.73 (291)	8.25 (8)	8.14 (7)	7.35 (17)
		$F=.435$, df=4, p=.783			

Table 6.5
Multivariate Regression Models with Criminal Procedure, Search and Seizure, and Rights of the Accused Scales as Dependent Variables

	Criminal Procedure		Search		Rights of Accused	
	b	Beta	b	Beta	b	Beta
Economic liberalism scale	.373*	.107	.201	.081	.146	.106
Racial liberalism scale	.200	.046	.037*	.012	.231*	.133
Criminal justice liberalism	.831**	.386	.488**	.315	.335**	.393
Region (base=South)						
New England	.496	.042	.293	.034	.126	.026
Mid Atlantic	.485	.076	.255	.056	.210	.083
West North Central	.479	.037	.018	.002	.197	.040
Mountain	-.022	-.002	-.036	-.004	.159	.032
Pacific	.273	.037	.272	.052	.039	.013
Area (base=suburb)						
Rural	.547	.063	.449	.072	.124	.038
City	.023	.004	-.053	-.012	.110	.047
Scared walking at night	.042	.007	-.042	-.010	.116	.050

	Criminal Procedure		Search		Rights of Accused	
	b	Beta	b	Beta	b	Beta
Marital status (base=married)						
Divorced/Separated	1.207**	.129	.944**	.140	.330	.090
Widowed	-.0029	.000	-.296	-.028	.419	.073
Never married	.693	.068	.633	.086	.029	.007
Religion (base=Protestant)						
Jewish	-.013	-.002	-.0054	-.001	.016	.005
Catholic	.272	.042	.127	.027	.192	.075
Atheist	1.009*	.092	.885**	.112	.143	.033
Race (base=white)						
Black	-.825	-.043	-.088	-.006	-.772*	-.099
Asian	1.073	.044	.822	.047	.231	.023
Hispanic	.788	.025	1.058	.047	-.299	-.024
Male	.297	.042	.242	.048	.0033	.001
Age	-.111	-.033	-.123	-.051	.026	.019
Ideology	-.410**	-.237	-.301**	-.243	-.076	-.111
Party	.246*	.163	.123*	.114	.096*	.161
Respect for police	.790**	.200	.776**	.244	-.040	-.023
Law practiced (base=general)						
Criminal	.362	.036	.277	.039	.045	.011
Corporate	.341	.023	.302	.029	-.132	-.024
Family	-.665	-.052	-.368	-.040	-.415	-.081
Retired	-.963	-.070	-.346	-.035	-.551*	-.107
Probate	-.619	-.045	-.042	-.004	-.670*	-.120
Out	-.686	-.045	-.628	-.062	-.043	-.007
Real estate	-.277	-.018	-.138	-.013	-.156	-.026
Civil	-.184	-.019	-.237	-.034	-.124	-.032
Personal injury	-.294	-.019	-.355	-.032	.024	.004
Tax	.695	.046	.616	.056	.017	.003
Business	-1.375**	-.097	-.641	-.063	-.839**	-.146
Criminal defense	.410	.029	.354	.035	.048	.009
Other	-.637	-.082	-.450	-.081	-.281	-.091
R^2	.493		.482		.352	
Adjusted R^2	.429		.417		.275	
F	7.707**		7.459**		4.584**	
N	339		343		359	

$*p<.05; **p<.01$

Note: The b's are unstandardized regression coefficients, the Betas are standardized coefficients.

Table 6.6
Multivariate Regression Models with Agreement with Court
as Dependent Variable

	b	Beta
Economic liberalism	-.128	-.059
Racial liberalism scale	.218	.080
Criminal justice liberalism	-.210**	-.156
Region (base=South)		
New England	-.242	-.033
Mid Atlantic	.015	.004
West North Central	-.193	-.024
Mountain	.273	.034
Pacific	-.123	-.027
Scared walking at night	.0020	.001
Area (base=suburb)		
Rural	-.313	-.058
City	.203	.055
Marital status (base=married)		
Divorced/Separated	-.958**	-.164
Widowed	.691	.076
Never married	-.935*	-.146
Religion (base=protestant)		
Jewish	-.065	-.013
Catholic	-.0085	-.002
Atheist	-.667	-.098
Race (base=white)		
Black	.028	.002
Asian	-.952	-.063
Hispanic	-1.673	-.086
Age	.042	.020
Ideology	.271*	.251
Party	-.123	-.131
Respect for police	-.841**	-.304
Law practiced (base=general)		
Criminal	-.509	-.082
Corporate	-.588	-.064
Family	.094	.012
Retired	-.076	-.009
Probate	-.462	-.054
Out	.371	.039
Real estate	-.333	-.035
Civil	.084	.014
Personal injury	-.036	-.004
Tax	-1.252*	-.132
Business	-.443	-.050
Criminal defense	-.556	-.063
Other	.047	.010

	b	Beta
R^2		.598
Adjusted R^2		.357
F		4.405**
N		339

*p<.05;**p<.01

Note: The b's are unstandardized regression coefficients, the Betas are standardized coefficients.

Table 6.7
Multivariate Regression Models with Economic Liberalism,
Radial Liberalism, and Criminal Justice Scales as Dependent Variables

	Criminal Justice		Racial Justice		Economic Justice	
	b	Beta	b	Beta	b	Beta
Region (base=South)						
New England	-.223	-.040	.266	.093	.392*	.113
Mid-Atlantic	.057	.019	.167*	.115	.154	.083
West North Central	.129	.022	.343*	.120	.294	.081
Mountain	-.099	-.017	.126	.044	.137	.039
Pacific	.115	.034	.266	.161	.190	.090
Scared walking at night	-.303*	-.111	-.081	-.008	-.045	-.026
Area (base=suburb)						
Rural	.289	.176	.207*	.107	-.034	-.014
City	.176	.063	.082	.060	-.001	.000
Marital status (base=married)						
Divorced/Separated	-.152	-.035	-.252*	-.116	-.211	-.077
Widowed	-.224	-.033	-.094	-.028	-.152	-.035
Never married	-.210	-.043	-.166	-.069	.064	.021
Religion (base=Protestant)						
Jewish	.239	.064	.041	.023	.131	.057
Catholic	.030	.010	-.001	.000	.101	.053
Atheist	.194	.038	-.115	-.046	.057	.018
Race (base=white)						
Black	1.184**	.126	.695**	.149	.197	.033
Asian	-.066	-.006	.149	.025	-.152	-.020
Hispanic	-.143	-.009	-.449	-.068	-.671	-.070

continued . . .

Table 6.7 (continued)

	Criminal Justice		Racial Justice		Economic Justice	
	b	Beta	b	Beta	b	Beta
Male	.122	.038	-.101	-.063	.100	.050
Age	-.036	-.023	-.006	-.008	-.015	-.015
Ideology	-.277**	-.341	-.126**	-.313	-.137**	-.270
Party	-.108*	-.152	-.031	-.089	-.062	-.141
Respect for police	-.023	-.011	.071	.069	.008	.007
Law practiced (base=general)						
Criminal	.737**	.156	.055	.024	.231	.078
Corporate	-.096	-.015	-.189	-.058	-.087	-.021
Family	-.024	-.004	.238	.077	.047	.012
Retired	-.446	-.075	.026	.099	-.033	-.009
Probate	-.368	-.056	.252	.078	.212	.052
Out	-.277	-.041	.230	.069	.023	.006
Real estate	-.173	-.024	.072	.021	-.355	-.082
Civil	.072	.016	.086	.038	-.018	-.006
Personal injury	-.144	-.021	.125	.036	.396	.091
Tax	-.420	-.059	-.182	-.051	-.163	-.035
Business	.058	.008	.082	.025	-.048	-.011
Criminal defense	.903**	.142	.369*	.117	.265	.067
Other	-.009	-.003	.292**	.166	-.024	.011
R^2	.392		.338		.258	
Adjusted R^2	.329		.271		.183	
F	6.293		5.074		3.441	
N	375		383		381	

*p<.05; **p<.01
Note: The b's are unstandardized regression coefficients, the Betas are standardized coefficients.

Table 6.8
Multivariate Regression Models with Party, Ideology, and Fear of Crime as Dependent Variables

	Party		Ideology		Fear of Crime	
	b	Beta	b	Beta	b	Beta
Region (base=South)						
New England	.131	.017	-.133	-.019	-.134	-.065
Mid-Atlantic	.403*	.097	-.329*	-.091	-.033	-.031
West North Central	-.070	-.009	.038	.005	-.158	-.074
Mountain	.120	.015	-.357	-.051	-.189	-.090
Pacific	.150	.032	-.081	-.020	-.105	-.085
Scared walking at night	-.177	-.046	.272*	.082		
Area (base=suburb)						
Rural	-.086	-.016	-.063	-.013	-.260**	-.180
City	-.080	-.020	-.073	-.021	.232**	.227
Marital status (base=married)						
Divorced/Separated	-.227	-.036	-.022	-.004	.068	.041
Widowed	-.210	-.022	.227	.027	-.117	.047
Never married	-.048	-.007	-.086	-.014	.125	.069
Religion (base=Protestant)						
Jewish	-.214	-.041	-.332*	-.074	.037	.027
Catholic	-.338*	-.079	.102	.027	.015	.013
Atheist	-.206	-.029	-.169	-.027	.064	.034
Race (base=white)						
Black	-.023	-.002	.089	.008	.064	.018
Asian	.226	.013	-.386	-.026	.087	.020
Hispanic	-.373	-.020	-.694	-.042	.171	.035
Male	.356*	.078	.060	.015	-.269**	-.227
Age	.070	.032	-.032	-.017	.022	.039
Ideology	.889**	.772			.060*	.199
Party			.647**	.745	-.028	-.109
Respect for police	.079	.027	-.168	-.066	-.013	-.108
Law practiced (base=general)						
Criminal	.354	.053	-.313	-.054	-.146	-.084
Corporate	.147	.016	-.086	-.011	-.016	-.006
Family	.280	.033	-.287	-.038	.019	.009
Retired	.254	.031	-.120	-.017	.046	.021
Probate	.779*	.084	-.496	-.062	.006	.003
Out	.264	.028	-.042	-.005	.038	.015
Real estate	.115	.012	-.003	-.013	.034	.013
Civil	.269	.042	-.316	-.057	-.024	-.014
Personal injury	-.090	-.010	-.426	-.050	.028	.011
Tax	.737*	.072	-.279	-.032	-.090	-.034

continued . . .

Table 6.8 (continued)

	Party		Ideology		Fear of Crime	
	b	Beta	b	Beta	b	Beta
Law practiced (continued)						
Business	-.030	-.003	.192	.023	.142	.057
Criminal defense	.148	.016	-.568*	-.072	.013	.005
Other	.250	.050	-.403*	-.092	.086	.065
R²		.674		.686		.235
Adjusted R²		.643		.655		.162
F	21.473			21.354		3.198	
N	387		387		387	

*p<.05; **p<.01
Note: The b's are unstandardized regression coefficients, the Betas are standardized coefficients.

Table 6.9
Multivariate Regression Models with Respect for Police
as Dependent Variable

	b	Beta
Region (base=South)		
New England	-.101	-.037
Mid Atlantic	.043	.030
West North Central	.147	.053
Mountain	.100	.037
Pacific	.141	.087
Scared walking at night	-.026	-.020
Area (base=suburb)		
Rural	-.033	-.017
City	.066	.050
Marital status (base=married)		
Divorced/Separated	.251*	.118
Widowed	.276	.085
Never married	-.028	-.012
Religion (base=Protestant)		
Jewish	-.004	-.002
Catholic	.021	.015
Atheist	.002	.001

	b	Beta
Race (base=white)		
Black	-.047	-.010
Asian	.018	.003
Hispanic	-.363	-.057
Male	-.161	-.104
Age	-.055	-.073
Ideology	-.070*	-.178
Party	.024	.071
Respect for police		
Law practiced (base=general)		
Criminal	-.118	-.052
Corporate	-.221	-.070
Family	-.314	-.107
Retired	-.335	-.120
Probate	-.349*	-.110
Out	.008	.003
Real estate	-.235	-.070
Civil	-.136	-.063
Personal injury	.161	.048
Tax	-.159	-.046
Business	-.050	-.015
Criminal defense	.302	.098
Other	-.039	-.022
R^2	.149	
Adjusted R^2	.067	
F	1.186	
N	387	

*$p < .05$; **$p < .01$

Note: The b's are unstandardized regression coefficients, the Betas are standardized coefficients.

Table 6.10
Path Analysis for the Survey of the Legal Elite

Results of Path

Political Ideology (-.341**) .... Criminal Liberalism Scale
Fear of Crime (-111*) .... Criminal Liberalism Scale
Race (Base=white) (Black=-.126) .... Criminal Liberalism Scale
Gender (base=female) (male=-.078) .... Party ID
Area (base=suburb) (rural=.180) .... Fear of Crime
Race (base=white) (black=.008) .... Political Ideology
Region (base=South) (Mid-Atlantic=.097*) .... Party ID
Religion (base=Protestant) (Catholic=-.079*) .... Party ID
Race (base=white) (black=.043) .... Overall Criminal Justice Scale
Gender (base=female) (male=.042) .... Overall Criminal Justice Scale
Area (base=suburb) (rural=.063) .... Overall Criminal Justice Scale
Region (base=South) (Mid-Atlantic=.076) ...... Overall Criminal Justice Scale
Religion (base=Protestant) (atheist=.092) .... Overall Criminal Justice Scale
Economic Scale (.107*) .... Overall Criminal Justice Scale
Respect for Police (.200**) .... Overall Criminal Justice Scale
Marital Status (base=married) (divorced=.129) ... Overall Criminal Justice Scale
Fear of Crime (.007) .... Overall Criminal Justice Scale
Racial Liberalism Scale (.046) .... Overall Criminal Justice Scale
Law Practiced (base=general practice)
                    (business=-.097**) .... Overall Criminal Justice Scale
Political Ideology (-.237**) .... Overall Criminal Justice Scale
Criminal Liberalism Scale (.386*) .... Overall Criminal Justice Scale

---

*p<.05; **p<.01

Chapter 7

Conclusion

This book has argued and offered evidence that the mass public as a whole is overall less civil libertarian than the legal profession. Within the mass public, individuals with greater levels of education and knowledge are more supportive of civil liberties than others. Differences in support for civil liberties between the mass public and the legal profession were large but not as great as one might have expected based upon media reports concerning the public's opinion regarding more salient issues such as the death penalty. Differences between the general mass public and those with more education and knowledge (the "attentive public") existed, but were not as large as those that occurred when comparing lawyers and nonlawyers. Larger differences among the mass public in support for civil liberties are related to race, gender, marital status, age, region, respect for the police, party, ideology, as well as community type, religion, income, role of the Court, and personal experience with crime. Also related are one's fear of crime, source of information regarding crime, and the amount of time one watches television per day. However, what was clearly most important in predicting one's opinion concerning civil liberties in the area of criminal procedure was the respondent's opinion regarding the root causes of crime, as well his or her opinion regarding the general state of the criminal justice system. The latter was true for both the public and lawyers.

Assuming that citizen support for civil liberties is an aim that society should strive to achieve, the question now becomes how can the mass public begin to appreciate the opinions of the legal elite, or, and at least how, can the opinions of the general population of the mass public begin to resemble those of the attentive public? It is taken as a given that certain factors cannot be changed: all members of the mass public do not obtain a legal education, nor will they ever become as knowledgeable in the intricacies of the law as are members of the legal profession. In addition, the entire general population is not going to obtain the highest levels of education. Also, many of the demographic variables such as race, gender, region, marital status, and age must be taken as a starting point.

However, it is a fact that the variables that can be changed are those that seem to have the greatest effect on opinion concerning civil liberties, especially opinions concerning the court system in general, as well as the root causes of crime in particular. In addition, though it might not be possible to change the public's source of information concerning crime, it might be possible to apply pressure to "at least make the media more self-conscious about slanted news and probably curb some of the more blatant excesses" (Page, 1996, p. 127). Another factor which can be improved upon is knowledge. This factor is quite important, as Delli Carpini and Keeeter (1996, p. 266) note: "tolerance is logically higher among citizens who are aware of constitutional provisions for civil liberties."

In sum, if the mass public can be helped in acquiring greater levels of political knowledge, through a mass media that would report on issues of criminal justice with great accuracy, it is possible that opinions regarding the root causes of crime would also change and accord more with those of the legal elite. A most positive scenario would be a mass media that allows legal experts representing different viewpoints to present their arguments to the American public in an uncensored forum, thus allowing the American public to formulate unbiased opinions. It is true that this sort of information is becoming more and more available with the proliferation of specialized cable outlets such as CNN and Court TV; however, one must look for possible institutional biases in the reporting, as well the need to sensationalize the reporting to attract viewers. These factors can quite possibly sway the public from positions they might otherwise adopt in an environment in which the only aim of members of the media was to educate the public.

MEDIA BIAS

I am not arguing, however, that the system in which information is disseminated in American society is totally lacking, and that the public does not have real or informed opinions. There are researchers such as Russell Neuman (also see Converse, 1964) who have argued that the public merely has "non-attitudes" or "pseudo-opinions." In fact, Neuman (1986, p. 23) says that "most respondents feel obliged to have an opinion, in effect, to help the interviewer out." Furthermore, Neuman argues that it is even the case that "when citizens are asked if they have thought about an issue enough to have an opinion, 80-90 percent of the population selects an alternative in response to most questions. In effect, opinions are invented on the spot." In contrast, more recent and comprehensive research by Page and Shapiro (1992, p. 391) offers evidence that "by the time national polls are taken, public opinion has often been 'refined and enlarged' through public debate. The system of collective deliberation could certainly be improved upon, as we will argue below. But it already works well enough to produce generally well-informed collective public opinion that responds to changing realities and new information, as our survey data reveals." In other words, though there are, of course, possibilities for improvement in the information provided to the mass public with which they form their opinions, the public's opinions are, collectively, quite rational. It is in the realm of helping the public find sources of information that will be educational that improvement is needed. This is especially pertinent, since the basic differences between the two publics were their opinions regarding the root causes of crime, an area in which one's opinion can easily be swayed by biases in the media.

THE MASS MEDIA/MEDIA BIAS

There has been much criticism of the mainstream media. Edward Herman and Noam Chomsky (1988, p. 306) argue that the "mass media of the United States are powerful ideological institutions that carry out a system-supported propaganda function by reliance on market forces, internalized assumptions, and self-censorship, and without significant overt coercion." Noted media critic Michael Parenti (1986, p. 9), explains that "the major distortions (in the media) are repeatable, systematic, and even systemic—the product not only of deliberate manipulation but of the ideological and economic conditions under which the media operate." Parenti concludes (p. 228) that "along with owners (of media outlets) and advertisers, political rulers exercise a substantial influence over what becomes news." Ben Bagdikian (1987) goes a step further, arguing that "it (the private media) robs the public of understanding the real world." In addition, as was explained in Chapter 1, Page and Shapiro (1992) point out the differences between educating, manipulating, and misleading the mass public. As noted above, many knowledgeable media observers would argue that the mainstream media at times manipulate and even mislead the public through distortions and occasionally even outright lies. One explanation, as mentioned, is the control various elite groups have over much of the content of the mass media, and their self-interest in promoting certain viewpoints. It is also plausible that there is a symbiotic relationship between the mass media and elected politicians in promoting certain viewpoints.

Applying these ideas to the area of criminal justice, many politicians might have a vested interest in making the "crime problem" appear larger than it is, so as to appear as "heroes" when they "solve" the problem. In addition, some might have an interest in highlighting certain crimes so that they will be given credit by their constituents when the crime is solved. As is known from the literature on the motivations of much of the activity of various members of Congress (Fenno, 1978; Fiorina, 1989), reelection is a high priority, if not *the* priority. If there is a chance for public "credit claiming," one can be sure a politician will be there.

This is not to argue that the members of the mainstream media do not themselves have an interest in making the crime problem to appear larger than it actually is. Audience and readership often rise when there is a sensational crime story. The more sensational the spin that the media can imprint on a particular crime story, the more they can count on viewers to sit glued to their sets watching daily updates. As cynical as the notion may sound, it would be interesting to see if there is a greater incidence of "crime" reported on the local nightly news, and especially sensational crime stories during the time periods popularly known as "sweeps." This is when advertising rates for particular time periods are set, based upon the ratings that TV stations obtain during the sweeps period. The media's persistent emphasis on crime, advertently or inadvertently, might cause many in society to be more fearful of crime, and therefore be more supportive of "tough" measures in the "war on crime."

It should also be remembered that since crime "makes" news, murders and other gruesome crimes will naturally become lead stories on the nightly news. Hence, individuals who receive their information from television will not even be aware of drops in crime, especially if they live in a large media market, such as New York, Los Angeles, or Chicago, unless a big drop in crime occurs and *that* becomes a major news story. Typically at least one or two murders, rapes, or burglaries per day have a very good chance of being the lead story on the nightly news (Frankel, 1997).

Lawyers, as well as the more educated and more knowledgeable, are most probably affected to a lesser degree by the mass media than the less educated and knowledgeable portion of the public, since they have acquired more in-depth information concerning crime. Their sources of information are more likely to include newspapers and magazines, as opposed to merely television. As was reported in Table 4.12, respondents who had higher levels of education and knowledge were almost twice as likely to list newspapers as their main source of information than those with lower levels of education and knowledge.

In sum, both the mainstream media, as well as many in the elite community, including politicians, have an incentive to exaggerate the crime problem. Given that, then, is there any possibility for the mass public to receive unadulterated information concerning crime.

SOLUTIONS?

How do we solve the media's slant or at times outright distortion of facts when it comes to crime and criminal justice? In his book *Who Deliberates?* (1996), Benjamin Page makes a number of suggestions. First, he suggests that "for individual media consumers . . . the answer is easy: be wary and shop around." He argues that it is now easier to obtain different opinions from different media outlets. He also argues that individuals can obtain information from CNN, C-Span, PBS, as well as talk radio. Furthermore, he argues that individuals should "exercise skepticism . . . figure out motivations and ideologies in the newspaper, magazine, or television show you are looking at; watch for its editorial thrust and for slants in the news or information it presents" (p. 126). A major problem with this strategy is that most individuals who would take the time to investigate the news to this degree are likely to be the more educated and more knowledgeable. Furthermore, according to C-Span's own data collected by Statistical Research Inc., viewers of C-Span are quite different demographically from the rest of the country. They are more informed than the average citizen and are more likely than the average citizen to have voted. Some 90% read a local newspaper (12% read *The Wall Street Journal* and 10% read *The New York Times*). Also, 90% of them voted in the last election. This is precisely the group whose members do not have as great a problem in obtaining accurate information.

Another medium of information that Page seems to believe can be put to use is the Internet. This source might also be used by many in the mass public to gather information. At least in the mid 1990s, when the Internet was still new, many who did not tune into C-Span or CNN might quite definitely have "surfed" the Web. Even for younger individuals, and even for many in the inner city, surfing the web for conversation and information is actually "cool," as evidenced by its usage on such cool sources of information as MTV, VH1, as well as the numerous Web-sites used by individuals who would not ordinarily tune in to stations such as CNN and C-Span. However, even here we run into problems. As Page points out, when wandering the Web "be warned about the lack of quality control: the facts you encounter may be fantasies" (p. 126). In other words, the medium of information most likely to attract younger citizens who would not be obtaining information from other sources, is also most likely to attract individuals who are in the business of disseminating outlandish theories to unsuspecting consumers. This is possible, because anyone can post anything on the Internet, unlike television, and to a greater degree newspapers or magazines, that have certain standards regarding the accuracy of what they report.

Another method of having the mass public educate themselves that has received some attention of late has been the concept of "deliberative democracy." Some concepts such as this suffer from similar flaws as the ideas expressed above. For example, one possibility is "Project Vote Smart," which Fishkin (1991, p. 115) states provides "an 800 number, advertised on CNN, which citizens could call to get nonpartisan information about candidate positions." Certain problems with this method immediately come to mind. First, as Fishkin himself notes, even an informational 800 number can be used as a means of disseminating false or misleading information to unsuspecting callers. Also, this again puts an added burden on overworked members of the public, who would be quite irrational to go out of their way to such a great extent in obtaining information. Another of Fishkin's ideas, the national deliberative opinion poll, would have a small number of individuals become extremely knowledgeable on a variety of issues. One of the hopes for the advocates of this is that the attention such events would arouse in the mass media would trickle down to members of the mass public, and help educate them. The catch, of course, is that there is still a problem with the degree to which average members of the mass public will pay attention to such special events. In addition, one must wonder whether or not the mainstream media would even cover such an event—and to what degree and for what length a time period. The massive amount of coverage that Fishkin believes could be provided might be nothing more than wishful thinking. Furthermore, what is needed is not a temporary solution, rather, a continuous incentive for the mass media to properly educate the mass public.

A more realistic idea as to how to diversify the sources of information, and assure more truthful dissemination of information to the mass public, would seem to begin with the elites, as opposed to the mass public. Since the elites would be more aware of the "truth," it is more likely to be this group, through various methods, who can pass along the information to the mass public. Of course, it must be remembered that "anything as vast and complicated as our whole information system is not easy to change" (Page, 1996, p. 127). Instead, what is more realistic are changes in the system, little by little. Page proposes the notion of "campaign truth squads" that can "at least make the media more self-conscious about slanted news and probably curb some of the most blatant excesses" (p. 127). In addition, he lauds media watchgroups, whether they be from the Right or Left.

Another solution focuses its attention not on the media, but on the members of the public themselves. If citizens become more involved in politics on a personal level, they will naturally have a greater interest in acquiring information regarding current political topics. Unfortunately, people in the United States, as opposed to other countries (see Dalton, 1992), look at voting as the highest form of participation. As Page and Shapiro (1992, p. 392) note, "perhaps the most conspicuous deficiency is the lack of opportunity for political learning through direct participation." They continue and explain that "in a country where only about half the eligible citizens vote in presidential elections, where town meetings are rare, where most workplaces are hierarchical, and where most citizens are not mobilized by a congenial issue-oriented party or political group, the educational potential of participation is not fully realized."

This problem of nonparticipation has the potential to be particularly acute in the area of criminal justice. As Page and Shapiro (p. 394) and others (also see Zaller, 1992) point out, it will be extremely hard at times for members of the mass public to obtain accurate information, since "there does seem to be substantial slippage in democratic responsiveness, a substantial discrepancy between what citizens want and what government does, which may result from a dim spotlight that does not direct public attention to unpopular policies—especially when there is bipartisan collusion of the sorts we have already alluded to, and when few or no dissenting elite voices speak up."

Applying these ideas to the area of criminal justice, the question becomes to what extent the mainstream media, as well as elected officials, have a vested interest in exaggerating the crime problem, and in only giving one side of the story in how society should be fighting crime. If one were to apply the ideas of John Zaller, who argues that the opinions of the mass public will become knowledgeable as long as there are two sides to elite opinion and debate, the question becomes: Where can members of the public obtain truthful information and become educated in the current state of affairs regarding issues of criminal justice? If both Democrats and Republicans have an incentive to exaggerate the crime problem and, of course, would not dare sound "soft" on crime, where can members of the mass public turn to obtain alternative opinions? As mentioned, the Internet might provide this, but the information is not trustworthy. Active participation in the political process, as well as the possibility of members of the mass public going well out of their way to obtain information is not probable and might not even be rational. Furthermore, the situation regarding news currently available on crime from the mainstream media might fall within the realm Page and Shapiro (p. 393) describe when they state that at times "the availability of key facts about certain public policies may be low, for reasons of chance or design; the public may have no way (no helpful cue givers, no free information on TV) to know what is going on—to know whether or not the government is doing what the citizens want, for example—and may, therefore have no way of enforcing its will and ensure responsiveness." In other words, even if the members of the mass public wanted to assess different angles to the crime problem, there might not be elite discourse from which to obtain alternative cues. This might help explain why the opinions of the public regarding the death penalty in recent years have become as one-sided as they are.

A possible solution to this particular problem might be to increase "media diversity." Page (p. 127) suggests that media diversity might be achieved by "help(ing) out non-money losing, nonmainstream journals, for example, by contributing, working, publicizing, or at least subscribing to them, and by making sure that neighbors, coworkers, fellow group members, and public officials know about them."

It would seem from the results of the two surveys of this study that members of the legal profession are in a perfect position, if they have the will, to provide diversity within the media. It can be assumed that lawyers, owing to their extensive legal training, would be more likely to have an in-depth understanding of the crime problem, reasons for civil liberties, as well as the connection between crime and the various social causes for crime. In the past few years, since the O.J. Simpson case began (as well as other high-profile cases including the Menendez case), we have seen a proliferation of programs hosted by lawyers, or programs on which lawyers have been billed as featured panelists or experts (e.g., *Burden of Proof* on CNN, *Rivera Live* on CNBC). If indeed lawyers are providing true information with which members of the attentive public can follow and become educated, and in turn educate the mass public, then the ideas Page put forth are beginning to take hold. However, if the lawyers are merely being used by the media in order to legitimize mainstream opinions, then the consequences can be dire indeed. As Page and Shapiro (p. 395) note, "corporations fund foundations and think tanks that produce research studies and support the 'experts' seen on TV, often, presumably (if businessmen behave in a rational fashion) serving corporate purposes." It would be questionable as to whether or not the mainstream media would allow true dissension from mainstream norms even among members of the legal community.

Nonetheless, there is evidence that minority legal opinions during the O.J. Simpson trial and during its aftermath were heard and given a reasonable amount of respect by the mainstream media. Though an overwhelming majority of the white community, including many white elites, believed Simpson to be guilty, most outlets that covered the trial had commentators who differed with each other. In fact, it can be argued that the civil liberties at stake in the case were actually brought forth and explained to the general public. Of course there were those among the public who followed the general flow of information emanating from the trial, yet did not understand the technicalities of the various search and seizure issues covered during the trial. However, as many political scientists have noted (see Popkin, 1991), individuals need not know the intricacies and technicalities of the various issues under discussion to become sufficiently knowledgeable in forming real and stable opinions.

In other words, the Simpson trial and the various talk shows it has spawned might have helped educate the public by causing the public to think about civil liberties and their importance, even if some might have had little interest in the technicalities of the case. As Samuel Popkin explains (1991), the public need not know the particularities of hard-to-follow issues, and yet be labeled rational. He explains (p. 214) that "people will use simplifying assumptions to evaluate complex information." In concluding his book *The Reasoning Voter* (p. 236), he explains that we must "ask not for more sobriety and piety from our citizens, for they are voters, not judges; offer them instead cues and signals which connect their world with the world of politics." Applying these notions to the evidence from the mass survey I conducted, one can hypothesize that if an average citizen were able to follow at least the general arguments during the O.J. Simpson trial, he or she should be able to form rational opinions concerning the specific issues covered by the survey. In addition, since many lawyers and legal scholars have begun appearing on television discussing crime and its societal implications, it is possible that the public might be closer to the time when a media that educates might help it obtain more truthful information.

In short, the public is now in a position where the mainstream TV media seem to be providing more in-depth coverage regarding legal issues. This is not to argue that watching the nightly news, with its continued emphasis on savage crimes, will not influence some opinions away from civil libertarian positions, and that newspapers and magazines do not provide more in depth coverage of crime and the root causes of crime. However, given that television is likely to stay as the number one source of information for many, this might be the best that can be hoped for. It is now in the hands of the lawyers to act as educators in their role as experts on the nightly news, talk shows, and special issue shows (e.g., *Nightline*, *Crossfire*, *Equal Time*). As curious and scary as it may sound to some members of the public, the public's very understanding of the crime problem and criminal justice may be—and ought to be—in the hands of members of the legal profession.

Appendix 1

Survey of the General Public

INTRODUCTION

Hello, I am calling from Columbia University in New York, and conducting a survey on public opinion about the criminal justice system in the United States.

I'm supposed to talk to the adult member of this household who had the most recent birthday—even if he or she isn't at home right now. Thinking only of the people living here who are at least 18 years old, can you tell me who was the last one to have a birthday? [IF INFORMANT DOESN'T KNOW ALL THE BIRTHDAYS] Well, of the ones you do know, who had the last birthday?

[IF INFORMANT DID NOT HAVE THE LAST BIRTHDAY] May I speak to that person, please? [WHEN DESIGNATED RESPONDENT COMES ON THE LINE, RE-INTRODUCE YOURSELF, IF NECESSARY, AND GO QUICKLY TO THE FIRST QUESTION. IF DESIGNATED RESPONDENT IS NOT AVAILABLE, TRY TO MAKE AN APPOINTMENT.]

Note: Responses of don't know and no answer are excluded from the computation of the mean and standard deviation, and therefore are also not included in the total N for all questions, whether or not the mean was computed.

First, I would like to ask your opinion on some issues.

1. Do you favor or oppose the death penalty for persons convicted of murder?

1. favor	Favor (1)	78%
2. oppose	Oppose (2)	20%
8. don't know	Don't know/NA	3%
9. no answer/refuse	Mean	1.20
	Standard Deviation	.40
	N	790

2. Do you favor or oppose the death penalty for persons convicted of rape?

    1. favor   Favor (1)   39%
    2. oppose   Oppose (2)   55%
    8. don't know   Don't know/NA   6%
    9. no answer/refuse   Mean   1.58
                                Standard Deviation   .49
                                N   764

Please tell me whether you favor or oppose the following.

3. Do you favor or oppose allowing the police to view a person's property, which can be viewed from the air, without a search warrant?

    1. favor   Favor (1)   51%
    2. oppose   Oppose (2)   47%
    8. don't know   Don't know/NA   2%
    9. no answer/refuse   Mean   1.48
                                Standard Deviation   .50
                                N   795

4. How about allowing the police who are investigating a crime to use methods such as flashing papers which look like search warrants?

    1. favor   Favor (1)   10%
    2. oppose   Oppose (2)   89%
    8. don't know   Don't know/NA   1%
    9. no answer/refuse   Mean   1.90
                                Standard Deviation   .31
                                N   807

5. What about allowing authorities to use dogs to sniff for drugs in all luggage entering the United States?

    1. favor   Favor (1)   91%
    2. oppose   Oppose (2)   8%
    8. don't know   Don't know/NA   1%
    9. no answer/refuse   Mean   1.08
                                Standard Deviation   .27
                                N   805

6. How about allowing searches of a citizen's trash, placed outside of the person's property, without a search warrant?

1. favor	Favor (1)	49%
2. oppose	Oppose (2)	50%
8. don't know	Don't know/NA	1%
9. no answer/refuse	Mean	1.51
	Standard Deviation	.50
	N	802

7. What about allowing authorities to search a suspect's private body parts for drugs?

1. favor	Favor (1)	55%
2. oppose	Oppose (2)	42%
8. don't know	Don't know/NA	2%
9. no answer/refuse	Mean	1.43
	Standard Deviation	.50
	N	793

8. How about allowing the government to detain a suspected criminal for more than 48 hours without being charged for a specific crime?

1. favor	Favor (1)	30%
2. oppose	Oppose (2)	68%
8. don't know	Don't know/NA	2%
9. no answer/refuse	Mean	1.69
	Standard Deviation	.46
	N	793

9. Do you favor or oppose allowing the police to search any closed containers in a car, during a routine traffic stop, without any strong belief that illegal items are inside the container?

1. favor	Favor (1)	44%
2. oppose	Oppose (2)	55%
8. don't know	Don't know/NA	1%
9. no answer/refuse	Mean	1.56
	Standard Deviation	.50
	N	804

10. How about allowing the police to board any ship or boat, to inspect any documents on board, when the ship is on the open seas?

1. favor	Favor (1)	66%
2. oppose	Oppose (2)	32%
8. don't know	Don't know/NA	2%
9. no answer/refuse	Mean	1.32
	Standard Deviation	.47
	N	795

11. How about allowing the police to stop a suspect who appears to be acting suspiciously, for example, pacing in front of a building at night?

1. favor	Favor (1)	82%
2. oppose	Oppose (2)	18%
8. don't know	Don't know/NA	.5%
9. no answer/refuse	Mean	1.18
	Standard Deviation	.38
	N	808

12. How about allowing the authorities to use undercover police to obtain an admission from a suspect when his lawyer is not present?

1. favor	Favor (1)	35%
2. oppose	Oppose (2)	62%
8. don't know	Don't know/NA	2%
9. no answer/refuse	Mean	1.64
	Standard Deviation	.48
	N	793

13. How about allowing a voluntary admission of a crime even when the suspect asks for a lawyer and the lawyer is not present?

1. favor	Favor (1)	52%
2. oppose	Oppose (2)	47%
8. don't answer	Don't know/NA	1%
9. no answer/refuse	Mean	1.48
	Standard Deviation	.50
	N	803

14. How about allowing evidence which was illegally obtained to be used to contradict witnesses for the defendant?

1. favor	Favor (1)	27%
2. oppose	Oppose (2)	72%
8. don't know	Don't know/NA	1%
9. no answer/refuse	Mean	1.73
	Standard Deviation	.44
	N	800

15. How about allowing the government to frisk (pat down) a suspect if there is probable cause (a good belief) to believe there is incriminating evidence?

1. favor	Favor (1)	81%
2. oppose	Oppose (2)	18%
8. don't answer	Don't know/NA	1%
9. no answer/refuse	Mean	1.18
	Standard Deviation	.39
	N	804

16. How about allowing a suspect who is mentally ill to waive his right to counsel?

1. favor	Favor (1)	17%
2. oppose	Oppose (2)	81%
8. don't know	Don't know/NA	1%
9. no answer/refuse	Mean	1.83
	Standard Deviation	.38
	N	791

Now I'd like to ask you a few questions about different parts of the government. [In all questions below, do not give the choice of none or other, just code as such if such is the case.]

17. Which branch of the federal government do you have the most confidence in: Congress, the Supreme Court, or the presidency?

1. Congress	Congress	19%
2. The Supreme Court	The Supreme Court	40%
3. The President	The President	13%
4. None	None	28%
8. don't know	Don't know/NA	.4%
9. no answer/refuse	N	808

Note: A question order effect experiment was performed with questions 18-24. Half of the respondents were assigned version 1, while the other half were assigned version 2.
Note: Results for questions 18-24 are reported in version 1 and combine the results for both versions of the survey.

Version 1:
18. In general (overall), how much confidence do you have in the federal government's ability to run its national programs? Would say a great deal of confidence, only some confidence, or hardly any confidence at all?

1. a great deal	A great deal (1)	9%
2. only some	Only some (2)	51%
3. hardly any	Hardly any (3)	40%
8. DK	Don't know/NA	1%
9. na/refuse	Mean	2.31
	Standard Deviation	.62
	N	805

19. In the case of <u>the military</u>, how much confidence do you have in the federal government's ability to run the military? A great deal of confidence, only some confidence or hardly any confidence at all?

1. a great deal	A great deal (1)	35%
2. only some	Only some (2)	42%
3. hardly any	Hardly any (3)	21%
8. DK	Don't know/NA	2%
9. na/refuse	Mean	1.86
	Standard Deviation	.74
	N	797

20. How about <u>Social Security</u>? (repeat as needed, how much confidence do you have . . . to run Social Security?)

1. a great deal	A great deal (1)	15%
2. only some	Only some (2)	36%
3. hardly any	Hardly any (3)	47%
8. DK	Don't know/NA	2%
9. na/refuse	Mean	2.32
	Standard Deviation	.73
	N	798

21. How about <u>environmental protection programs</u>? (how much confidence . . . to run environmental protection programs?)

1. a great deal	A great deal (1)	13%
2. only some	Only some (2)	48%
3. hardly any	Hardly any (3)	37%
8. DK	Don't know/NA	3%
9. na/refuse	Mean	2.25
	Standard Deviation	.67
	N	787

22. How about <u>Medicare</u>? (how much confidence . . . to run Medicare?)

1. a great deal	A great deal (1)	13%
2. only some	Only some (2)	40%
3. hardly any	Hardly any (3)	43%
8. DK	Don't know/NA	4%
9. na/refuse	Mean	2.31
	Standard Deviation	.69
	N	776

23. How about <u>assistance to poor families</u>? (how much confidence . . . programs to assist poor families?)

1. a great deal	A great deal (1)	9%
2. only some	Only some (2)	39%
3. hardly any	Hardly any (3)	51%
8. DK	Don't know/NA	2%
9. na/refuse	Mean	2.43
	Standard Deviation	.65
	N	797

24. Missing Question

Version 2:

18. Missing Question

19. How much confidence do you have in the federal government's ability to run the <u>military</u>? Would you say a great deal of confidence, only some confidence, or hardly any confidence at all?

1. a great deal
2. only some
3. hardly any
8. DK
9. na/refuse

20. How about <u>Social Security</u>? How much confidence do you have in the federal government's ability to run Social Security? Would you say a great deal of confidence, only some confidence, or hardly any confidence at all?

1. a great deal
2. only some
3. hardly any
8. DK
9. na/refuse

21. How about <u>environmental protection programs</u>? (repeat as needed, how much confidence . . . to run environmental protection programs?)

    1. a great deal
    2. only some
    3. hardly any
    8. DK
    9. na/refuse

22. How about <u>Medicare</u>? (how much confidence . . . to run Medicare?)

    1. a great deal
    2. only some
    3. hardly any
    8. DK
    9. na/refuse

23. How about <u>assistance to poor families</u>? (how much confidence . . . programs to assist poor families?)

    1. a great deal
    2. only some
    3. hardly any
    8. DK
    9. na/refuse

24. <u>In general</u> (overall), how much confidence do you have in the federal government's ability to run its national programs? (A great deal of confidence, only some confidence or hardly any confidence at all?)

    1. a great deal
    2. only some
    3. hardly any
    8. DK
    9. na/refuse

25. Which of the following comes closest to what you believe to be the role of the Supreme Court in society? Do you believe the Supreme Court should follow the wishes of society or what the Court believes to be right?

    1. The Supreme Court should
       follow the wishes of society.　　　Follow society　　　39%

2. The Supreme Court should follow
   what it believes to be right.   Follow own views   50%
3. depends   Depends   10%
8. don't know   Don't know/NA   .5%
9. no answer/refuse   N   807

26. Do you believe that when people violate a ruling of the Supreme Court,
    they are always wrong, usually wrong, usually not wrong, or never wrong?

1. always   Always (1)   16%
2. usually   Usually (2)   56%
3. usually not   Usually not (3)   24%
4. never   Never (4)   2%
8. don't know   Don't know/NA   2%
9. no answer/refuse   Mean   2.12
                             Standard Deviation   .69
                             N   796

27. How often do you believe that the Constitution gives the police the right to
    enter one's home without a warrant: always, usually, usually not, or never?

1. always   Always (1)   2%
2. usually   Usually (2)   20%
3. usually not   Usually not (3)   27%
4. never   Never (4)   50%
8. don't know   Don't know/NA   1%
9. no answer/refuse   Mean   3.26
                             Standard Deviation   .69
                             N   801

28. Do you believe that reading a suspected criminal his legal rights is always
    a burden (helps cause criminals to go free) on the criminal justice system,
    usually a burden on the criminal justice, usually not a burden on the crim-
    inal justice system, or never a burden on the criminal justice system?

1. always   Always (1)   9%
2. usually   Usually (2)   12%
3. usually not   Usually not (3)   13%
4. never   Never (4)   66%
8. don't know   Don't know/NA   .1%
9. no answer/refuse   Mean   3.37
                             Standard Deviation   1.00
                             N   801

29. How much respect do you have for police in your area—a great deal, some, or hardly any?

1. a great deal of respect	A great deal (1)	64%
2. some respect	Only some (2)	27%
3. hardly any respect	Hardly any (3)	8%
8. don't know	Don't know/NA	1%
9. no answer/refuse	Mean	1.43
	Standard Deviation	.64
	N	804

GENERAL KNOWLEDGE
[All in this area will be open-ended questions.]

Now I would like to ask you some questions of general knowledge. Please do not feel uncomfortable if you do not know the answers. Most of the people questioned do not.

30. Can you tell me who is the chief justice of the United States Supreme Court?

1. William Rhenquist	Wrong answer (0)	92%
2. Other justice	Rhenquist (1)	8%
3. Other name	Don't know/NA	------
8. don't know	Mean	.08
9. no answer/refuse	Standard Deviation	.27
	N	811

31. Can you tell me the name of the only black member on the current United States Supreme Court?

1. Clarence Thomas	Wrong answer (0)	68%
2. Thurgood Marshall	Thomas (1)	32%
3. William Rhenquist	Don't know/NA	------
4. Other justice	Mean	.32
5. Other name	Standard Deviation	.47
6. remembered later when Thomas was mentioned in question 33	N	811
8. don't know		
9. no answer/refuse		

32. How many members are there currently on the United States Supreme Court?

1. 5 or less	Wrong answer (0)	75%
2. 6	Nine justices (1)	25%
3. 7	Don't know/NA	------
4. 8	Mean	.25
5. 9	Standard Deviation	.43
6. 10	N	811
7. 11 or more		
8. don't know		
9. no answer/refuse		

33. Do you believe Clarence Thomas has had a liberal or conservative voting record since joining the Supreme Court?

1. Liberal	Wrong answer (0)	63%
2. Conservative	Conservative (1)	37%
8. don't know	Don't know/NA	------
9. no answer/refuse	Mean	.37
	Standard Deviation	.48
	N	811

34. Do you happen to know what job or political office is now held by Al Gore?

1. Vice-President	Wrong answer (0)	18%
2. Senator	Vice-President (1)	82%
3. Congressperson	Don't know/NA	------
4. Supreme Court Justice	Mean	.82
5. Other position	Standard Deviation	.38
8. don't know	N	811
9. no answer/refuse		

35. Whose responsibility is it to determine if a law is constitutional or not, is it the president, the Congress, or the Supreme Court?

1. President	Wrong answer (0)	38%
2. Congress	Supreme Court(1)	62%
3. Supreme Court	Don't know/NA	------
8. don't know	Mean	.62
9. no answer/refuse	Standard Deviation	.49
	N	811

36. How much of a majority is required for the U.S. Senate and House to over-ride a presidential veto?

1. majority	Wrong answer (0)	52%
2. 2/3s majority	2/3s majority (1)	48%
3. 100%	Don't know/NA	------
4. other amount	Mean	.48
8. don't know	Standard Deviation	.50
9. no answer/refuse	N	811

37. Do you happen to know which party had the most members in the House of Representatives in Washington before the election this past November?

1. Republican	Wrong answer (0)	23%
2. Democrat	Democrat (1)	77%
8. don't know	Don't know/NA	------
9. no answer/refuse	Mean	.77
	Standard Deviation	.42
	N	811

38. Would you say that one of the parties is more conservative than the other at the national level? Which party is more conservative?

1. Republicans	Wrong answer (0)	34%
2. Democrat	Republicans (1)	66%
8. don't know	Don't know/NA	------
9. no answer/refuse	Mean	.66
	Standard Deviation	.48
	N	811

BACKGROUND INFORMATION

For each of the following please tell me whether or not you believe it is a very important factor causing crime today:

39. The lack of income equality

1. yes	Yes (1)	53%
2. no	No (2)	47%
8. don't know	Don't know/NA	.4%
9. no answer/refuse	Mean	1.47
	Standard Deviation	.50
	N	808

40. A legal system that is too lenient on criminals

1. yes	Yes (1)	82%
2. no	No (2)	17%
8. don't know	Don't know/NA	1%
9. no answer/refuse	Mean	1.18
	Standard Deviation	.38
	N	803

41. Liberal Supreme Court decisions that have hurt the efforts of law enforcement

1. yes	Yes (1)	64%
2. no	No (2)	34%
8. don't know	Don't know/NA	2%
9. no answer/refuse	Mean	1.35
	Standard Deviation	.48
	N	795

42. Money being spent on social programs instead of on building prisons

1. yes	Yes (1)	30%
2. no	No (2)	68%
8. don't know	Don't know/NA	2%
9. no answer/refuse	Mean	1.69
	Standard Deviation	.46
	N	793

43. The lack of economic opportunities for the poor and for members of minority groups.

1. yes	Yes (1)	57%
2. no	No (2)	43%
8. don't know	Don't know/NA	.4%
9. no answer/refuse	Mean	1.43
	Standard Deviation	.49
	N	808

44. The media's emphasis on the rights of the accused and not on the rights of the victim

1. yes	Yes (1)	57%
2. no	No (2)	43%
8. don't know	Don't know/NA	.4%
9. no answer/refuse	Mean	1.30
	Standard Deviation	.46
	N	803

45. With regard to the death penalty, would you say blacks have generally been treated the same as whites, less well than whites, or better than whites?

1. the same as whites	Less well (1)	39%
2. less well than whites	The same (2)	53%
3. better than whites	Better than (3)	7%
8. don't know	Don't know/NA	1%
9. no answer/refuse	Mean	1.67
	Standard Deviation	.60
	N	803

46. In general, do you believe that blacks are accused and convicted of criminal acts more than whites, simply because they are black?

1. yes	Yes (1)	39%
2. no	No (2)	60%
8. don't know	Don't know/NA	1%
9. no answer/refuse	Mean	1.61
	Standard Deviation	.49
	N	806

47. Where do you usually get <u>most</u> of your information on crime in the United States? From the newspapers, radio, television, magazines, talking to people, or where?
[Only <u>one</u> answer should be accepted. If respondent gives more than one answer repeat question with an emphasis on the word most.]

1. papers	Papers	21%
2. radio	Radio	10%
3. television	Television	60%
4. magazines	Magazines	2%
5. talking to people	Talking to people	5%
6. other	Other	3%
8. don't know	Don't know/NA	.1%
9. no answer/refuse	N	810

48. On the average day, about how many hours do you personally watch television? [Ask as open-ended question. If "none," skip to 50.]

1. none	none (1)	8%
2. 1 hour	1 hour (2)	31%
3. 2 hours	2 hours (3)	28%
4. 3 hours	3 hours (4)	16%

5. 4 hours	4 hours (5)	9%
6. 5 hours or more	5 hours or more (6)	8%
8. don't know	Don't know/NA	------
9. no answer/refuse	Mean	3.12
	Standard Deviation	1.37
	N	811

49. Do you believe that watching television news makes you more sympathetic toward the rights of those accused of the crime or the rights of those who are victims of crime, or does television news not influence your opinions either way?

1. sympathetic toward the accused	Sympathetic toward the accused	7%
2. sympathetic toward the victim	Sympathetic toward the victim	39%
3. not at all	Not at all	54%
8. don't know	Don't know/NA	1%
9. no answer/refuse	N	740

50. On the average day, about how many hours do you personally read the newspapers? [Ask as open-ended question. If "none," skip to 52.]

1. none	none (1)	32%
2. 1 hour	1 hour (2)	57%
3. 2 hours	2 hours (3)	11%
4. 3 hours	3 hours (4)	.7%
5. 4 hours	4 hours (5)	.1%
6. 5 hours or more	5 hours or more (6)	------
8. don't know	Don't know/NA	------
9. no answer/refuse	Mean	1.81
	Standard Deviation	1.05
	N	811

51. Do you believe that reading the newspaper makes you more sympathetic toward the rights of the accused or towards the rights of the victim, or does reading the newspaper not influence your opinion either way?

1. sympathetic toward the accused	Sympathetic toward the accused	5%
2. sympathetic toward the victim	Sympathetic toward the victim	28%
3. not at all	Not at all	36%
8. don't know	Don't know/NA	.2%
9. no answer/refuse	N	550

52. Do you spend any time listening to talk and call-in shows on the radio?

1. yes [go to 53]	Yes (1)	39%
2. no [go to 55]	No (2)	62%
8. don't know	Don't know/NA	------
9. no answer/refuse	Mean	1.62
	Standard Deviation	.49
	N	811

53. On the average day, about how many hours do you personally listen to talk and call-in shows on the radio?

1. 1 hour	1 hour (1)	19%
2. 2 hours	2 hours (2)	12%
3. 3 hours	3 hours (3)	4%
4. 4 hours	4 hours (4)	1%
5. 5 hours or more	5 hours or more (5)	1%2
8. don't know	Don't know/NA	------
9. no answer/refuse	Mean	1.81
	Standard deviation	1.05
	N	312

54. Due to these radio talk show hosts, do you find yourself becoming more sympathetic toward the rights of the accused, or more sympathetic towards the victim, or do these hosts not influence your opinion either way.

1. sympathetic toward accused	Sympathetic toward the accused	4%
2. sympathetic toward victims	Sympathetic toward the victim	44%
3. not at all	Not at all	53%
8. don't know	Don't know/NA	.1%
9. no answer/refuse	N	311

55. Would you call the area you live in a part of the city, suburb of a city, or nowhere near a big city?

1. city	City	38%
2. suburb	Suburb	33%
3. rural	Rural	29%
8. don't know	Don't know/NA	------
9. no answer/refuse	N	811

56. Is there any area near where you live—that is, within a mile—where you would be afraid to walk alone at night?

1. yes	Yes (1)	42%
2. no	No (2)	58%
8. don't know	Don't know/NA	------
9. no answer/refuse	Mean	1.58
	Standard Deviation	.49
	N	811

57. How about at home at night—do you feel safe and secure or not?

1. yes	Yes (1)	92%
2. no	No (2)	8%
8. don't know	Don't know/NA	------
9. no answer/refuse	Mean	1.09
	Standard Deviation	.28
	N	811

58. In general, do you think the courts in your area deal too harshly, about right, or not harshly enough with criminals?

1. too harshly	Too harshly (1)	4%
2. about right	About right (2)	37%
3. not harshly enough	Not harshly enough (3)	58%
8. don't know	Don't know/NA	1%
9. no answer/refuse	Mean	2.54
	Standard Deviation	.58
	N	804

59. What, if any, is the worst crime that has been committed against you or your immediate family? [first ask open-ended, if "none" continue] vandalism of your car, being mugged, a robbery in your home, physical assault, murder.

1. vandalism of your car	Vandalism of car	11%
2. being mugged	Mugged	5%
3. a robbery in your home	Robbery in home	20%
4. physical assault	Physical assault	7%
5. murder	Murder	5%
8. don't know	Rape	4%
9. no answer/refuse	None	48%
	Don't know/NA	-----
	N	811

60. What is your religious preference? Is it Protestant, Catholic, Jewish, some other religion or no religion?

1. Protestant	Protestant	58%
2. Catholic	Catholic	26%
3. Jewish	Jewish	3%
4. Atheist	Atheist	8%
5. Muslim	Muslim	.2%
6. Other	Other	4%
8. don't know	Don't know/NA	.2%
9. no answer/refuse	N	805

61. Generally speaking, do you usually think of yourself as a Republican, a Democrat, an Independent or what?

1. Republican [go to 62]	Democrat (1)	30%
2. Democrat [go to 63]	Independent (2)	35%
3. Independent [go to 64]	Republican (3)	33%
4. Other	Other	.5%
8. don't know	Don't know/NA	2%
9. no answer/refuse	Mean	2.04
	Standard deviation	.80
	N	799

62. Would you call yourself a strong Republican or a not very strong Republican?

1. strong Republican	Strong Republican (1)	51%
2. not very strong Republican	Not very strong Republican (2)	49%
8. don't know	Don't know/NA	------
9. no answer/refuse	Mean	1.49
	Standard Deviation	.50
	N	274

63. Would you call yourself a strong Democrat or a not very strong Democrat?

1. strong Democrat	Strong Democrat (1)	34%
2. not very strong Democrat	Not very strong Democrat (2)	66%
8. don't know	Don't know	------
9. no answer/refuse	Mean	1.67
	Standard Deviation	.47
	N	242

64. Do you think of yourself as closer to the Republican party or Democratic party?

1. Republican party	Republican party	18%
2. Democratic party	Democratic party	20%
3. Neither party	Neither party	62%
4. don't know	Don't know	.4%
9. no answer/refuse	N	280

Based upon questions 61-64, a seven-point scale measuring partisan identification was created:

Strong Democrat (1)	9%
Democrat (2)	20%
Independent, closer to Democrats (3)	7%
Independent (4)	22%
Independent, closer to Republicans (5)	6%
Republican (6)	17%
Strong Republican (7)	17%
NA	2%
Means	4.15
Standard deviation	2.02
N	796

65. In general, when it comes to politics, do you usually think of yourself as a liberal, a conservative, a moderate, or what?

1. liberal [go to 66]	Liberal (1)	17%
2. conservative [go to 67]	Moderate (2)	42%
3. moderate [go to 68]	Conservative (3)	36%
4. other	Other	.1%
8. don't know	Don't know/NA	4%
9. no answer/refuse	Mean	2.20
	Standard deviation	.72
	N	780

66. Do you think of yourself as a strong liberal or a not very strong liberal?

1. strong liberal	Strong liberal (1)	36%
2. not very strong liberal	Not very strong liberal (2)	64%
8. don't know	Don't know/NA	------
9. no answer/refuse	Mean	1.64
	Standard Deviation	.48
	N	141

67. Do you think of yourself aş a strong conservative or a not very strong conservative?

1. strong conservative	Strong conservative (1)	36%
2. not very strong conservative	Not very strong conservative (2)	64%
8. don't know	Don't know/NA	------
9. no answer/refuse	Mean	1.64
	Standard Deviation	.48
	N	295

68. Do you think of yourself as more like a liberal or more like a conservative?

1. more like a liberal	More like a liberal	22%
2. more like a conservative	More like a conservative	24%
3. neither	Neither	54%
8. don't know	Don't know/NA	------
9. no answer/refuse	N	344

Based upon questions 65-68, a seven-point scale measuring political ideology was created:

Strong liberal (1)	6%
Liberal (2)	11%
Moderate, closer to liberal (3)	9%
Moderate (4)	23%
Moderate, but closer to conservative (5)	10%
Conservative (6)	23%
Strong conservative (7)	13%
NA	4%
Means	4.47
Standard deviation	1.79
N	780

69. What kind of work do you do?
    If not answered ask, what is your job called? [PROBE] What do you actually do on the job? [PROBE] Tell me, what are some of the main duties? [PROBE] What kind of work place do you work for? [FIRST ASK AS OPEN-ENDED QUESTION—ONLY PRY IF NECESSARY.]

    1. Not in workforce (student, homemaker, etc.)
    2. Major executive, management, and administrative
    3. Owner (small retail store, business or farm)
    4. Advanced professional (engineer, architect, lawyer, journalist)
    5. White collar, clerical (nonsupervisory)
    6. Skilled or semiskilled labor
    7. Unskilled labor

8. don't know
9. no answer/refuse

Not in workforce	24%
Executive or management	.4%
Owner	4%
Advanced professional	14%
Skilled or semiskilled labor	25%
Unskilled labor	33%
Don't know/NA	1%
N	810

70. Are you currently: married, widowed, divorced, separated, or have you never been married?

1. married	Married	57%
2. widowed	Widowed	10%
3. divorced	Divorced	11%
4. separated	Separated	2%
5. never been married	Never been married	20%
8. don't know	Don't know/NA	------
9. no answer/refuse	N	811

71. If married, how many people, including your spouse, live in the household?

1. Two	One	20%
2. Three	Two	31%
3. Four or more	Three	20%
8. don't know	Four or more	29%
9. no answer/refuse	Don't know/NA	.1%
	N	810

72. How old were you on your last birthday? [Ask as open-ended question. Only give choices if necessary.]

		Lock '95	SSI*
1. 18 to 24	18 to 24 (1)	12%	14%
2. 25 to 33	25 to 33 (2)	19%	22%
3. 34 to 43	34 to 43 (3)	23%	21%
4. 44 to 64	44 to 64 (4)	30%	26%
5. 65 or over	65 or over (5)	17%	17%
8. don't know	Don't know/NA	------	
9. no answer/refuse	Means	3.20	
	Standard deviation	1.26	
	N	811	

*SSI—Survey Sampling Inc.

73. What race or ethnic group do you consider yourself? [If necessary: we mean white, black, Asian, Hispanic, Native-America, or what?]

		Lock '95	NORC*
1. White	White	85%	84%
2. Black	Black	11%	9%
3. Asian	Asian	1%	1%
4. Hispanic	Hispanic	4%	4%
5. Native-American	Native-American	1%	
6. All others (please specify)	All others	.2%	.6%
8. don't know	Don't know/NA	------	
9. no answer/refuse	N	801	

*NORC—National Opinion Research Center

74. What is the highest grade of school or year of college you completed? [Ask as open-ended question.]

1. Grade school education (completed 8th grade)
2. Some high school education (completed 9th to 11th grade)
3. High school graduate (completed 12th grade)
4. Completed one to three years of college (13 to 15 years of education)
5. College graduate (completed 16 years of education)
6. Some graduate work (completed more than 17 years of education)
7. Graduate degree
8. don't know
9. no answer/refuse

	Lock '95	NORC
Grade school education (1)	4%	5.6%
Some high school education (2)	10%	10.5%
High school graduate (3)	34%	33.7%
Completed one to three years of college (4)	24%	21.9%
College graduate (5)	17%	14.7%
Some graduate work (6)	3%	10.9%*
Graduate degree (7)	8%	2.7%
Don't know/NA	------	
Means	3.83	
Standard deviation	1.46	
N	811	

*Variations are caused by different methods used to code M.A.

75. [Only ask if necessary] What sex are you?

		Lock '95	CACI Marketing
1. Male	Male	51%	48%
2. Female	Female	49%	52%
8. don't know	Don't know/NA	------	
9. no answer/refuse	N	811	

76. If you added together the yearly incomes of all the members of your family living at home last year, would the total of all their incomes be less than $20,000, or more than $40,000, or somewhere in-between?
[IF LESS THAN $20,000] Would the total of all their incomes be less than $10,000?
[IF IN BETWEEN] Would the total of all their incomes be less than $30,000 or more than $30,000?
[IF MORE THAN $40,000] Would the total of all their incomes be between $40,000 and $50,000, or between $50,000 and $60,000, or more than that?

		Lock '95	NORC
1. Less than $10,000	Less than $10,000 (1)	10%	11.9%
2. $10,000 to $19,999	$10,000 to $19,999 (2)	20%	17.1%
3. $20,000 to $29,999	$20,000 to $29,999 (3)	19%	17.3%
4. $30,000 to $39,999	$30,000 to $39,999 (4)	16%	16.4%
5. $40,000 to $49,999	$40,000 to $49,999 (5)	12%	13.0%
6. $50,000 to $60,000	$50,000 to $60,000 (6)	6%	8%
7. More than $60,000	More than $60,000 (7)	14%	16.3%
8. don't know	Mean	3.76	
9. no answer/refuse	Don't know/NA	3%	
	Standard Deviation	1.89	
	N	789	

77. Have you or a family member ever been accused or convicted of a crime? *Asked of half the survey.*

1. Yes	Yes (1)	19%
2. No	No (2)	80%
	Mean	1.81
	Standard deviation	.39
	N	303

Thank you for participating in our survey.

Appendix 2

Survey of Legal Elite (Lawyers)

December 1994

Dear Attorney,

We are conducting a study concerning legal experts' attitudes toward issues of criminal justice. Your responses will be kept strictly confidential. The study's results will be reported only as aggregate statistics. Your response is important to assure that we obtain a broad and representative sample of expert opinion. There is a check-off box on the last page of the survey, if you would like a copy of the study's results. If you have any questions concerning the survey, you can call Shmuel Lock at (718) 338-0553 or Professor Robert Y. Shapiro at (212) 854-3944. We have provided a stamped envelope for your convenience. We thank you in advance for taking part in our survey.

Sincerely yours,
Shmuel Lock

Note: Responses of don't know and no answer are excluded from the computation of the mean and standard deviation, and therefore are also not included in the total N for all questions, whether or not the mean was computed.

For each of the following, please indicate the choice that comes closest to your opinion.

1. The death penalty for persons convicted of murder.
   favor ___ oppose ___

Favor (1)	57%
Oppose (2)	42%

NA   1%
Mean   1.43
Standard deviation   .50
N   406

2. The death penalty for persons convicted of rape.
   favor ___ oppose ___

   Favor (1)   20%
   Oppose (2)   78%
   NA   2%
   Mean   1.79
   Standard deviation   .40
   N   403

3. Allowing the police to view a person's property, which can be viewed from
   the air, without a search warrant.
   favor ___ oppose ___

   Favor (1)   62%
   Oppose (2)   37%
   NA   2%
   Mean   1.37
   Standard deviation   .48
   N   404

4. Allowing the police who are investigating a crime to use methods such as
   flashing papers, which look like search warrants.
   favor ___ oppose ___

   Favor (1)   5%
   Oppose (2)   94%
   NA   1%
   Mean   1.95
   Standard deviation   .22
   N   406

5. Allowing authorities to use dogs to sniff for drugs in all luggage entering the
   United States.
   favor ___ oppose ___

   Favor (1)   86%
   Oppose (2)   13%
   NA   .2%

Mean	1.14
Standard deviation	.34
N	409

6. Allowing searches of a citizen's trash, placed outside of the person's property, without a search warrant.
   favor ____ oppose ____

Favor (1)	64%
Oppose (2)	36%
NA	------
Mean	1.36
Standard deviation	.48
N	410

7. Allowing authorities to search a suspect's private body parts for drugs.
   favor ____ oppose ____

Favor (1)	43%
Oppose (2)	54%
NA	3%
Mean	1.56
Standard deviation	.50
N	396

8. Allowing the government to detain a suspected criminal for more than 48 hours without being charged for a specific crime.
   favor ____ oppose ____

Favor (1)	12%
Oppose (2)	87%
NA	1%
Mean	1.88
Standard deviation	.33
N	405

9. Allowing the police to search any closed containers in a car, during a routine traffic stop, without any strong belief that illegal items are inside the container.
   favor ____ oppose ____

Favor (1)	10%
Oppose (2)	90%
NA	.2%

Mean	1.90
Standard deviation	.30
N	405

10. Allowing the police to board any ship or boat, to inspect any documents on board, when the ship is on the open seas.
    favor ___ oppose ___

Favor (1)	35%
Oppose (2)	62%
NA	3%
Mean	1.64
Standard deviation	.48
N	399

11. Allowing the police to stop a suspect who appears to be acting suspiciously, for example, pacing in front of a building at night.
    favor ___ oppose ___

Favor (1)	64%
Oppose (2)	35%
NA	1%
Mean	1.35
Standard deviation	.48
N	406

12. Allowing the authorities to use undercover police to obtain an admission from a suspect when his/her lawyer is not present.
    favor ___ oppose ___

Favor (1)	25%
Oppose (2)	73%
NA	2%
Mean	1.75
Standard deviation	.44
N	403

13. Allowing a voluntary admission of a crime even when the suspect asks for a lawyer and the lawyer is not present.
    favor ___ oppose ___

Favor (1)	29%
Oppose (2)	71%
NA	.7%

Mean   1.71
Standard deviation   .45
N   407

14. Allowing evidence which was illegally obtained to be used to contradict witnesses for the defendant.
favor ___ oppose ___

Favor (1)   32%
Oppose (2)   67%
NA   1%
Mean   1.67
Standard deviation   .47
N   406

15. Allowing the authorities to frisk (pat down) a suspect if there is probable cause (a good belief) to believe there is incriminating evidence.
favor ___ oppose ___

Favor (1)   79%
Oppose (2)   20%
NA   1%
Mean   1.20
Standard deviation   .40
N   405

16. Allowing a suspect who is mentally ill to waive right to counsel.
favor ___ oppose ___

Favor (1)   8%
Oppose (2)   90%
NA   2%
Mean   1.92
Standard deviation   .28
N   404

17. Which branch of the federal government do you have the most confidence in?
Congress ___ The Supreme Court ___ The President ___

Congress   8%
Supreme Court   74%
President   8%
None   8%
NA   1%
N   405

18. Which of the following comes closest to what you believe to be the role of the Supreme Court in society?
The Supreme Court should follow the wishes of society ___
The Supreme Court should follow what it believes to be right ___

Society	12%
Court	77%
Neither	3%
Law	2%
Constitution	5%
NA	2%
N	403

19. Do you believe that when people violate a ruling of the Supreme Court they are:
always wrong ___ usually wrong ___ usually not wrong ___
never wrong ___

Always (1)	14%
Usually (2)	75%
Usually not (3)	5%
Never (4)	1%
NA	5%
Means	3.17
Standard deviation	.53
N	388

20. How often do you believe that the constitution gives the police the right to enter one's home without a warrant?
always ___ usually ___ usually not ___ never ___

Always (1)	1%
Usually (2)	5%
Usually not (3)	70%
Never (4)	22%
NA	2%
Means	3.17
Standard deviation	.53
N	403

21. Do you believe that reading a suspected criminal his legal rights is a burden on the criminal justice system?
always ___ usually ___ usually not ___ never ___

Always (1)	4%
Usually (2)	5%
Usually not (3)	38%
Never (4)	53%
NA	.5%
Means	3.40
Standard deviation	.76
N	408

22. How much respect do you have for police in your area?
    a great deal of respect ___ some respect ___ hardly any respect ___

Great deal (1)	43%
Only some (2)	46%
Hardly any (3)	10%
NA	.7%
Means	1.66
Standard deviation	.65
N	407

For each of the following, please indicate whether or not you believe it is a very important factor causing crime today.

23. The lack of income equality
    yes ___ no ___

Yes (1)	52%
No (2)	48%
NA	.7%
Means	1.48
Standard deviation	.50
N	407

24. A legal system that is too lenient on criminals
    yes ___ no ___

Yes (1)	51%
No (2)	48%
NA	1%
Means	1.48
Standard deviation	.50
N	405

25. Liberal Supreme Court decisions that have hurt the efforts of law enforcement.

yes ___ no ___

Yes (1)	30%
No (2)	69%
NA	1%
Means	1.70
Standard deviation	.46
N	405

26. Money being spent on social programs, instead of on building prisons.

yes ___ no ___

Yes (1)	24%
No (2)	74%
NA	2%
Means	1.76
Standard deviation	.43
N	402

27. The lack of economic opportunities for the poor and for members of minority groups.

yes ___ no ___

Yes (1)	65%
No (2)	33%
NA	2%
Means	1.34
Standard deviation	.47
N	402

28. The media's emphasis on the rights of the accused and not on the rights of
the victim.

yes ___ no ___

Yes (1)	37%
No (2)	62%
NA	2%
Means	1.63
Standard deviation	.48
N	402

29. With regard to the death penalty, would you say blacks have generally been treated:
    the same as whites ___ less well than whites ___ better than whites ___

Less well (1)	62%
Same as (2)	32%
Better than (3)	4%
NA	2%
Mean	1.42
Standard deviation	.58
N	404

30. In general, do you believe that blacks are accused and convicted of criminal activities more than whites simply because they are black?
    yes ___ no ___

Yes (1)	37%
No (2)	62%
NA	1%
Means	1.62
Standard deviation	.49
N	406

31. What would you call the area you live in?
    city ___ suburb ___ rural ___

City	39%
Suburb	48%
Rural	13%
NA	.2%
N	409

32. Is there any area near where you live—that is, within a mile—where you would be afraid to walk alone at night?
    yes ___ no ___

Yes (1)	44%
No (2)	55%
NA	.5%
Means	1.62
Standard deviation	.49
N	409

33. How about at home at night—do you feel safe and secure or not?
    yes ___ no ___

Yes (1)	91%
No (2)	9%
NA	.5%
Means	1.09
Standard deviation	.28
N	408

34. In general, do you think the courts in your area deal with criminals:
    too harshly ___ about right ___ not harshly enough ___

Too harsh (1)	8%
About right (2)	60%
Not harsh enough (3)	30%
NA	2%
Mean	2.22
Standard deviation .58	
N	401

35. What if any, is the worst crime that has been committed against you or your immediate family?
    vandalism of your car ___ being mugged ___ a robbery in your home ___
    physical assault ___ murder ___ other ___

Car	34%
Mugged	9%
Robbery in home	32%
Physical assault	9%
Murder	3%
Rape	2%
None	11%
Other	1%
NA	.5%
N	403

36. Generally speaking, do you think of yourself as a:
    Strong Democrat ___ Democrat ___
    Independent, but closer to Democrat ___ Independent ___
    Independent, but closer to Republican ___
    Republican ___ Strong Republican ___

Strong Democrat (1)	12%
Democrat (2)	16%
Independent, closer to Democrat (3)	16%
Independent (4)	9%
Independent, closer to Republicans (5)	19%
Republican (6)	19%
Strong Republican (7)	8%
NA	1%
Means	3.96
Standard deviation	1.89
N	405

37. In general, when it comes to politics, do you think of yourself as a:
    Strong liberal ___ Liberal ___ Moderate, but closer to a liberal ___
    Moderate ___ Moderate, but closer to a conservative ___
    Conservative ___ Strong conservative ___

Strong Liberal (1)	8%
Liberal (2)	10%
Moderate, but closer to liberal (3)	21%
Moderate (4)	17%
Moderate, but closer to conservative (5)	20%
Conservative (6)	17%
Strong Conservative (7)	5%
NA	1%
Means	4.07
Standard deviation	1.65
N	404

38. What is your religious preference?
    Protestant ___ Catholic ___ Jewish ___ Atheist ___ Muslim ___
    Other ___

	Lock '95	McGuire '93
Protestant	43%	53%
Catholic	27%	29%
Jewish	16%	12%
Atheist	8%	
Muslim	------	
Other	5%	6%*
NA	1%	
N	406	

*McGuire combined Atheists and Others

39. What kind of law do you practice?
    See Table 6.1 for frequencies.

40. Are you currently:
    married ___ widowed ___ divorced ___ separated ___
    never been married ___

Married	78%
Widowed	4%
Divorced	9%
Separated	1%
Never been married	8%
NA	.2%
N	409

41. If married, how many people, including your spouse, live in the household?
    two ___ three ___ four or more ___

One	20%
Two	33%
Three	13%
Four or more	34%
NA	.2%
N	409

42. How old were you on your last birthday?
    18 to 24 ___ 25 to 33 ___ 34 to 43 ___ 44 to 64 ___ 65 or over ___

25-33 (2)	8%
34-43 (3)	29%
44-64 (4)	43%
65- (5)	21%
NA	.2%
Means	3.77
Standard deviation	.87
N	409

43. What race or ethnic group do you consider yourself?
    White ___ Black ___ Asian ___ Hispanic ___ Native-American ___
    Other ___

	Lock '95	McGuire '93
White	94%	
Black	2%	2%
Asian	1%	
Hispanic	2%	2%
Native-American	1%	
Other	------	
NA	.2%	
N	409	

44. Gender?
male ___ female ___

	Lock '95	Martindale Hubbell
Male	78%	82%
Female	22%	18%
NA	.2%	
N	409	

If you wish to receive a copy of the summary of the survey's findings, please mark here. _____

Yes	66%
No	34%
N	409

Appendix 3

Summary of the Law: Criminal Procedure

This Appendix provides a basic background to the areas of the law covered by the survey. Full citations of the cases are presented in the Bibliography.

1. Arrest, search and seizure.
   a. Which areas should not be protected by the fourth amendment, and therefore eliminate the need for a warrant to be obtained before a search is performed?

   Katz—person must have actual and reasonable expectations of privacy. (1967)

   Oliver—open fields beyond one's curtilage (i.e., close proximity to home, steps made to ensure its privacy) are not protected by the fourth amendment (no reasonable expectation of privacy). (1984)

   Dow Chemical Co.—property may fall within the curtilage for physical trespass, yet not for aerial observation (i.e., no warrant needed to view fields from plane). (1986)

   Knotts—use of an electronic beeper to monitor defendants movements on public roads does not violate a driver's expectations of privacy. (1983)

   Place—it is not a fourth amendment search when dogs perform "sniff tests" to search for drugs in luggage. (1983)

   Smith—police need not obtain a warrant to install a pen register (i.e., one has no reasonable expectation of privacy in the numbers he calls, even from own home). (1979)

   Miller—no reasonable expectation of privacy on items or information transferred to third persons (e.g., checks or financial statements given to bank). (1976)

   Jacobsen—when search of said property is performed by a private individual, expectation of privacy disappears. (1984)

Greenwood—trash, placed outside of one's property, may be searched without a warrant. (1988)

Hudson—no legitimate expectation of privacy in one's prison cell. (1984)

Olson—overnight guest has expectation of privacy (hence police need permission of owner or warrant to search). (1990)

b. How much probable cause is needed for a search to be conducted?

Wong Sun—it must be more likely than not that the arrest or search is justified, even under a warrantless situation. (1963)

Garrison—if police erroneously, but reasonably and honestly, believe false information was given to a magistrate to obtain a warrant, the warrant is not invalid. (1987)

c. How much information is needed to obtain a warrant and how specific must the warrant be?

Gates—identity of informant not necessary. Courts look at totality of circumstances. (1983)

Winston—interest of individual in privacy balanced against society's interest. (1985)

Montoya de Hernandez—it may be reasonable to pump a suspected defendant's alimentary canal. (1985)

2. Warrantless arrests and searches.

a. What type of circumstances allow for a warrantless arrest and search?

Payton—without exigent circumstances the police may not enter a private home. (1980)

Welsh—seriousness of offense can be considered in determining exigency. (1984)

Riverside—postarrest probable cause hearing should be made within forty-eight hours. (1991)

Garner—use of deadly force to arrest fleeing suspect is unreasonable when suspect poses no immediate threat to anyone. (1985)

b. What is the extent of the warrantless search that may be conducted?

Chadwick—there must be some possibility that suspect can reach area being searched (i.e., to destroy evidence or to harm officers). (1977)

Belton—during custodial arrest, the entire passenger compartment of car contents and contents of container in the compartment can be searched. (1981)

Maryland v. Buie—when arrest takes place in home, protective sweep of entire home is possible under certain circumstances (officers fear for safety due to possible dangerous person on premises). (1990)

Lafayette—no exception needed when police conduct inventory of prisoner's possessions, even if it was possible to obtain warrant. (1983)

c. How exigent must the circumstances be to do away with the warrant?

Cupp—must be in imminent danger of losing evidence due to defendant's destruction of the evidence. (1973)

Steagald—police may not enter one's private dwelling to arrest another unless they are in hot pursuit. (1981)

d. What areas should be called "in plain view" of officers, and hence nullify the need for the warrant?

Arizona v. Hicks—at moment of sight police must have probable cause that object is incriminating. (1987)

Dickerson—at moment police touch the defendant, they must have probable cause to believe that item felt is incriminating. (1993)

e. Should all the ordinary rules apply to an automobile?

Chambers—there is a looser standard for cars, as opposed to houses (e.g., once police have taken driver and his car to police station, they may search his car without a warrant). (1970)

Ross—if search of car is permitted, search of closed containers is also permitted. (1982)

Acevedo—police may purposefully wait till defendant caries container into his car, in order to be allowed to search it without warrant. (1991)

Class—during traffic stop, officers allowed to reach into car to enable himself to read the VIN number, when defendant has exited the car. (1986)

Colorado—inventory search of impounded vehicle allows one to search closed containers as well (protects police from false claims of theft). (1987) But, *Wells* states that search must not be merely trick to discover incriminating evidence. (1990)

f. What actions are needed by the defendant to show that he or she consents to the search?

Schneckloth—one need not necessarily know that he had a right to refuse his consent, to validate his consent (such knowledge is only one factor among many to be considered). (1973)

Mendenhall—defendant's subjective beliefs are what is relevant (did he intend to consent?). (1980)

Jimeno—when scope of consent is unclear, and thing to be searched is a car, the search of closed containers is assumed. (1991)

g. When may third persons consent to the search of another?

Rodriguez—if police reasonably but mistakenly believe that person consenting has authority to do so, search is valid. (1990)

Coolidge—irrelevant that consenter knows not the purpose of the search. (1971)

h. When are stop and frisk stops permissible (i.e., when actual probable cause is not in existence)?

Sokolow—modest amount of suspicion is enough to justify a stop (number of acts together make suspect look like drug dealer). (1989)

White—look at totality of the circumstances in judging an informant's tip. (1971)

Montoya de Hernandez—detention of traveler for forty-eight hours to find drugs in her rectum is justified due to law enforcement's needs. (1985)

   i. Should the same rules apply to regulatory searches?

Villamonte-Marquez—even where probable cause is lacking, authorities may board any vessel, and inspect any documents on board, when ship is headed on high seas. (1983)

Sitz—police may set up checkpoint on highway to test drivers for drunkenness without any suspicion about any particular driver. (1990)

Griffen—those on parole or probation are subject to occasional search, even without probable cause. (1987)

3. Electronic surveillance and undercover agents.

   a. Should wiretapping ever be allowed?

Goldman—microphone placed against wall of private office not physical trespass. (1942)

Katz—rejected *Goldman*; there is a search and seizure even if conversations are intangible, hence, fourth amendment protects people's speech. (1967)

Scott—though government must make effort, when wiretap approved, to minimize intercepting innocent conversations, rarely will a violation be found for failing to attempt to minimize the eavesdropping of innocent talk. (1978)

   b. Should undercover agents ever be allowed?

Lewis—unbugged secret agents are okay. It's defendant's fault for misplacing his trust. (1966)

   c. What constitutes entrapment?

Russell—there is no constitutional angle on entrapment, state law rules. (1973)

4. Confessions and police interrogations.

   a. When is one in custody, and hence triggers the need for Miranda warnings?

Berkemer—stops of motorists for minor traffic violations are not custodial. (1984)

Perkins—even if defendant is in jail and he does not know that he is talking to an undercover agent there, he is not in custody (no police-dominated atmosphere). (1990)

   b. Under what conditions does the public safety exception to the Miranda rule apply?

Quarles—Court stated that Miranda rules are not constitutional rights but merely are prophylactic measures. Hence, one can take a cost-benefit perspective. When officer has reasonable concern for public safety, warnings may be overlooked. (1984)

   c. What type of warnings are required under Miranda?

Duckworth—even ambiguous warnings containing phrases such as "we have no way of giving you a lawyer, but one will be appointed for you, if you wish, if and when you go to court," will be acceptable. (1989)

d. What actions are needed by the defendants to show that he has waived his Miranda rights?

Moran—use of trickery by police to discourage client from seeing lawyer, even deliberate deception is allowed. (1986)

Connelly—even if suspect's waiver is caused by his mental illness, absent police coercion, waiver is valid, no matter how irrational the decision is. (1986)

Spring—even if at time of waiver suspect believes that police are focusing on minor crime, while really there is a focus on a major crime, waiver allowed. (1987)

Minnick—if suspect asks for and consults with a lawyer, and thereafter is interrogated by police without the lawyer, the defendant's rights are deemed violated. (1990)

Harvey—if defendant asks for lawyer during arraignment, but police initiate questioning anyway, his words may be entered for impeachment purposes but not for substantive use. (1990)

McNeil—requesting a lawyer is charge specific (if one asks for A lawyer for charge a he can still be questioned about charge B). (1991)

e. Should grand jury witnesses receive any protection from Miranda?

Dionisio—rights do not apply and it is not a custodial environment. (1973)

Mandujano—just because warnings are not given, perjury will still be punished. (1976)

f. Even if Miranda applies to a particular interrogation, should the poisoned testimony be allowed for impeachment purposes?

Doyle—defendant's silence at time of arrest may not be used to impeach his testimony at trial. (1976)

Greer—however, prosecution may strategically bring up defendant's silence yet not have the trial reversed. (1987)

5. Lineups and other pretrial identification procedures.

a. When does the privilege against self-incrimination take hold?

Schmerber—an involuntary blood test is not self-incrimination since it is not testimonial or communicative. (1966)

Neville—if defendant refuses to take blood test, prosecutor can comment upon this at trial. (1983)

b. When does the right to counsel take hold?

Kirby—no right to counsel before formal proceedings begin (e.g., at lineups). (1972)

6. The exclusionary rule.

a. Who should have standing to assert this rule?

Alderman—only those whose rights were violated by the search itself— not those hurt by the introduction of the damaging evidence. (1969)

Rawlings—defendant must have a legitimate expectation of privacy on items seized; mere ownership is not enough. (1980)

Olson—an overnight guest can object to a search where he is staying even though he does not own the premises. (1990)

Padilla—membership in a conspiracy does not give members an automatic right to object to the search of another member. Each must show that he had an expectation of privacy. (1993)

b. When should the rule apply?

Harris—evidence can always be use to impeach the defendant's trial testimony. (1971)

James—illegally obtained evidence cannot be used to impeach testimony of defense witnesses other than defendant himself. (1990)

c. When should the good-faith exception be applied?

Sheppard—as long as judge claims he will amend warrant, officer can rely on such assurances. (1984)

Leon—reasonable reliance on search warrant, which turns out to be unsupported by probable cause, does not invalidate search. (1984)

7. The right to counsel.

a. Which procedures should this right be attached to?

Argersinger—all indigent misdemeanor defendants faced with a possible jail sentence have a right to counsel. (1972)

Baldasar—if defendant is convicted for misdemeanor where right to counsel does not attach, this conviction cannot increase a subsequent sentence for a different crime. (1980)

b. At which stages should this right apply?

Coleman—right attaches at preliminary hearing, though reversal not needed if denial was harmless error. (1970)

Estelle—psychiatric examination to determine one's need for death sentence requires counsel. (1981)

c. What is needed to waive this right?

Brewer—waiver must be knowing and intelligent. (1977)

Connelly—state must prove waiver by a preponderance of the evidence. (1986)

d. What quality of service is guaranteed by this right?

Strickland—to require reversal, defendant must show his counsel was both deficient and probably caused the result. (1984)

Morris—defendant has no right to specific attorney (e.g., if attorney is hospitalized the case must go on). (1983)

Moulton—evidence which would be legal in one case, yet illegal in another case cannot be used in the second case. (1985)

I will now list the areas of criminal procedure which I have included in my study. In parentheses are the cases which are applicable to the stated areas of the law. The cases also show how the law has evolved over time.

1. Arrest, search and seizure.
   a. Which areas should be protected by the fourth amendment? (*Katz, Dunn, Oliver, Dow Chemical Co., Ciraolo*)
   b. How much probable cause is needed for a search to be conducted? (*Wong Sun, Garrison, Mallory*)
   c. How much information is needed to obtain a warrant and how specific must the warrant be? (*Aguilar, Gates, Alabama, Harris, Zurcher, Ker, Bowers, Horton, Montoya de Hernandez*)
2. Warrantless arrests and searches.
   a. What type of circumstances allow for a warrantless arrest and search? (*Watson, Payton, Welsh, Tennessee*)
   b. What type of crimes allow for the "search incident to arrest" exception to apply? (*Rabinowitz, Chimel, Chadwick, Belton, Maryland*)
   c. How exigent must the circumstances be to do away with the warrant? (*Cupp, Steagald*)
   d. What areas should be called in "plain view"? (*Arizona, Horton*)
   e. Should all the ordinary rules apply to an automobile as well? (*Chambers, Cardwell, Ross, New York, Colorado*)
   f. What action are needed for consent? (*Schneckloth, Mendenhall*)
   g. When may third persons consent to the search of another? (*Matlock, Rodriguez*)
   h. Should the same rule apply to regulatory searches? (*Camara, Michigan, Villamonte-Marquez, Michigan Department of Police*)
3. Electronic surveillance and undercover agents.
   a. Should wiretapping ever be allowed? (*Goldman, Katz, Scott*)
   b. Should undercover agents ever be allowed? (*Lee, Lopez, White*)
   c. What constitutes entrapment? (*Russell*)
4. Confessions and police interrogation.
   a. What is a voluntary confession? (*Brown, Spano, Escobedo*)
   b. When should the Miranda rule apply? (*Miranda*)
   c. When is one in custody? (*Illinois, Beckwith, Berkemer*)
   d. Under what condition should the public safety apply? (*Quarles*)
   e. what actions are needed by the defendant to show that he has waived his Miranda rights? (*Fox, Duckworth, Moran, Connelly, Harvey*)
   f. Should grand jury witnesses receive any protection from Miranda? (*Dionisio, Mandujano*)
   g. Even if Miranda applies, should the poisoned testimony be allowed for impeachment purposes? (*Greer, Doyle*)

5. Lineups and other pretrial identification procedures.
   a. When does the privilege against self-incrimination take hold? (*Schmerber*, *Neville*)
   b. When does the right to counsel take hold? (*Gilbert*, *Moore*)
6. The exclusionary rule.
   a. Who should have standing to assert this rule? (*Alderman*, *Rawlings*, *Olson*)
   b. When should the rule apply? (*Harris*, *James*)
   c. Should the good faith exceptions be applied? (*Leon*, *Sheppard*)
7. The right to counsel.
   a. Which procedures should this right be applied to? (*Argersinger*, *Baldasar*)
   b. At which stages should this right apply? (*Moran*, *Coleman*, *Estelle*)
   c. What is needed to waive this right? (*Brewer*, *Connelly*)
   d. What quality of service is guaranteed by this right? (*Strickland*, *Morris*, *Moulton*)

Appendix 4

The National Surveys

The national survey data reported here were obtained from a survey of the general public that was conducted by telephone from December 26, 1994, through January 16, 1995. In all, there were 811 completed interviews, which on average took fifteen minutes.

THE SAMPLE

The sample of telephone numbers was obtained from Survey Sampling Inc. (SSI), One Post Road, Fairfield, CT 06430. According to its documentation, SSI starts with a computer bank comprising over 60 million directory-listed households. Using area code and exchange data regularly obtained from the telephone company and proprietary database, this file of listed telephone numbers is subjected to an extensive cleaning and validation process to ensure that all exchanges are currently valid, assigned to the correct area code, and fall within an appropriate set of zip codes.

Telephone exchanges and working blocks which contain three or more listed residential telephone numbers are considered valid and represented on the SSI database. A block is the set of 100 contiguous numbers identified by the first two digits of the suffix in a telephone number.

Exchanges are assigned to a single county on the basis of listed residential telephone households. Nationally, about 70% of all exchanges appear to fall totally within single county boundaries. For those overlapping county and/or state lines, the exchanges are assigned to the county of plurality, or to the county with the highest number of listed residency within the exchange. This assignment prevents any overrepresentation of these exchanges.

STRATIFICATION TO COUNTIES

To equalize the probability of telephone household selection from anywhere in the area sampled, samples are first systematically stratified to all counties in the survey area in proportion to each county's share of telephone households.

To obtain reasonable estimates of telephone households by county, SSI developed a special database beginning with the 1980 Census data for residential telephone incidence. These percentages are then applied to current projections of households by county, as published annually by *Sales and Marketing Management* magazine.

After a geographic area has been defined as a combination of counties, the sum of the estimated telephone households is calculated and divided by the desired sample size to produce a sampling interval.

The database is sorted by state and county FIPS Codes. Using the interval and the estimated telephone households of each county in the sample area, a quota by county is calculated. Any county whose population of estimated telephone households equals or exceeds the sampling interval is included in proportion to its share of telephone households. To ensure equal and random probability of selection for smaller counties, the computer generates a random starting point within the first interval.

SELECTION OF NUMBERS WITHIN COUNTIES

For each county in the sample, the required quota of unique telephone numbers is selected by systematically sampling from among all working blocks of numbers in all telephone exchanges assigned to that county. The database is sorted by county of assignment, area code, exchange, and working block.

A sampling interval is calculated by dividing the number of possible random phone numbers for the county (total number of working blocks times 100) by the quota allocated to that county. Each exchange will have a probability of selection equal to its share of active blocks.

SELECTION AMONG WORKING BLOCKS

Using a random start within the first interval for each county, exchanges and working blocks are systematically selected. Within each selected block, the final two digits of the phone number are randomly chosen from the range 00-99. Before this phone number is selected for the sample, its eligibility is verified. If the number is found to be ineligible, subsequent numbers are sequentially checked and the first eligible number encountered is selected for the sample. The search never leaves the block.

Numbers are also considered ineligible if they are marked by SSI's Protection System. Virtually every SSI Random Digit Sample is marked on the database to protect against re-use for a period of up to a year. If as number is marked as protected, it is considered ineligible for selection. However, the system will override and select a protected number in order to preserve the integrity of the sample. SSI's Protection System provides fresher respondents and less chance for overlap with other research projects.

The survey reported here was then conducted and completed using the SSI sample of likely valid phone numbers.

THE SURVEY

The survey began on December 26, 1994, and was completed on January 16, 1995. The survey was administered by telephone using the random digit dialing method described above. To ensure random representation within households, the last birthday method was utilized. The response rate (nonrefusals) was 65.3%: 811 out of 1,241 English-speaking, residential dwellings respondents completed their interviews.

Attempts to reach respondents began at 9 a.m. and continued until 10 p.m., Monday through Friday; 12 p.m. until 10 p.m. on Sundays; and 7 p.m. until 10 p.m. on Saturdays, within the time zone of the respondent. Calls were made until 1 a.m. Eastern time, which would correspond to 10 p.m. Pacific time. This was to avoid overrepresentation from within the Eastern time zone. If a respondent could not be reached during the day (e.g., 1 p.m.), an attempt made to recontact the respondent in the evening (e.g., 7 p.m.), and again later that night (e.g., 10 p.m.). In addition, if the respondent could not be reached during an ordinary weekday, at least one attempt was made to reach the respondent during the weekend. Four phone calls were made to each respondent, of which at least one phone call was made within each of the time periods mentioned above. On average, the length of the survey was fifteen minutes. The interview time ranged from 10 to 25 minutes over all respondents.

The survey was administered by Lock and three other interviewers. Lock trained the interviewers using an interviewer manual that was developed for this survey, which is described later in this Appendix.

REPRESENTATIVENESS AND CHARACTERISTICS OF SAMPLE

The demographic characteristics of the respondents compared closely with typical national telephone samples. A few questions were included in the survey that had been asked about the same time in other national surveys; the distributions of responses to these questions were not significantly different from those in the other surveys (conducted by the Gallup organization, *The New York Times/CBS News*, and the 1994 NORC General Social Survey, NES surveys—see "Comparison to Past Surveys" section later in this Appendix). Since Lock's survey was performed immediately following the Republican takeover of Congress in 1994, the public was slightly more up to date on some of the questions concerning political knowledge that were related to the relative ideology of the two major political parties and control of Congress.

Because none of the interviewers had the ability to speak Spanish, sixteen respondents who did not have the ability to speak English were unable to participate in the survey. These responses were not counted as refusals, rather, they were included with those whom the interviewers had not been able to reach. Included within this group were a few instances in which the interviewer made the decision not to complete the interview, because of a total lack of comprehension on the part of the respondent.

Prior to the survey, interviewers were trained in the intricacies of survey technique. An interviewer manual was read by each of the interviewers.

INTERVIEWER MANUAL

You will be conducting a random telephone survey. The main objective will be to receive honest and complete answers to all the questions being asked. It is vital to conduct the survey in an efficient and professional manner, so that proper responses are received.

1. Speak clearly. It is important that the respondent understand that this a random survey, that their answers are important to the survey and if asked, they can be reassured that their responses will be confidential. This will help assure honest answers. The interviewer should also be aware that speaking slowly and clearly is vital, because many people may not have previously thought of these issues. It is important that the respondent understand the question the first time it is asked so that the survey can be completed expediently. We do not want questions asked twice, since that may cause people to hang up in the middle of the survey. But, above all, be polite and patient.

2. Avoid sounding monotonous. Once the respondent has begun to answer, you should keep up a steady pace of questioning. Do not sound like you are bored by the survey, even if you have asked these questions many times previously. Every time you speak to a different respondent, conduct the interview as if it was your first one. Make the questions sound interesting and vital. If the respondent wishes to hang up, remind them that this survey is important to the public at large and that the survey will only take a few minutes longer. If you make the survey sound important, they will believe the survey is important.

3. Keep to the words of the text. Every question must be read exactly the way it is written. Changing even one word to sound more "interesting" may change the entire context of the question and invalidate the entire survey. Each question has been carefully composed and should be read exactly as it is written. Again, do not deviate from the words in the questions.

4. Look to the parentheses to explain ambiguities. The additions in the parentheses are merely there as explanations for people who may not understand the questions as written. Do not offer the information in the parentheses if it is

not asked for. Do not change the wording in the parentheses. Since reading the explanations in the parentheses can become very time-consuming, it is important not to offer this information unless it is asked for.

5. Attempt to elicit all answers, yet do not appear pushy or prying. For example, if a person seems persistent in not wanting to answer a question, first remind the respondent that no names are being used. Reassurances should be given, if respondent acts hesitantly. If the person is still persistent, move on to the next question and complete the rest of the survey. The goal is to have complete, accurate, and honest surveys.

6. Each interviewer will be given a special survey answer key. Be prepared when conducting the survey. Have survey questions, answer key, and marker all prepared before making the phone calls. The answers should be marked the moment the answer is given, so that the next question can be immediately given to the respondent. In this manner the survey will be conducted efficiently and expediently.

7. It is important to follow the guidelines on the telephone answer sheet. Across the line of every phone number there are boxes for four attempted phone calls. You must write in the date and time of every attempt in the provided boxes. Do not leave messages on answering machines. If the respondent does not answer the phone, hang up and try again the next day, following the schedule I will now give. [See Thomas Piazza, 1993. "Meeting the Challenge of Answering Machines," *Public Opinion Quarterly* 57 (1993):219-231.] The best time to reach people with answering machines is Monday through Thursday, 1-10 p.m. Therefore, following the advice of Piazza, between 1 and 6 p.m. we will be calling people with no previous machine answers, while between 6 and 10 p.m. we will be calling back those who previously had their machines answer. If the respondent answers but asks if you can call back at a different time, write the date and time when you will call back in the next box. If the respondent merely hangs up on you without any response, do not call back again. When you have exhausted all possibilities of the phone number, completed the survey, no reply, etc., use the explanation code at the bottom of the page and write your result at the end of each line.

8. On the sheet entitled "survey sampling," you should write your name on top of the column in the box entitled "name." You should also write the time and date of each call attempted. In addition, in the column "entitled" result place the result of the phone call based on the self-explanatory codes listed on the bottom of each page. Also, on top of each answer sheet, copy the page number found on the top left-hand corner of the survey sampling sheet onto the top of the answer sheet. In addition, copy the telephone and code found under the telephone number onto the top of the answer sheet.

9. Coding: For each and every interview, the following preparations were performed:

The interviewer used a minisample of 25 respondents as prepared by Survey Sampling Inc. and dialed all the numbers on the list. The interviewer then entered one of the codes from the bottom of the sheet, so as to assure the ability to follow the respondent. The 12 codes were:

a. TM, if the call was terminated by the respondent after the interview had begun.

b. RF, if the respondent terminated the interview before the interview began. These numbers were not dialed again.

c. CM, if the interview was completed.

d. NA, if there was no answer and no answering machine. A return phone call was made at a different time of the day and week. All numbers were dialed on a weekday afternoon, evening and weekend.

e. CB, if the respondent asked to be called back at a different time. When this occurred, the time to return the phone call was written in the column entitled "2nd attempt."

f. OQ, numbers that would not have been used if we had been over our quota. This did not occur, and all numbers were used.

g. BZ, if the number dialed was busy. When this occurred calls were tried again within a short period of time, since it was known that someone was home.

h. AM, if an answering machine was reached. These numbers were redialed at a different time of day or week, unless it was obvious that we had reached a government office or private business.

i. DS, if the number dialed was disconnected.

j. BG, if the number reached was a business or government office. Calls were immediately terminated if this occurred.

k. DL, if the respondent was deaf or did not understand or speak English. Sixteen interviews were terminated for this reason.

l. FX, if the number dialed was a fax machine. In addition, many numbers are now set aside for one's modem. This situation exists in both private homes and businesses. As usage of the home computer spreads, it is probable that more numbers will have to be used to complete a survey of this size.

10. Final results:

Completions: 811

Not completed due to

 Terminated/Refusals: 430

 Business/Government: 334

 Deaf/Language: 39

 Fax machines: 153

 No answer: 63

 Disconnected: 647

 Answering machine: 38

COMPARISONS TO PAST SURVEYS

1. Is there any area—that is, within a mile—where you would be afraid to walk at night?

	Yes	No
Lock 1994-95	42%	58%
Gallup 1993	43%	56%
NORC-GSS 1994	47%	52%

2. How about at home at night—do you feel safe and secure or not?

Lock 1994-95	91%	9%
Gallup 1992	89%	11%

3. Do you favor or oppose the death penalty for those convicted of murder?

Lock 1994-95	78%	20%
NORC-GSS 1994	74%	19%
Gallup 1994	80%	16%

4. How much respect do you have for police in your area: a great deal, some, or hardly any?

	Great deal	Some	Hardly Any
Lock 1994-95	64%	27%	8%
Gallup 1991	60%	32%	7%

5. Do you happen to know what job or political office is now held by Al Gore (NES—insert Dan Quayle in place of Al Gore)?

	% Correct
Lock 1994-95	82%
NES 1990-91	84%

6. Whose responsibility is it to determine if a law is constitutional or not: it the president, the Congress, or the Supreme Court?

Lock 1994-95	62%
NES 1990-91	68%

7. How much of a majority is required for the U.S. Senate and House to override a presidential veto?

	% Correct
Lock 1994-95	48%
NES 1990-91	37%

8. Do you happen to know which party had the most members in the House of Representatives in Washington before the election this past November?

Lock 1994-95	77%
NES 1990-91	55%

9. Would you say that one of the parties is more conservative than the other at the national level? Which party is more conservative?

Lock 1994-95	65%
NES 1990-91	57%

THE LAWYER SURVEY

The respondents for the survey of lawyers were purchased from List Strategies Inc., 1290 Avenue of the Americas, New York, New York 10104-1499. The lawyers were chosen from the Martindale-Hubbell Law Directory. All lawyers within the United States are located within this directory. Respondents were mailed a questionnaire listing the identical questions asked of the mass public. Three hundred and sixty four out of a possible of 931 lawyers responded after the first mailing. Another 46 lawyers responded to a second mailing. In all, 410 lawyers responded, for a response rate of 45%. Interestingly, the lawyers who responded to the questionnaire, came from a broad cross section of specializations.

Appendix 5

Factor Analysis for Survey of Legal Elite and Mass Public by Education and Knowledge

Factor analysis was also performed separately for respondents with different levels of knowledge and education. This was done in order to detect possible differences in the structure of the attitudes produced by having more knowledge and education, as well as exposure to information. As Tables A.1 thru A.6 reveal, factor analysis results differ based upon the one's level of education and knowledge. The number of factors ranges from two, for individuals who fall within the middle level of education, to four for the individuals with low and high levels of knowledge, as well as for respondents with high levels of education. Table A.7 presents the results to the factor analysis performed on the responses given by the lawyers. One can see that there were three factors for the responses given by members of the legal elite.

Interestingly, the structures of the opinions differ based upon education and knowledge. The structures are not identical to these for the entire mass sample. The pattern which occurred for the entire survey of the mass public still substantially holds for respondents with different levels of education and knowledge and for lawyers. Also, the results are comparably reliable, valid, and plausible.

Table A.1
**Rotated Factor Solution for Attitudes Toward Criminal Procedures
by Education (Education=Low)**

	Factor 1	Factor 2	Factor 3
Search property from air	.18043	.12028	**.61363**
Dogs sniff for drugs	-.09464	**.38495**	.09402
Search trash off property	.13592	.17066	**.33468**
Search body parts for drugs	.17433	**.50528**	.15430
Search closed container in car	**.51576**	.17158	.06648
Search ship for documents	.29021	.25400	.08623
Stopping suspicious person	.00589	**.72235**	-.09141
Frisk suspect if probable cause	.11704	**.50180**	-.05048
Detain suspect 48 hrs before charge	**.63432**	.14197	-.38788
Undercover agents obtain admission	**.78831**	-.14781	.17126
Admission w/o lawyer after request	**.48888**	.23177	-.01929
Evidence illegally obtained contradicts defendants witnesses	**.46029**	-.06669	.14629

Correlation between factors 1 and 2 = .43999
Correlation between factors 2 and 3 = .21551
Correlation between factors 1 and 3 = .23422

Oblique/oblimin rotation from principal axis factoring. Excludes items dealing with police using fake papers and a mentally ill individual waiving the right to counsel. Factor Pattern Matrix (N=112).

Table A.2
Rotated Factor Solution for Attitudes Toward Criminal Procedures by Education (Education=Mid)

	Factor 1	Factor 2
Search property from air	.09621	**-.47239**
Dogs sniff for drugs	.00877	**-.39666**
Search trash off property	.01513	**-.61752**
Search body parts for drugs	.20110	-.19534
Search closed container in car	**.50881**	-.14544
Search ship for documents	**.53221**	.05797
Stopping suspicious person	-.03737	**-.49382**
Frisk suspect if probable cause	**.32319**	-.03884
Detain suspect 48 hrs before charge	**.42700**	.01189
Undercover agents obtain admission	**.47109**	-.11888
Admission w/o lawyer after request	**.54083**	.07969
Evidence illegally obtained contradicts defendants witnesses	**.33271**	-.15925

Correlation between factors =-.64558

Oblique/oblimin rotation from principal axis factoring. Excludes items dealing with police using fake papers and a mentally ill individual waiving the right to counsel. Factor Pattern Matrix (N=275).

Table A.3

**Rotated Factor Solution for Attitudes Toward Criminal Procedures
by Education (Education = High)**

	Factor 1	Factor 2	Factor 3	Factor 4
Search property from air	-.02725	-.03642	**-.76997**	.00866
Dogs sniff for drugs	.11386	.03848	**-.21669**	.08417
Search trash off property	-.02053	.03907	**-.47501**	-.02491
Search body parts for drugs	.10883	-.06731	-.23000	**.33947**
Search closed container in car	**.42842**	.09179	-.18859	.08470
Search ship for documents	**.62592**	.00408	.03513	.13511
Stopping suspicious person	.14196	.09804	-.08973	**.36650**
Frisk suspect if probable cause	.08549	.03773	.01225	**.57458**
Detain suspect 48 hrs before charge	.14538	**.55150**	.02538	-.13833
Undercover agents obtain admission	-.16012	**.44919**	-.06207	.19144
Admission w/o lawyer after request	-.06882	**.44570**	.01504	.13749
Evidence illegally obtained				
contradicts defendants witnesses	.10474	**.38722**	-.12179	-.07220

Correlation between factors 1 and 2 = .21985
Correlation between factors 1 and 3 = -.40593
Correlation between factors 1 and 4 = .28308
Correlation between factors 2 and 3 = -.38328
Correlation between factors 2 and 4 = .26912
Correlation between factors 3 and 4 = -.45796

Oblique/oblimin rotation from principal axis factoring. Excludes items dealing with police using fake papers and a mentally ill individual waiving the right to counsel. Factor Pattern Matrix (N = 424).

Table A.4
Rotated Factor Solution for Attitudes Toward Criminal Procedures by Knowledge (Knowledge = Low)

	Factor 1	Factor 2	Factor 3	Factor 4
Search property from air	**.51561**	-.16541	.15839	.06865
Dogs sniff for drugs	.20761	.23219	.23465	-.13181
Search trash off property	**.75185**	.10724	-.14565	-.05248
Search body parts for drugs	**.41813**	-.02154	.06316	.09083
Search closed container in car	.32636	.04170	**.34553**	.12779
Search ship for documents	.12932	.05499	**.66348**	-.17591
Stopping suspicious person	**.22389**	.06182	.14581	.13663
Frisk suspect if probable cause	-.05477	-.03663	**.43023**	.15168
Detain suspect 48 hrs before charge	-.04351	**.76112**	-.04356	.07268
Undercover agents obtain admission	.24891	.05206	-.06619	**.58801**
Admission w/o lawyer after request	-.01533	.22601	.23104	**.38702**
Evidence illegally obtained contradicts defendants witnesses	**.27195**	.11322	.07873	.13312

Correlation between factors 1 and 2 = .33303
Correlation between factors 1 and 3 = .48131
Correlation between factors 1 and 4 = .31688
Correlation between factors 2 and 3 = .24483
Correlation between factors 2 and 4 = .18437
Correlation between factors 3 and 4 = .30988

Oblique/oblimin rotation from principal axis factoring. Excludes items dealing with police using fake papers and a mentally ill individual waiving the right to counsel. Factor Pattern Matrix (N = 233).

Table A.5
Rotated Factor Solution for Attitudes Toward Criminal Procedures by Knowledge (Knowledge=Mid)

	Factor 1	Factor 2	Factor 3
Search property from air	**.66303**	-.03661	-.02063
Dogs sniff for drugs	**.40238**	.06538	.14220
Search trash off property	**.38700**	-.00503	-.13850
Search body parts for drugs	**.37188**	.05772	-.14672
Search closed container in car	.13614	.07321	**-.52710**
Search ship for documents	.11107	.06919	**-.45984**
Stopping suspicious person	**.46584**	.05374	-.08411
Frisk suspect 48 hrs before charge	**.35972**	.04688	-.19320
Undercover agents obtain admission	.11218	**.56117**	.02901
Admission w/o lawyer after request	.03564	**.41839**	.07757
Evidence illegally obtained contradicts defendants witnesses	.09020	**.36243**	-.02225

Correlation between factors 1 and 2 = .48933
Correlation between factors 1 and 3 = -.34704
Correlation between factors 2 and 3 = -.35351

Oblique/oblimin rotation from principal axis factoring. Excludes items dealing with police using fake papers and a mentally ill individual waiving the right to counsel. Factor Pattern Matrix (N=334).

Table A.6
**Rotated Factor Solution for Attitudes Toward Criminal Procedures
by Knowledge (Knowledge=High)**

	Factor 1	Factor 2	Factor 3	Factor 4
Search property from air	.27926	-.04043	**.42470**	.00216
Dogs sniff for drugs	-.13111	-.05428	**.44982**	-.13474
Search trash off property	.11690	-.03737	**.52013**	.09090
Search body parts for drugs	-.01526	-.09793	**.25832**	-.23271
Search closed container in car	.25604	-.14521	.04929	**-.43235**
Search ship for documents	.02583	.01526	-.00871	**-.59504**
Stopping suspicious person	-.05938	**-.88013**	.02931	.08385
Frisk suspect if probable cause	.05159	**-.43189**	.05729	-.08293
Detain suspect 48 hrs before charge	**.43101**	-.16686	-.13781	-.06879
Undercover agents obtain admission	**.59514**	-.01045	.04446	.08735
Admission w/o lawyer after request	**.38088**	-.00858	.05834	-.15281
Evidence illegally obtained contradicts defendants witnesses	**.5066**	.10869	.11990	-.08766

Correlation between factors 1 and 2 =-.27414
Correlation between factors 1 and 3 =.28753
Correlation between factors 1 and 4 =-.32325
Correlation between factors 2 and 3 =-.30842
Correlation between factors 2 and 4 =.36670
Correlation between factors 3 and 4 =-.35603

Oblique/oblimin rotation from principal axis factoring. Excludes items dealing with police using fake papers and a mentally ill individual waiving the right to counsel. Factor Pattern Matrix (N=244).

Table A.7

Rotated Solution for Attitudes of Lawyers Toward Criminal Procedures

	Factor 1	Factor 2	Factor 3
Search property from air	.21592	.03772	**-.54322**
Dogs sniff for drugs	**.52672**	-.05510	-.15084
Search trash off property	.28677	.00741	**-.51869**
Search body parts for drugs	**.59360**	.04827	.03814
Search closed container in car	-.01087	**.60490**	.06799
Search ship for documents	.18120	**.39853**	.05226
Stopping suspicious person	**.50247**	.16160	-.00583
Frisk suspect if probable cause	**.48909**	.01391	-.02739
Detain suspect 48 hrs before charge	.06376	**.46814**	.12293
Undercover agents obtain admission	.09528	**.41260**	-.19730
Admission w/o lawyer after request	-.12385	**.53826**	-.30944
Evidence illegally obtained contradicts defendants witnesses	.09557	**.47634**	-.02739

Correlation between factors 1 and 2 = .50163
Correlation between factors 1 and 3 = -.42712
Correlation between factors 2 and 3 = -.27606

Oblique/oblimin rotation from principal axis solution. Excludes items dealing with police using fake papers and a mentally ill individual waiving the right to counsel. Factor Pattern Matrix (N=410).

Bibliography

Abramson, Paul R., John Aldrich, and David W. Rohde. 1995. *Change and Continuity in the 1992 Elections*. Washington, D.C.: Congressional Quarterly Press.

Adamany, David W., and Joel B. Grossman. 1983. Support for the Supreme Court as a National Policy Maker. *Law and Policy Quarterly* 5:405-437.

Alwin, Duane F., Ronald L. Cohen, and Theodore M. Newcomb. 1991. *Political Attitudes Over the Life Span: The Bennington Women After Fifty Years*. Madison: The University of Wisconsin Press.

Bacharach, Peter, and Morton S. Baratz. 1962. Two Faces of Power. *American Political Science Review* 56:947-952.

Backstrom, Charles H., and Gerald Hursh-Cesar. 1986. *Survey Research*. New York: John Wiley.

Bagdikian, Ben H. 1987. *The Media Monopoly*. Boston: Beacon.

Banfield, E.C. 1970. *The Unheavenly City*. Boston: Little, Brown.

Belknap, George, and Angus Campbell. 1951. Party Identification and Attitudes Toward Foreign Policy. *Public Opinion Quarterly* 15:601-623.

Bentham, J. 1843. *The Works of Jeremy Bentham*, ed. Jay Browning. Edinburgh: Tait.

Berelson, Bernard. 1952. Democratic Theory and Public Opinion. *Public Opinion Quarterly* 16:313-330.

Black, Charles, Jr. 1960. *The People and the Court*. New York: Macmillan.

Bobo, Lawrence, and Fredrick C. Licarri. 1989. Education and Political Tolerance: Testing the Effects of Cognitive Sophistication and Target Group Affect. *Public Opinion Quarterly* 53:285-308.

Caldeira, Gregory A. 1977. Children's Images of the Supreme Court: A Preliminary Mapping. *Law and Society Review* 11:851-870.

———. 1986 Neither the Purse Nor the Sword: The Dynamics of Public Confidence in the United States Supreme Court. *American Political Science Review* 80:1209-1226.

———. 1987. Public Opinion and the Supreme Court: FDR's Court Packing Plan. *American Political Science Review* 81:1139-1154.

Campbell, Angus, Philip E. Converse, Warren E. Miller, and Donald E. Strokes. 1960. *The American Voter*. New York: John Wiley.

Carmines, Edward G., and James A. Stimson. 1982. Racial Issues and the Structure of Mass Belief Systems. *Journal of Politics* 44:2-20.

———. 1989. *Issue Evolution: Race and the Transformation of American Politics*. Princeton, N.J.: Princeton University Press.

Casey, Gregory. 1974. The Supreme Court and Myth: An Empirical Investigation. *Law and Society Review* 8:385-419.

———. 1976. Popular perceptions of Supreme Court Rulings. *American Politics Quarterly* 4:3-35.

Chomsky, Noam, and Edward Herman. 1979. *The Washington Connection and Third World Fascism*. Boston: South End Press.

Converse, Philip E. 1964. The Nature of Belief Systems in Mass Public. In *Ideology and Discontent*, ed. David E. Apter. New York: Free Press, 206-261.

Cook, Beverly B. 1977. Pubic Opinion and Federal Judicial Policy. *American Journal of Political Science* 21:567-600.

Corwin, Edward S. 1936. The Constitution as Instrument and as Symbol. *American Political Science Review* 30:1071-1075.

Dahl, Robert A. 1956. *A Preface to Democratic Theory*. Chicago: University of Chicago Press.

Dalton, Russell J. 1992. *Citizen Politics in Western Democracies*. Chatham, N.J.: Chatham House Publishers, Inc.

Dawson, Michael C. 1994. *Behind the Mule: Race and Class in African American Politics*. Princeton, N.J.: Princeton University Press.

Delli Carpini, Michael X. 1986. *Stability and Change in American Politics: The Coming of Age of the Generations of the 1960s*. New York: New York University Press.

Delli Carpini, Michael X., and Scott Keeter. 1991. Stability and Change in the U.S. Public's Knowledge of Politics. *Public Opinion Quarterly* 55:583-612.

———. 1996. *What Americans Know About Politics and Why It Matters*. New Haven, Conn.: Yale University Press.

de Tocqueville, Alexis. 1945. *Democracy in America*. New York: Vintage Books (originally published in 1835).

Diamond, Edwin, and Stephen Bates. 1992. *The Spot*. Cambridge, Mass.: MIT Press.

Dolbeare, Kenneth M., and Philip M. Hammond. 1968. The Political Party Basis of Attitudes Toward the Supreme Court. *Public Opinion Quarterly* 32:16-30.

Downs, Anthony. 1957. *An Economic Theory of Democracy*. New York: HarperCollins.

Easton, David, and Jack Dennis. 1969. *Children in the Political System: Origins of Political Legitimacy*. New York: McGraw-Hill.

Eisenstein, James, and Herbert Jacob. 1977. *Felony Justice: An Organizational Analysis of Criminal Courts*. Boston: Little, Brown.

Elkins, David J. 1993. *Manipulation and Consent: How Voters and Leaders Manage Complexity*. Vancouver: University of British Columbia Press.

Epstein, Lee, Thomas G. Walker, and William J. Dixon. 1989. The Supreme Court and Criminal Justice Dispute: A Neo-Institutional Perspective. *American Journal of Political Science* 33:825-841.

Erickson, Robert S., and Kent L. Tedin. 1992. *American Public Opinion: Its Origins and Impact*. New York: Macmillan.

Fenno, Richard F. 1978. *Home Style: House Members in Their Districts*. New York: HarperCollins.

Fiorina, Morris P. 1981. *Retrospective Voting in American National Elections*. New Haven, Conn.: Yale University Press.

———. 1989. *Congress: Keystone of the Washington Establishment*. New Haven, Conn.: Yale University Press.

Fishkin, James. 1991. *Democracy and Deliberation: New Directions for a Democratic Reform*. New Haven, Conn.: Yale University Press.

———. 1992. *The Dialogue of Justice: Toward a Self-Reflected Society*. New Haven, Conn.: Yale University Press.

Frankel, Max. 1997. Live at 11: Death. *The New York Times Magazine*, June 15, p. 20.

Funkhauser, G. Ray. 1973a. The Issues of the Sixties: An Exploratory Study in the Dynamics of Public Opinion. *Public Opinion Quarterly* 37:62-75.

———. 1973b. Trends in Media Coverage of the Issues of the Sixties. *Journalism Quarterly* 50:533-558.

Geddes, Barbara, and John Zaller. 1989. Sources of Popular Support for Authoritarian Regimes. *American Journal of Political Science* 33:319-347.

Gibson, James L. 1988. Political Intolerance and Political Repression During the McCarthy Red Scare. *American Political Science Review* 82:512-529.

Graebner, Diane. 1973. Judicial Activity and Public Attitudes. *Buffalo Law Review* 23:465-498.

Greeley, Andrew M. 1989. *Religious Change in America*. Cambridge, Mass.: Harvard University Press.

———. 1990. *The Catholic Myth: The Behavior and Beliefs of American Catholics*. New York: Scribners.

Grofman, Bernard, Lisa Handley, and Richard G. Niemi. 1992. *Minority Representation and the Quest for Voting Equality*. New York: Cambridge University Press.

Hacker, Andrew. 1992. *Two Nations: Black and White, Separate, Hostile, Unequal*. New York: Scribners.

Handberg, Roger, and William S. Maddox. 1982. Pubic Support for the Supreme Court in the 1970s. *American Politics Quarterly* 10:333-346.

Herman, Edward, and Noam Chomsky. 1988. *Manufacturing Consent: The Political Economy of the Mass Media*. New York: Pantheon Books.

Hirsh, Herbert, and Lewis Donohew. 1968. A Note on Black-White Differences in Attitudes Toward the Supreme Court. *Social Science Quarterly* 49:557-562.

Hyman, Herbert H., and Charles R. Wright. 1979. *Education's Lasting Influence on Values*. Chicago: University of Chicago Press.

Iyengar, Shanto, and Donald R. Kinder. 1987. *News That Matters: Television and American Opinion*. Chicago: University of Chicago Press.

Jackman, Robert W. 1972. Political Elites, Mass Publics, and Support for Democratic Principles. *Journal of Politics* 54:753-773.

Jordan, Donald L. 1993. Newspaper Effects on Policy Preferences. *Public Opinion Quarterly* 57:191-204.

Kessel, John H. 1966. Pubic Perceptions of the Supreme Court. *Midwest Journal of Political Science* 10:167-191.

Key, V.O. 1961. *Public Opinion and American Democracy*. New York: Knopf.

Kluger, Richard. 1975. *Simple Justice*. New York: Vintage Books.

LaFave, Wayne, and Jerold Israel. 1992. *Criminal Procedure*. St Paul: West Publishing Co.

Lehne, Richard, and John Renyolds. 1978. The Impact of Judicial Activists on Public Opinion. *American Journal of Political Science* 22:896-904.

Lerner, Max. 1936. Constitution and Court as Symbols. *Yale Law Review* 46:1290-1319.

Locke, John. 1960. *Two Treatises of Government*, ed. Peter Laslett. New York: Cambridge University Press.

Lukes, Steven. 1975. *Power: A Radical View*. New York: Humanities Press.

Marshall, Thomas. 1987. The Supreme Court as an Opinion Leader. *American Politics Quarterly* 15:147-168.

———. 1989. *Public Opinion and the Supreme Court*. New York: Longman.

McClosky, Herbert. 1964. Consensus and Ideology in American Politics. *American Political Science Review* 58:361-382.

McClosky, Herbert, and Alida Brill. 1983. *Dimensions of Tolerance: What Americans Believe About Civil Liberties*. New York: Russell Sage Foundation.

McClosky, Herbert, and John Zaller. 1984. *The American Ethos: Public Attitudes toward Capitalism and Democracy*. Cambridge, Mass.: Harvard University Press.

McGuire, Kevin T. 1993. *The Supreme Court Bar: Legal Elites in the Washington Community*. Charlottesville: University of Virginia Press.

Milburn, Michael A. 1991. *Persuasion and Politics: The Social Psychology of Public Opinion*. Belmont, Calif.: Wadsworth.

Mill, J.S. 1965. *Collected Works*, ed. J.M. Robson. Toronto: University of Toronto Press (originally published in 1849).

Miller, Arthur Selwyn. 1965. Some Pervasive Myths About the United States Supreme Court. *Saint Louis University Law Review* 10:153-189.

Miller, Arthur. 1974. Political Issues and Trust in Government. *American Political Science Review* 68:951-972.

Mishler, William, and Reginald S. Sheehan. 1993. The Supreme Court as a Counter-majoritarian Institution? The Impact of Pubic Opinion on Supreme Court Decisions. *American Political Science Review* 87:87-101.

Mueller, Carol M. 1990. *The Politics of the Gender Gap*. Newbury Park, Calif.: Sage.

Myerson, Allen R. 1996. America's Quiet Rebellion Against McDonaldization. *The New York Times Week in Review*, p. 5.

Neuman, W. Russell. 1986. *The Paradox of Mass Politics: Knowledge and Opinion in the American Electorate*. Cambridge, Mass.: Harvard University Press.

Newsweek. 1994. The Myth of Generation X. June 6, p. 62.

Nie, Norman, Sidney Verba, and John Petrocik. 1976. *The Changing American Voter*. Cambridge, Mass.: Harvard University Press.

Nunn, Clyde A., Harry J. Crockett, Jr., and J. Allan Williams. 1978. *Tolerance for Non-conformity: A National Survey of Changing Commitment to Civil Liberties*. San Francisco: Jossey-Bass.

Page, Benjamin. 1996. *Who Deliberates?: Mass Media in Modern Democracy*. Chicago: University of Chicago Press.

Page, Benjamin I., and Robert Y. Shapiro. 1992. *The Rational Public: Fifty Years of Trends in Americans' Policy Preferences*. Chicago: University of Chicago Press.

Page, Benjamin I., Robert Y. Shapiro, and Glenn R. Dempsey. 1987. Television News and Changes in Americans' Policy Preferences. *American Political Science Review* 83:23-44.

Parenti, Michael. 1986. *Inventing Reality: The Politics of the Mass Media*. New York: St. Martin's Press.

Popkin, Samuel. 1991. *The Reasoning Voter: Communication and Persuasion in Presidential Campaigns*. Chicago: University of Chicago Press.

Price, Vincent, and John Zaller. 1993. Who Gets the News? Alternative Measures of News Reception and Their Implications for Research. *Public Opinion Quarterly* 57:133-164.

Prothro, James W., and Charles M. Grigg. 1960. Fundamental Principles of Democracy: Bases of Agreement and Disagreement. *Journal of Politics* 22:276-294.

Pruet, George W., Jr., and Henry R. Glick. 1986. Social Environment, Public Opinion, and Judicial Policy Making. *American Politics Quarterly* 14:5-33.

Radin, Solomon. 1978. The Jurisprudence of Death: Evolving Standards for the Cruel and Unusual Punishment Clause. 126 *University of Pennsylvania Law Review* 989-990.

Richardson, Richard J., and Kenneth N. Vines. 1970. *The Politics of Federal Courts*. Boston: Little, Brown.

Rosenberg, Gerald N. 1991. *The Hollow Hope: Can Courts Bring About Social Change?* Chicago: University of Chicago Press.

Rousseau, J.J. 1953. *Rousseau, Political Writings*, ed. R. Watkins. London: Nelson (originally published in 1762).

Schattschneider, E.E. 1960. *The Semisovereign People*. Hinsdale, Ill.: Dryden Press.

Schuman, Howard, Charlotte Steeh, and Lawrence Bobo. 1985. *Racial Attitudes in America: Trends and Interpretations*. Cambridge, Mass.: Harvard University Press.

Schumpeter, J.A. 1943. *Capitalism, Socialism and Democracy*. New York: Harper and Row.

Segal, Jeffery A., and Albert Cover. 1989. Ideological Values and Votes of U.S. Supreme Court Justices. *American Political Science Review* 83:557-565.

Sigelman, Lee. 1979. Black-White Differences in Attitudes Toward the Supreme Court: A Replication in the 1970s. *Social Science Quarterly* 60:113.

Sigelman, Lee, and Susan Welch. 1991. *Black Americans' Views of Racial Inequality*. New York: Cambridge University Press.

Shapiro, Martin. 1990. The Supreme Court from Early Burger to Early Rehnquist. In *The New American Political System*, ed. Anthony King. Washington, D.C.: United Press of America.

Shapiro, Robert Y., and Harpeet Mahajan. 1986. Gender Differences in Public Policy Preferences: A Summary of Trends from the 1960s to the 1980s. *Public Opinion Quarterly* 50:42-61.

Sniderman, Paul M., Richard A. Brody, and Philip E. Tetlock. 1991. *Reasoning and Choice: Explorations in Political Psychology*. New York: Cambridge University Press.

Sniderman, Paul, M., Thomas Piazza, Philip E. Tetlock, and Ann Kendrick. 1991. The New Racism. *American Journal of Political Science* 35:423-447.

Stimson, James A. 1991. *Public Opinion in America: Modes, Cycles, and Swings*. Boulder, Colo.: Westview Press.

Stouffer, Samuel A. 1955. *Communism, Conformity, and Civil Liberties*. New York: Doubleday.

Sullivan, John L., James E. Piereson, and George E. Marcus. 1982. *Political Tolerance and American Democracy*. Chicago: University of Chicago Press.

Tannenhaus, Joseph, and Walter F. Murphy. 1981. Patterns of Public Support in the Supreme Court: A Panel Study. *Journal of Politics* 43:23-39.

Wahlke, John C. et al. 1962. *The Legislative System*. New York: John Wiley.

Wald, Kenneth M. 1992. *Religion and Politics in America*. Washington, D.C.: Congressional Quarterly.

Walker, Samuel. 1989. *Sense and Nonsense About Crime*. Belmont, Calif.: Wadsworth.

Weil, Fredrick L. 1985. The Variable Effects of Education on Liberal Attitude: A Comparative Historical Analysis of Anti-Semitism Using Public Opinion. *American Sociological Review* 50:458-474.

Wilson, James Q. 1983. *Thinking About Crime*. New York: Basic Books.

Wilson, James Q., and Richard J. Herrnstein 1985. *Crime and Human Nature: The Definitive Study of the Causes of Crime*. New York: Simon and Schuster.

Woodward, Bob, and Scott Armstrong. 1979. *The Brethren: Inside the Supreme Court*. New York: Simon and Schuster.

Zaller, John. 1992. *The Nature and Origin of Mass Opinion*. New York: Cambridge University Press.

Zaller, John, and Stanley Feldman. 1992. A Simple Theory of the Survey Response: Answering Questions Versus Revealing Preferences. *American Journal of Political Science* 36:579-616.

CASES USED TO FORMULATE SURVEY

Acevdo, California v., 111 S. Ct. 1982 (1991).

Adams v. Williams, 407 U.S. 143 (1972).

Aguilar v. Texas, 378 U.S. 108 (1964).

Alabama v. White, 58 U.S.L.W. 4747 (1990).

Alderman v. U.S., 394 U.S. 165 (1969).

Almeida-Sanchez v. U.S., 413 U.S. 266 (1973).

Argersinger v. Hamlin, 407 U.S. 25 (1972).

Arizona v. Hicks, 480 U.S. 321 (1987).

Baldasar v. Illinois, 446 U.S. 222 (1980).

Belton, New York v., 453 U.S. 454 (1981).

Beckwith v. U.S., 425 U.S. 341 (1976).

Belton, New York v., 453 U.S. 454 (1981).

Berkemer v. McCarty, 468 U.S. 420 (1984).

Bertine, Colorado v., 479 U.S. 367 (1987).

Bowers, Commonwealth v., 274 A.2d 546 (Pa. Super. Ct. 1970).

Brewer v. Williams, 430 U.S. 387 (1977).

Brown v. Mississippi, 297 U.S. 278 (1936).

Butler, North Carolina v., 441 U.S. 369 (1979).

Camara v. Municipal Court, 387 U.S. 523 (1967).

Cardwell v. Lewis, 417 U.S. 583 (1974).

Carney, California v., 471 U.S. 386 (1985).

Carroll v. U.S., 267 U.S. 132 (1925).

Chadwick, U.S. v., 433 U.S. 1 (1977).

Chambers v. Maroney, 399 U.S. 42 (1970).

Chimel v. California, 339 U.S. 752 (1969).

Ciraolo, California v., 476 U.S. 227 (1986).

Class, New York v., 475 U.S. 106 (1986).
Coker v. Georgia, 433 U.S. 584 (1977).
Coleman v. Alabama, 399 U.S. 1 (1970).
Connelly, Colorodo v., 479 U.S. 157 (1986).
Coolidge v. New Hampshire, 403 U.S. 443 (1971).
Cupp v. Murphy, 412 U.S. 291 (1973).
Dickerson, Minnesota v., 113 S. Ct. 2130 (1993).
Dionisio, U.S. v., 410 U.S. 1 (1973).
Dow Chemical Co. V. U.S., 476 U.S. 227 (1986).
Doyle v. Ohio, 426 U.S. 610 (1976).
Duckworth v. Eagan, 109 S. Ct. 2875 (1989).
Dunn, U.S. v., 480 U.S. 294 (1987).
Escobedo v. Illinois, 378 U.S. 478 (1964).
Estelle v. Smith, 451 U.S. 454 (1981).
Fox, U.S. v., 403 F.2d 97 (2d Cir. 1968).
Furman v. Georgia, 408 U.S. 238 (1972).
Garner, Tennessee v., 471 U.S. 1 (1985).
Garrison, Maryland v., 480 U.S. 79 (1987).
Gates, Illinois v., 462 U.S. 213 (1983).
Gilbert v. California, 388 U.S. 218 (1967).
Goldman, U.S. v., 316 U.S. 129 (1942).
Greenwood, California v., 486 U.S. 35 (1988).
Greer v. Miller, 483 U.S. 756 (1987).
Gregg v. Georgia, 428 U.S. 153 (1976).
Griffen v. Wisconsin, 483 U.S. 868 (1987).
Harris, U.S. v., 403 U.S. 573 (1971).
Harvey, Michigan v., 58 U.S.L.W. 4288 (1990).
Horton v. California, 58 U.S.L.W. 4694 (1990).
Hudson v. Palmer, 468 U.S. 517 (1984).
Havens, U.S. v., 446 U.S. 620 (1980).
Illinois v. Perkins, 58 U.S.L.W. 4737 (1990).
Jacobsen, U.S. v., 466 U.S. 109 (1984).
James v. Illinois, 58 U.S.L.W. 4115 (1990).
Jimeno, Florida v., 111 S. Ct. 1801 (1991).
Katz v. U.S., 389 U.S. 347 (1967).
Ker v. California, 374 U.S. 23 (1963).
Kirby v. Illinois, 406 U.S. 682 (1972).
Knotts, U.S. v., 460 U.S. 276 (1983).
Lee, U.S. v., 343 U.S. 747 (1952).
Leon, U.S. v., 468 U.S. 897 (1984).
Lewis v. U.S., 385 U.S. 206 (1966).
Lopez, U.S. v., 385 U.S. 206 (1966).
Mallory v. U.S., 354 U.S. 449 (1957).
Mandujano, U.S. v., 425 U.S. 564 (1976).
Martinez-Fuerte v. U.S., 428 U.S. 543 (1976).
Maryland v. Buie, 58 U.S.L.W. 4218 (1990).
Mathiason, Oregon v., 429 U.S. 492 (1977).
Matlock, U.S. v., 415 U.S. 164 (1974).
McNeil v. Wisconsin, 111 S. Ct. 2204 (1991).

Mendenhall, U.S. v., 446 U.S. 544 (1980).
Michigan v. Clifford, 464 U.S. 287 (1984).
Michigan Department of State Police v. Sitz, 58 U.S.L.W. 478 (1990).
Miller, U.S. v., 425 U.S. 435 (1976).
Mimms, Pennsylvania v., 434 U.S. 106 (1977).
Minnick v. Mississippi, 498 U.S. 146 (1990).
Miranda v. Arizona, 384 U.S. 436 (1966).
Montoya de Hernandez, U.S. v., 473 U.S. 531 (1985).
Moore v. Illinois, 434 U.S. 220 (1977).
Moran v. Burbine, 475 U.S. 412 (1986).
Morris v. Slappy, 461 U.S. 1 (1983).
Moulton, Maine v., 474 U.S. 159 (1985).
Neville, South Dakota v., 459 U.S. 553 (1983).
New York v. Class, 475 U.S. 106 (1986).
Oliver v. U.S., 466 U.S. 170 (1984).
Olson, Minnesota v., 58 U.S.L.W. 4464 (1990).
Opperman, South Dakota v., 428 U.S. 364 (1976).
Padilla, U.S. v., 113 S. Ct. 1936 (1993).
Payton v. New York, 445 U.S. 573 (1980).
Perkins, Illinois v., 496 U.S. 292 (1990).
Place, U.S. v., 426 U.S. 6196 (1983).
Prouse, Delaware v., 440 U.S. 648 (1979).
Quarles, N.Y. v., 467 U.S. 649 (1984).
Rabinowitz, U.S. v., 339 U.S. 56 (1950).
Rawlings v. Kentucky, 448 U.S. 98 (1980).
Riverside, County of v. McLaughlin, 111 S. Ct. 1661 (1991).
Rodriguez, Illinois v., 58 U.S.L.W. 4892 (1990).
Ross, U.S. v., 456 U.S. 798 (1982).
Russell, U.S. v., 411 U.S. 423 (1973).
Schmerber v. California, 384 U.S. 757 (1966).
Schneckloth v. Bustamonte, 412 U.S. 218 (1973).
Scott, U.S. v., 436 U.S. 128 (1978).
Sharpe, U.S. v., 470 U.S. 675 (1985).
Sheppard, Massachusetts v., 468 U.S. 981 (1984).
Sitz, Michigan Department of State Police v., 496 U.S. 444 (1990).
Smith v. Maryland, 442 U.S. 735 (1979).
Sokolow, U.S. v., 490 U.S. 1 (1989).
Spano, N.Y. v., 360 U.S. 315 (1959).
Spring, Colorado v., 479 U.S. 564 (1987).
Stansbury v. California, 511 U.S. 318 (1994).
Steagald v. U.S., 451 U.S. 204 (1981).
Strickland v. Washington, 466 U.S. 688 (1984).
Tennessee v. Garner, 471 U.S. 1 (1985).
Terry v. Ohio, 392 U.S. 1 (1968).
Vale v. Louisiana, 399 U.S. 30 (1970).
Villamonte-Marquez, U.S. v., 462 U.S. 579 (1983).
Watson, U.S. v., 423 U.S. 411 (1976).
Wells, Florida v., 495 U.S. 1 (1990).
Welsh v. Wisconsin, 466 U.S. 740 (1984).

White, U.S. v., 401 U.S. 745 (1971).
Winston v. Lee, 470 U.S. 753 (1985).
Wong Sun v. U.S., 371 U.S. 171 (1963).
Zurcher v. The Stanford Daily, 436 U.S. 547 (1978).

Index

About the Author

SHMUEL LOCK is Assistant Professor in the Department of Law, Police Science, and Criminal Justice Administration at the John Jay College of Criminal Justice. His current research interests are in the area of public opinion regarding issues of criminal justice.

ISBN 0-275-96432-9

90000>

HARDCOVER BAR CODE